CALIFORNIA'S

BEST - LOVED

DRIVING

TOURS

Simon & Schuster Macmillan

Written by Robert Holmes

First published 1997

Edited, designed and produced by AA Publishing.

Published by AA Publishing

Published in the United States by Macmillan Travel
A Simon & Schuster Macmillan Company
1633 Broadway, New York, NY 10019

Macmillan is a registered trademark of Macmillan, Inc

ISBN 0-02861565-4

Cataloging-in-Publication Data is available from the Library of Congress.

Color separation: Daylight Colour Art, Singapore

Printed and bound by G. Canale & C. s.p.a., Torino, Italy

Right: *satisfied customer, Fisherman's Wharf*

CONTENTS

ABOUT THIS BOOK

This book is not only a practical touring guide for the independent traveler, but is also invaluable for those who would like to know more about California.

It is divided into 8 regions, with city and driving tours. The driving tours start and finish in those cities which we consider to be the most interesting centers for exploration. There are special features on theme parks, the Wine Country, the Gold Country and California's missions.

Each tour has details of the most interesting places to visit en route. Boxes catering for special interests follow some of the main entries – for those whose interest is in history or walking or those who have children. There are also boxes which highlight scenic stretches of road and which give details of special events, crafts and customs.

The simple route directions are accompanied by an easy-to-use map at the beginning of each tour, along with a chart showing how far it is from one town to the next in miles and kilometers. This can help you decide where to take a break and stop overnight. (All distances quoted are approximate.)

Before setting off it is advisable to check with the information center listed at the start of the tour for recommendations on where to break your journey and for additional information on what to see and do, and when best to visit.

For information on driving in California see pages 163–4.

INFORMATION FOR NON-U.S. RESIDENTS

Banks

Banking hours in California have traditionally been from 9am to 3pm, Monday to Friday (except national holidays), but recent competition has resulted in longer hours of business (9am–6pm), and even Saturday opening (9am–2pm). Most banks do not offer foreign exchange facilities but it is possible to exchange money at the airport or some hotels. It is better to take U.S. dollar travelers' cheques, which are accepted as currency in most shops, hotels and restaurants, and can be replaced if lost or stolen.

Credit Cards

Major credit cards are accepted almost anywhere and their use is often the best way to take advantage of the most favorable exchange rates.

Currency

The U.S. dollar bill is available in denominations of 1, 5, 10, 20, 50 and 100. There is a two-dollar bill, but it is rarely seen. Coins come in denominations of 1 cent (penny), 5 cents (nickel), 10 cents (dime) and 25 cents (quarter).

Customs Regulations

Personal allowances include up to one litre of alcoholic beverages (for visitors of 21 or over), 200 cigarettes, 1.4kg tobacco, or 50 cigars plus $100 worth of gifts. In practice, most of these items are far cheaper within the U.S. than at airport duty free shops, so there is little point in importing them.

A host of golden pumpkins at the Half Moon Bay Pumpkin Festival

There is no restriction on the amount of currency imported or exported, but anything over $10,000 must be declared. U.S. customs are particularly concerned about drugs, animals, meat (both fresh and processed), plants and fresh fruit. Penalties are severe.

Emergency Telephone Numbers
For police, fire and ambulance dial 911 from any telephone.

Entry Regulations
Visas are required for all visitors to the U.S., except for Canadian citizens or nationals of Britain, France, Germany, Italy, the Netherlands, Sweden, Switzerland or Japan visiting the U.S. for business or tourist purposes, for a stay not exceeding 90 days, and provided that a return or onward ticket is held. In these instances a passport only is required. The type and validity of U.S. visas varies considerably, so seek advice from the nearest U.S. Embassy or Consulate. U.S. immigration is very strict and passengers whose travel documents are not in order will not be admitted under any circumstances.

Health
The standard of health care in California is extremely high – but so are the costs. It is essential to have a good health insurance policy. Many doctors and hospitals will refuse to give treatment unless proof of insurance can be given. Most major hospitals have 24-hour emergency rooms. Information on doctors can be obtained from hotels.

California does not have any specific health problems but it is a rabies risk area. If bitten, seek a doctor immediately. Tap water is drinkable, but if hiking in the back country do not drink from streams, which often carry the parasite Giardia.

AIDS is a continuing concern, particularly in the San Francisco area, where the AIDS Hotline number is 415 863 2437/1-800 367 2437 from anywhere in California. Safe sex is advisable.

Post Offices
Post office opening hours can vary, so it is always best to double-check. Stamps may be purchased from vending machines in a range of different places, such as hotels, motels, drugstores and transport terminals, but they cost more at these outlets than they do if you buy them at the post offices.

Telephones
Telephones are everywhere, and most of them are in working order. All public telephones accept 5, 10 and 25 cent coins, with 20 cents being the minimum charge. Hotels usually charge a high premium for calls from rooms. Always check rates, to avoid an unpleasant surprise.

Dial 0 for a local operator or 00 for a long-distance operator. For diect-dialing international calls, dial 011, the country code and then the number. International codes are:
Australia 61
Canada 1
New Zealand 64
UK 44

Time
California is on Pacific Standard Time, which is eight hours behind GMT.

Sombreros for sale in Olvera Street market, Los Angeles

GREATER LOS ANGELES & THE INLAND EMPIRE

In all America, nowhere is the car more important than in this giant metropolis. The size of Los Angeles is difficult to comprehend until you try driving from one neighborhood to another. It is impossible to tell where LA begins or ends. Los Angeles County has a population of over 11 million and covers an area of 4,083 square miles (10,575 sq km) with 88 incorporated cities, but the continuous urban sprawl goes way beyond this. Development stretches from Ventura County in the north to Orange County in the south, and from the Pacific coast to Riverside County and the Inland Empire in the east.

This five-county area is bigger than any state excluding California, New York or Texas. Altogether there are over 16 million people in an area of 34,149 square miles (88,446 sq km). As you would expect, an area of this size has it all except clean air. Only on rare days, when the Santa Ana winds flush away the smog, can you see the spectacular backdrop of the Inland Empire's San Bernardino mountains. The region has beaches, mountains, desert and some of the world's best entertainment. On the same day it is possible to swim in the Pacific and ski in the mountains, returning in the evening for dinner in one of America's great restaurants.

Los Angeles was founded by a group of settlers in 1781 on the banks of the Los Angeles River, but it was not until the sunshine lured film-makers in the early 1900s that the city achieved its present prominence and Hollywood become the movie capital of the world. On any day, somewhere on the city streets, there will be a film crew out shooting – although today it is often for television rather than the cinema. This emphasis on show business has helped Los Angeles become the barometer of popular culture in the nation and the city likes to think it is on the cutting edge of fashion. There is nothing modest here. Everything is larger than life and the more flamboyant the attitude the greater the respect – or so it often seems.

This is a city of acceptance. Anything goes, and you will be greeted equally whether you are in jeans and a T-shirt or a tuxedo, although jeans and a tuxedo may give you an edge! It is a cosmopolitan city in the greatest sense.

A large Asian population has grown up over the last few years and whole neighborhoods have distinct ethnic characteristics. Koreans, Vietnamese, Chinese and Filipinos represent a high percentage of the population that is reflected most noticeably in the proliferation of ethnic restaurants. This is a true Pacific Rim community. Unfortunately, not all of Los Angeles is equally safe, and although the dangers are often exaggerated by the press, some of the neighborhoods, particularly South Central and the Downtown area at night, are best avoided or visited with care.

Tour 1

Drive the freeways of this great city to visit the most interesting sites, from the glamour of Hollywood to the splendor of the Queen Mary at Long Beach. The freeways are as much part of Los Angeles as the sites. Without them the place would come to a standstill; at rush hour it often does come to a standstill, even with them! Locals spend a good percentage of their lives on these urban arteries so to get a feel for the real Los Angeles, join them on their home ground and include several of the most interesting attractions for good measure. Visit the city's best beaches along the Pacific, from Hermosa to Santa Monica, and on the way stop at some of its great museums, art galleries and shops.

Tour 2

To experience the real LA, walk along the boardwalk at Venice Beach. The street life, from roller bladers and body builders to jugglers and acrobats, provides a continuous theatre. This is the one beach that should be on everyone's itinerary. It is a microcosm of everything visitors to Los Angeles would expect. Bikini-clad beauties, muscle-bound hunks and every weird and wonderful form of humanity

Left: Mann's Chinese Theater, where the stars leave their marks

A portrait of America's past at the Gene Autry Western Heritage Museum, Griffith Park

in between. On top of all this there is sand, sun and the sea – although these seem to take second place to the more exotic activities on land. At the southern end of the beach is an area of graceful canals modelled on Venice, Italy, where you can enjoy a quiet stroll, watch the world go by, or feed the ducks.

Tour 3

The Inland Empire is a dormitory extension of the sprawling mass of Los Angeles. Every morning traffic fills the freeways as commuters head into the business districts, but they are leaving behind some of the most unexpected landscape in Greater Los Angeles. Drive along Route 66 through the orange groves and Victorian mansions of Redlands to the alpine lakes of Big Bear and Arrowhead. During the winter this is an important winter sports area, attracting thousands of Los Angeles ski fanatics at weekends and in the summer the lakes provide all kinds of water activities, from fishing to water-skiing. One of the more attractive aspects of the area comes from its high elevation. Even when smog is descending on downtown Los Angeles, clean, fresh air can be found only a few miles' drive away in these delightful mountains.

Los Angeles

Los Angeles is overwhelming. This tour can take a long day, as a broad introduction to the city's attractions, or several days, visiting sites *en route*. Covering LA County's valleys and beaches, it involves a considerable amount of freeway driving: an important part of LA lifestyle.

1/3 DAYS • 129 MILES • 208KM

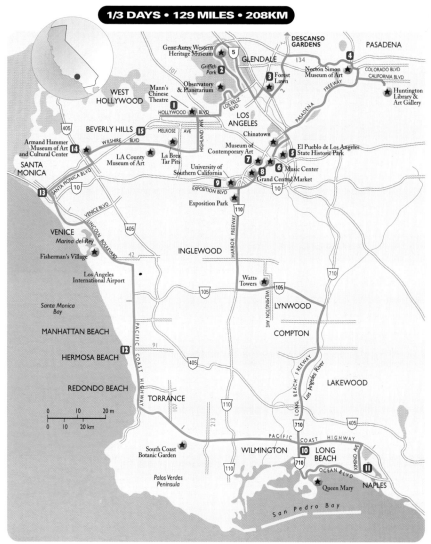

ⓘ *Tourist information Center, Hollywood Chamber of Commerce, 7000–7018 Hollywood Boulevard, Suite 1*

▶ *Start at Hollywood Boulevard.*

❶ Hollywood Boulevard

The glamour of Hollywood soon evaporates when you set foot in this seedy street. A few minutes of dodging panhandlers and empty bottles is usually enough for most people. Apart from the stars whose dubious honour it has been to have their names embedded in the dirty Hollywood Boulevard pavement, the other major attraction is Mann's Chinese Theater, where the hand- and foot-prints of several generations of Hollywood stars have been preserved in cement since it opened in 1927. Over 200 stars have been immortalized here, from Mary Pickford and Douglas Fairbanks to Arnold Schwarzenegger and Whoopi Goldberg.

The name that has drawn many a starry-eyed hopeful – and thousands of tourists

SCENIC ROUTES

Just north of Hollywood, take Mulholland Drive west off 101 north and climb up into the Hollywood Hills and Santa Monica mountains for spectacular views over Hollywood and Los Angeles. The drive is scattered with the palatial homes of many film and television stars.

▶ *Continue east on Hollywood Boulevard to Western Avenue and turn north. Western veers right into Los Feliz and continues up into Griffith Park.*

❷ Griffith Park

This 4,400-acre (1,619-hectare) oasis of greenery sits astride the Hollywood Hills. It provides outdoor recreational facilities for the neighborhood, including an 18-hole golf course, more than 53 miles (85km) of jogging, hiking and bridle trails, and pony rides for youngsters. It even has a polo ground and cricket pitch, and is the home of several major attractions.

Off Western Drive, turn right onto West Observatory Drive for Griffith Observatory. Although it is doubtful whether the telescopes could now penetrate more than a few feet of Los Angeles smog, the observatory is still the major landmark of Griffith Park. On a clear day the views of Hollywood and downtown Los Angeles are spectacular. The 1930s architecture has provided a backdrop for many Hollywood films, most notably for James Dean in Rebel Without a Cause. The Hall of

Sciences has displays on astronomy and meteorology, and the planetarium is probably the only way to view stars at the observatory these days.

Continue down East Observatory Drive to Vermont and back to Los Feliz and turn east, then turn north on Crystal Springs Drive to reach the Gene Autry Western Heritage Museum, on the northeastern edge of the park. This impressive museum, dedicated to the Wild West, opened in 1988. Anyone with even the slightest interest in cowboys will be fascinated by the two floors of exhibits of historic artifacts and Western film memorabilia, such as the jacket worn by Robert Redford in Butch Cassidy and the Sundance Kid or John Wayne's gun belt. Film clips from old Westerns can be seen throughout the museum.

Pasadena's elegant City Hall, a world away from downtown LA

FOR CHILDREN

Travel Town, in Griffith Park, is a transportation museum with just about every form of vehicle possible represented. There are more than 30 steam engines and railroad cars, an 1849 circus wagon and a horse-drawn milk cart. Particularly popular is the narrow-gauge railway that takes children on a circuit of the park.

ⓘ *Visitor Center, 4730 Crystal Springs Drive (24-hours)*

▶ *Take I-5 south to the Glendale East exit. Continue along South Glendale Avenue.*

❽ Forest Lawn

Cemeteries may not be a normal tourist attraction, but Forest Lawn on South Glendale Avenue is said to have in excess of a million visitors a year. There you will be able to find the final resting places of stars such as Clark Gable and Jean Harlow. This perfectly manicured park is also home to larger-than-life-

sized reproductions of some of the world's great masterpieces, including Michelangelo's David and Leonardo da Vinci's Last Supper in stained glass. You can also see the world's largest religious painting on canvas, Jan Stryka's *The Crucifixion*. The 300 acres (121 hectares) of lush lawns are a popular, if macabre picnic site.

▶ *Take the Glendale Freeway north to Hwy 134 East and exit onto Fairoaks Avenue. Head south to Colorado Boulevard.*

❹ Pasadena

This small, wealthy community came to prominence in the 1930s because of its agreeable climate. It is only 20 minutes from downtown Los Angeles by freeway but, sitting at the foot of the San Gabriel Mountains, feels like a different part of the country. The historic town centre known as Old Town has been restored, preserving many of the fine old Victorian façades.

At 411 West Colorado Boulevard is an unusual' modern group of buildings housing the Norton Simon Museum of Art, a

collection that spans 2,500 years, including paintings by Rembrandt, Raphael and Rubens, drawings by Goya, sculpture by Rodin and Henry Moore and works by Cézanne, Van Gogh and Degas. The biggest display is of French art, from Poussin and Wateau through to the Impressionists and on to the Cubists, with important works by most of the major artists of each movement. One whole gallery is devoted to 88 works by Degas.

From Colorado Boulevard take Fairoaks south and turn left onto California Boulevard. At Allen Avenue turn right and go two blocks to the gates of Huntington Library. It would be difficult to find a more impressive collection of paintings and manuscripts anywhere. Of the four million items in the library, many are unique and invaluable. *The Ellesmere Manuscript* from *Chaucer's Canterbury Tales* dates back to 1410. There is a two-volume Gütenberg Bible printed on parchment in 1455, a Shakespeare folio edition and

Audubon's original edition of Birds of America. The collection of American art is impressive, but you will also find Gainsborough's Blue Boy and Thomas Lawrence's Pinkie among the paintings. As if this is not enough, the grounds of the Huntington match the galleries in interest, with several different gardens, each devoted to a different theme. The Japanese Garden is the most popular, but there is also a herb garden, a rose garden, a sub-tropical garden and a Shakespeare garden, where only the plants that existed in the playwright's time are grown. The Huntington deserves far more time than can be allocated on a driving tour, and is well worth a return visit.

BACK TO NATURE

The Descanso Gardens lie at the junction of I-210 and the Glendale freeway just to the north of Pasadena. Once a private estate, these 165-acre (67-hectare) gardens contain 100,000 camellias from throughout the world, and from October to May they present a riot of colour. From May to December the roses are in bloom and April is the peak month for lilacs and outdoor orchids.

▶ *Return to the Pasadena Freeway and go south to Cesar Chavez Parkway; follow it to Olvera Street.*

6 El Pueblo de Los Angeles State Historic Park
Downtown Los Angeles is generally considered to be a cultural desert. First impressions certainly suggest that the centre of the city consists of high-rise offices and little else, but this seemingly sterile area should not be dismissed: it has more to offer than many other parts of the Los Angeles conurbation.

The cutting edge of contemporary sculpture on display at MOCA

RECOMMENDED WALKS

Los Angeles Chinatown, although nowhere near as extensive as the Chinatown in San Francisco, consists of several blocks of intriguing shops filled with wares from exotic foods to oriental antiques. Several good restaurants offer moderately priced meals and serve tank-fresh seafood. The most authentic section is North Spring Street, south of the tourist zone. Walking maps of the area can be obtained from the Chinese Historical Society of Southern California at 970 North Broadway or 982 Gin Ling Way.

At the very heart of Los Angeles there remains a block of buildings dating back to the birth of the city. The Pueblo de Los Angeles State Historic Park preserves the area that was first settled in 1781. The Avila Adobe is the oldest building in the city and was constructed around 1818. Other buildings line either side of Olvera Street, a walkway that is a permanent Mexican marketplace, with craft shops and cafés almost obscuring the historic buildings behind them. It gives a very strong flavour of early Spanish California.

▶ *Go a few blocks west from Olvera Street to reach Grand Avenue and First Street.*

6 Music Center
Three performance spaces combine to form an impressive arts complex that is home to companies such as the Joffrey Ballet and the Los Angeles Philharmonic. The Dorothy Chandler Pavilion provides the concert hall; the Mark Taper Forum is for contemporary theater and the Ahmanson Theater is a 2,000-seat auditorium for traditional drama. The three buildings are linked by landscaped malls with fountains.

▶ *From the Music Center go south on Grand Avenue into what appears to be a canyon of high-rise office buildings.*

7 Museum of Contemporary Art (MOCA)
Nestling at the feet of the office blocks is a striking red sandstone and glass structure designed by Japanese architect, Arata Isozaki. This is the Museum of Contemporary Art, which, surprisingly for one of the most trendy cities on earth, did not open until 1986. It houses a small permanent collection from major modern movements, particularly artists who have

A cruise ship turned floating hotel: the *Queen Mary*, Long Beach

worked in California, such as Mark Rothko and Clyfford Still, but it is the special exhibits that have generated the attention of the art world. They are often so cutting-edge that they beg description.

▶ *Head two blocks east of the MOCA to Broadway and Third Street.*

8 Grand Central Market

A huge covered market – one of the most colorful and vibrant in California – sells all manner of food here, and although there is a strong Central American atmosphere you can find produce from all over the world.

▶ *Leave the downtown area on Figueroa and travel south to Exposition Boulevard.*

9 Exposition Boulevard

This south Los Angeles neighborhood is dubious at best, but on the corner of Figueroa and Exposition is one of the finest – and most expensive – universities in the state. The film school

here is particularly strong and has produced the likes of George Lucas, who is now a major benefactor. The campus is quite beautiful and the classical

---

FOR HISTORY BUFFS

Travel south of Exposition Park along the Harbor Freeway and take Wilmington Avenue north off I-105 to East 107th Street to see a bizarre group of 99-foot (30m)-high towers constructed from concrete-coated steel rods and encrusted with shells, tile, pottery and glass. It took Simon Rodia 33 years to complete the towers, which stand as a monumental example of true folk art. They were completed in 1954 and have since been designated a State Historic Park. The Watts Towers Art Center is next door, sponsoring exhibits and cultural events. This area of Los Angeles is not the safest, and care should be taken when travelling from the freeway to the towers.

---

buildings have frequently been used as Hollywood film locations. Tours of the campus are available.

Directly across the road from the University is the Los Angeles Coliseum, site of both the 1932 and the 1984 Olympics (surrounding areas can be dangerous), and next to the Coliseum, at Exposition Park, are two of the best museums in the city. The Natural History Museum is the biggest of its kind in the West. Apart from the usual dioramas of stuffed animals in their habitats there are very good exhibits of artifacts from Mayan, Aztec and Incan civilizations; bird and insect halls; and an exceptional collection of rocks, minerals and gems. The Cenozoic Hall has an intriguing exhibit chronicling the evolution of the horse through fossil remains.

The adjacent Californian State Museum of Science and Industry extends thorough several buildings, with displays on subjects as diverse as AIDS and earthquakes. This is a hands-on museum and many exhibits are interactive. Visitors can finger-paint on a computer, walk through a space shuttle and take a spin on a General Motors test track. The Aerospace Complex houses a collection of aircraft and spacecraft and also an Imax theatre screening the latest spectacles in 70mm surround vision.

▶ *Take the Harbor Freeway South (I-110) to I-105 East and then the Long Beach Freeway South (I-710) to Long Beach. Exit at the end of the freeway.*

10 Long Beach

Long Beach is so far from central Los Angeles that it is difficult to think of it as part of the same county. It sits on the Pacific coast by one of the world's biggest natural harbors, and the major attraction in town is the

Queen Mary. This majestic ship is now operated as a hotel, but visitors can tour the public areas of the ship.

The big event of the year in Long Beach occurs during the second week of April, when the whole town center is closed off for the Long Beach Grand Prix.

▶ *Follow Ocean Boulevard east to Naples.*

⓫ Naples
South of downtown Long Beach is Naples, built around a network of canals, complete with gondolas and serenading gondoliers.

▶ *Take Ximeno Avenue north to the Pacific Coast Highway and drive west to Redondo Beach.*

⓬ The Beaches
The Pacific Coast Highway (the PCH) hugs the coast, as its name suggests, and passes close to all the beach resorts of southern California. To see the beaches themselves, turn off the PCH and head a couple of blocks west. Just north of Long Beach the older seaside resorts of Redondo, Hermosa and Manhattan Beach have little of the glamour of Venice or Santa Monica, but they are usually hopping with young people surfing, playing volleyball, roller-blading or just hanging out. All three resorts have public piers that allow fishing.

▶ *Continue north on the PCH, which changes to Sepulveda Boulevard, past the Los Angeles Airport to Marina del Rey, the largest small craft harbor in the world. (To reach the visitor center turn west on Mindanao Way to 4701 Admiralty.) Continue north on Hwy 1, which becomes Lincoln Boulevard, and turn west onto Venice Boulevard. Continue to the end; go north on Pacific Avenue, which becomes Main Boulevard, to Santa Monica.*

⓭ Santa Monica
This trendy coastal resort was originally developed to funnel goods by railroad out of the rapidly expanding Los Angeles area: the Santa Monica piers were, in fact, railroad piers. Eventually the beautiful expanse of sandy beaches became the main attraction, and established Santa Monica as the premier resort area of the city. The pier is the most famous landmark in town. It was built in 1909 and is best known for its fully restored, turn-of-the-century carousel featured in The Sting. The 1930s ambience of the pier has resulted in its being a popular location for several other films. The pier is the best place to view the multitude of activities on the splendid beach. The rest of Santa Monica is filled with chic boutiques, art galleries and some of the finest restaurants in Los Angeles.

▶ *Drive east on Santa Monica Boulevard and turn north on Westwood Boulevard to the junction with Wilshire.*

⓮ Armand Hammer Museum of Art and Cultural Center
At 10889 Wilshire is an innovative new museum that houses Hammer's personal collection of art from Western Europe. On

Santa Monica's turn-of-the-century carousel silhouetted at sunset

display is the only Leonardo da Vinci *Codex* in the western hemisphere and more than 10,000 works by Daumier. The museum also presents major travelling exhibitions and prints, drawings, photographs and artists' books from the UCLA Grunwald Center for the Graphic Arts.

▶ *Continue east on Wilshire across Santa Monica Boulevard to Beverly Hills.*

🄱 Beverly Hills

The very name conjures up images of the rich and famous. Santa Monica Boulevard passes through the heart of the area and, for a glimpse of the high life (what can be seen of it, through gated driveways and over high walls), you can take Beverly Drive north and just meander through some of the immaculate streets. Return to Santa Monica Boulevard and exit south onto

Rodeo Drive, arguably the most exclusive shopping street in north America. Drive past the Rolls Royces and Mercedes to see virtually every designer name in the fashion industry displaying their very best wares.

Behind the façade of a modern glass-fronted structure, reflecting the palm trees that line Wilshire Boulevard, is one of the great art collections of North America in the largest museum in the West. The Los Angeles County Museum of Art covers the history of art from pre-Columbian gold ornaments to late 20th-century paintings. It is a museum of international importance, occupying four main buildings around a central courtyard. The recently added Pavilion for Japanese Art houses the Shin'enkan collection of Japanese paintings and *objets d'art*. The Ahmanson Building houses an outstanding collection of Indian and Buddhist art, along with collections from Africa, the South Seas and Egypt and some of the great masterpieces of the Renaissance.

Sitting incongruously next to the clean architecture of the LA County Museum of Art, 6 miles (10km) east of Beverly Hills, on Wilshire, are La Brea Tar Pits, bubbling with black ooze. During the Pleistocene era over 200 different kinds of animal were trapped in this primordial ooze, which perfectly preserved their skeletons. As a result, these are still being discovered by palaeontologists in one of the richest fossil deposits that has ever been found.

Adjacent to the tar pits is the George C. Page Museum, where many of the Ice Discoveries have been put on display, including the impressive skeletons of mastodons, mammoths and ancient horses.

▶ *Take Highland Avenue north off Wilshire to Melrose Avenue, where ultra-trendy boutiques, fashionable restaurants and beautiful people make a walk a fun interlude. Return north on Highland Avenue to Hollywood Boulevard.*

The smooth glass façade of the LA County Museum of Art

Venice
Walk

Venice was developed by tobacco magnate Abbot Kinney in 1904, as part of an attempt to create a cultural renaissance in America. For over 20 years it was a thriving centre of entertainment, built on a series of canals modelled after Venice in Italy. It was Kinney's intention to go even further and have gondolas ferrying people around, but by the end of the 1920s the area had fallen into decline and most of the canals had been filled in. In recent years Venice has undergone a remarkable recovery, reclaiming its unique character. Most of the Los Angeles beach resorts are relaxing; Venice is not. This must be the liveliest spot on the coast and any walk here can never fail to be entertaining.

2 HOURS

[i] *Tourist Information Center, Hollywood Chamber of Commerce, 7018 Hollywood Boulevard*

▶ *Start at Windward Avenue, turning west off Pacific Avenue.*

❶ Windward Avenue

In Kinney's day the avenue was lined with grand hotels. For a glimpse of the old days, visit the Italian-style colonnades near Pacific Avenue – one of the few surviving elements of old Venice. Today's commercial enterprises are a little less grand. The inevitable T-shirt shops rub shoulders with tattoo parlours and body-piercing establishments. Parking is not easy in this area, but there are some private lots at the end of Windward that are relatively inexpensive. Just follow the dubious-looking kids that are touting for business. Do not leave your valuables on display, and you should not have any problems.

North of Windward are several good sidewalk cafés, where the floorshow is free, as all kinds of entertainers perform on Ocean Front Walk. The quintessential Venice café is The Sidewalk Café at 1401 Ocean Front Walk. The food is really an afterthought, as you sit watching the sun set over the Pacific behind some of the best street entertainers in the country.

▶ *Walk south to 18th Avenue to Muscle Beach, past some of the murals which reflect the level of artistic talent here. The Rebirth of Venus, on the old St. Mark's Hotel at Windward and Ocean Front, is a particularly fine parody of Botticelli's masterpiece.*

❷ Muscle Beach

This is perhaps the most well-known spot in Venice, where narcissistic body-builders can be seen almost every day, posing on the outdoor apparatus outside the Muscle Beach Gym. The whole section down to the beach is littered with parallel bars,

A surfer prepares to join the throng of Venice fun-seekers

rings and other instruments of torture, where these sun-bronzed Adonises impress the mortal passers-by, swinging and pulling with the greatest of ease.

▶ *Continue south along Ocean Front Walk.*

❸ Ocean Front Walk

A stroll along the Walk guarantees a thoroughly entertaining display of wild Los Angeles. Try to avoid bikini-clad roller bladers zooming past, and take in the continuous street circus being played out daily. Jugglers, magicians and musicians, fire-eaters and fortune-tellers all try to out-do each other and to direct a few more dollars into the hat. All the way along are more cafés and shops, where you can break your journey if the entertainment

The daily promenade continues along Ocean Front Walk

starts to pall. It would seem that this is the junk food capital of the country, by the number of pizza, hot dog and hamburger vendors lining Ocean Front Walk. Don't come here for the food: the cafés all face west, so this is a perfect afternoon and evening location to stop and nurse a drink for an hour or two and enjoy the Californian sunset.

▶ *Continue to South Venice Boulevard and turn inland across Pacific Avenue to a small bridge on the south side of the road that crosses the Grand Canal. Steps lead down to a footpath that runs along the side of the canal.*

FOR CHILDREN

Venice is really a grown-ups' playground, but young children will be kept amused for hours by the multitude of performers along Ocean Front Avenue. Jugglers, conjurers and acrobats seem to be particularly popular with most children and for a few dollars in tips this is the cheapest entertainment in town.

❹ The Canals

This quiet, residential neighborhood is a total contrast to the frenetic activity of Ocean Front Walk – yet it is only two blocks away. This is the sole surviving area of Abbot Kinney's canals. Originally there were 16 miles (26km) of canals; now only this one section, centering on the Grand Canal, remains. Wander along the banks and cross the bridges that link four smaller canals, running at right angles to the Grand Canal. The houses are an interesting mix of modest cottages and mini palazzos. They are now far too expensive for the Bohemian fringe who used to occupy this area and they have been replaced by latter-day yuppies with artistic inclinations. The attraction of the area is obvious as you stroll along the footpaths. Where else in this mega-metropolis can you find the quiet, European atmosphere provided by this turn-of-the-century dream?

BACK TO NATURE

This urban carnival is hardly the place for an intense wildlife experience, but the peaceful canals at the end of the walk have a resident community of water fowl, and feeding the ducks is a popular activity for locals wanting to avoid the craziness a few blocks away.

▶ Take Dell Avenue to Washington Street and turn west towards the ocean.

❺ Venice Pier

The 1,100-foot (335m)-long Venice Pier anchors the south end of Venice Beach. It provides a great vantage point for a detached look back at the frenetic activity of Ocean Front Walk – and it also allows fishing at no cost. Certain areas in Venice are dangerous and should be avoided.

▶ Return to Windward Avenue along Ocean Front Walk.

There's never any shortage of color or curiosities in Venice

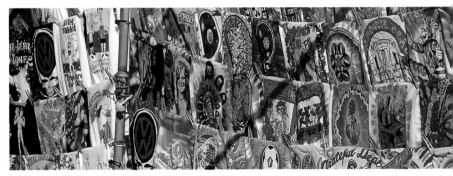

THEME PARKS

Southern California is second only to Orlando, Florida as the world theme park capital. California may no longer be king, but it is the birthplace of the greatest attraction of them all. Built in 1955, Disneyland was the world's first fantasy playground and it led to healthy competition from neighbouring Knott's Berry Farm, which grew from a 1920s roadside stand selling berries and rhubarb into a 150-acre (60-hectare) theme park rivalling its Magic Kingdom neighbor. Hollywood got onto the bandwagon through Universal Studios, where 420 acres (170 hectares) are devoted to giving the public a behind-the-scenes glimpse of the world of television and film production.

Disneyland

The Magic Kingdom is the theme park to end all theme parks. The very name has become synonymous with fantasy. Even the statistics are fantastic: during the summer more than 9,000 employees look after the needs of guests; the car park covers 102 acres (41 hectares) and can accommodate over 15,000 cars. There are over 60 major attractions, 39 restaurants and 61 shops, visited by over 10 million people a year. In fact, its popularity is its weakness. Go during the busy season and you will spend more time in lines and traffic than meeting Mickey Mouse. The best time to visit is between Thanksgiving and Christmas, but the crowds are generally thinner from September to May – excluding holidays. Avoid weekends at any time.

It really needs more than one day to experience Disneyland. If possible two days should be allocated, particularly during the peak season. Careful planning can help maximise your time in the park. The first rule is to arrive early. Plan to be at the gate about half an hour before the official opening time and make sure that you all have a good breakfast before you get there. The less time spent eating, the better. If you need to eat, try to do so outside the normal meal times, when the lines will be shorter. Finally, make a plan of attack. Decide which attractions to see and

make an itinerary to avoid aimless wandering.

Disneyland is divided into eight separate theme areas, spread over 80 acres (32 hectares). Main Street USA is a replica of the archetypal American main street from the 'good old days'. It forms the main entrance to the park and you have to walk down it to reach the other attractions. This is a real street and the buildings house real shops, all very willing to part you from your hard-earned cash. Start your visit at City Hall to pick up maps, entertainment and dining schedules. The Walt Disney Railroad offers an 18-minute circuit, stopping at four of the theme lands. One of four turn-of-the-century trains leaves the Main Street station every five to ten minutes. Adventureland is a world of steaming jungles and exotic sounds. Riverboats navigate a simulated jungle, and the Indiana Jones Adventure, takes travelers to the Temple of the Forbidden Eye.
New Orleans Square is perhaps the prettiest theme area, depicting New Orleans as it was 100 years ago, complete with strolling Dixieland musicians, French shops and sidewalk cafés. It is also home to two of the most popular attractions: Pirates of the Caribbean and the Haunted Mansion.
Critter Country is the backwoods setting for Splash Mountain, which hurls participants down a five-story moun-

tain waterfall. The other main attraction here is the Country Bear Playhouse.
Frontierland is a recreation of the Wild West, where the Big Thunder Mountain Railroad travels through bat-infested caverns, raging waterfalls and other hazards.
Mickey's Toontown is the closest it's possible to get to inhabiting the set of a Disney cartoon. Everything here is off-kilter, from the buildings to the Jolly Trolley that transports visitors on a weaving route through town.
Fantasyland is dominated by Sleeping Beauty Castle. There are more attractions here than any other 'land': 18 in all, and it is usually the most crowded area in the park. The Matterhorn is the highest structure in the park, usually the first visible sign of Disneyland to people arriving on the freeway. Sleds plummet from its peak on a hair-raising roller coaster ride. A five-minute aerial ride, Skyway to Tomorrowland, gives superb views of the park.
Tomorrowland has two rides that push amusement park technology to its limits. The Star Speeder lurches and banks through space, throwing passengers around as it takes wrong turns or blasts through clouds of ice crystals, and Space Mountain is a roller coaster ride in the dark through meteor showers and gaseous nebula.

Knott's Berry Farm

Knott's Berry Farm has a much more down-home feel to it than Disneyland. It is almost twice the area of its Anaheim neighbor, but the lower density of the attractions makes it easy to cover the park in a single day and not feel the same pressure of crowds. As with Disneyland, try not to visit during holiday periods and the peak summer months.
Unlike Disneyland, the Farm, as it is known locally, is based more

The stomach-churning Sky Jump Parachute: from above …

THEME PARKS

... and from below – one of the favorites at Knott's Berry Farm

on reality than fantasy. A refreshing aspect of the park is its commitment to culture and education. Many of the exhibits are of genuine historic value: the Old Trails Hotel in Ghost Town, for example, was relocated board by board from Prescott, Arizona. A strong emphasis is placed on the heritage of the American West, and this is successfully combined with the 168 rides to make the whole experience thoroughly entertaining. There is even a palaeontologist and a naturalist on hand to answer questions relating to a couple of the attractions that are primarily just good, plain fun.

The Farm is divided into eight main areas.

California Marketplace is a large area to the left of the entrance, with over 20 shops and dining establishments that are more interesting than they sound. You can visit this area without having to pay to enter the park.

Ghost Town is an almost totally authentic group of old buildings, relocated here by Walter Knott. Unlike Disneyland, the buildings here really are as old as they look. Even the narrow gauge railroad was brought to the farm in 1952. Knott bought the engines, rolling stock and even the rails of the Denver & Rio Grande, the last operating narrow gauge railroad in America. A genuine 100-year-old stagecoach gives tours of the farm.

The Timber Mountain Log Ride is billed as the oldest log flume ride in America. The hollowed-out log boats float through a saw mill before plunging down a 70-foot (21m) waterfall. The Calico Mine Train recreates the feeling of a real mine train in the old West. The two shows are a Wild West Stunt Show and a classic Western melodrama in the Birdcage Theater.

Wildwater Wilderness is the smallest theme area of the farm, and the Bigfoot Rapids are its sole attraction. A sign at the entrance says 'You WILL get wet' – and they mean it. This feels as authentic as any white water rafting trip.

Roaring 20s features the Kingdom of the Dinosaurs, one of the park's most popular attractions. Two-person cars take you on a journey through prehistoric time, narrowly avoiding the jaws of remarkably life-like animated dinosaurs. For thrills of a more physical nature, try the Boomerang. You are dropped from an 11-story height, to be catapulted through three loops that both flip you upside down and twist at the same time. When you think it's all over, you do the same thing in reverse. Next door is the Sky Jump Parachute, that drops a narrow cage 235 feet (72m) to earth. It is worth taking part for the views of the park from the top, but the ride is far less exciting than it looks.

Fiesta Village is home to Montezooma's Revenge, which catapults riders to 55mph (88kph) in three seconds, loops upside down and then repeats the process. There are a number of considerably less exciting rides in this theme area, much more suitable for younger children.

Camp Snoopy is a great area for children under six. A number of safe but fun rides, together with personal appearances by many of characters from the Peanuts comic strip, an outdoor theatre and a petting zoo, make this a perennial family favorite.

Indian Trails is a cultural exhibit devoted to Native Americans. Many tribes are represented and there are hands-on exhibits and demonstrations by a wide range of Indian craftsmen. There is even Indian food available, such as Navajo fry bread and buffalo stew.

Reflection Lake is the site for The Incredible Waterworks Show. This sound and light show, where hundreds of jets of water are choreographed to music, is particularly entertaining at night, when the extravaganza is enhanced by colored lights.

Universal Studios

The romance of Hollywood never fails to draw crowds, eager to see behind the scenes and maybe spot a star. Universal Studios is a fully operational film studio and tours were offered here even in the days of silent movies. The advent of sound put an end to that, but in 1964 the idea was resurrected, allowing a tour company to drive buses through the lot. In 1965 the Entertainment Center opened, with stunt shows and screen tests, and became the model for Universal Studio tours as they are today.

Studio Tram Tour offers an overview of the studios. Try to do this early in the day, before the crowds arrive. The 45-minute ride is the only way to see the back lots where there are sets used for films as diverse as Spartacus and Back to the Future. Up on a hill is Norman Bates' house from Hitchcock's Psycho. (Part of the fun is matching the set to the movie.) The highlight of the tram tour is Earthquake – The Big One, that provides three frightening minutes a little too close to reality for comfort for many California residents. The tour also provides intimate meetings with both King Kong and Jaws. Studio Center has three major attractions. Backdraft is a remarkable special-effects display from the film, in which you will be engulfed by flames and molten metal. To cool off stop by the ET Adventure and take an airborne bicycle ride through space with the Extra Terrestrial. To see how all this is done, go to the World of Cinemagic, where there are graphic demonstrations of how many of Hollywood's effects are produced. This is a fascinating show for anyone interested in the technical side of film-making.

Entertainment Center is the main area of the studios, and The Streets of the World is the main thoroughfare. Stroll down Baker Street in London or wander through the America of the 1950s while deciding which shows to visit next. This area has the greatest concentration of attractions. The most popular, with inevitable long lines, is Back to the Future. Eight riders in each time machine take a five-minute journey back through centuries at supersonic speed. The special effects and simulated speed make this a very rough ride, definitely not recommended to anyone with a queasy stomach. Two shows that are far less participatory, but a lot of fun, demonstrate the stuntman's art. Miami Vice and The Wild, Wild, Wild West Show both feature dozens of spectacular stunts from two very different genres of film-making. The Animal Actors' Stage introduces the audience to animal stars such as Beethoven the St Bernard, and shows how animals are put through their paces to produce winning performances in films such as Steel Magnolias and Batman Returns. Smaller children will enjoy An American Tail Show, featuring the characters from Fievel Goes West. The characters are remarkably true to their cartoon personas. Next to the theater is a New York dockside set, where children can experience a mouse-sized world.

An intimate moment with Jaws!

The Inland
Empire

The Inland Empire is rarely taken seriously as a visitor destination. Its grandiose name certainly does not reflect the urban sprawl and smog that plagues this commuter outpost of Los Angeles. Compared with most of California, this is certainly a low priority destination. But where else is it possible to drive from the beaches of Los Angeles and, within a couple of hours, be skiing in high mountains in clear air above the smog level? The tour includes several places of considerable interest in the cities of the Inland Empire and also includes the beautiful San Bernardino mountains, which rise up to 11,499 feet (3,505m).

2 DAYS • 267 MILES • 429KM

ITINERARY

LOS ANGELES	► **Redlands** (67m-108km)
REDLANDS	► **Big Bear Lake** (59m-95km)
BIG BEAR LAKE	► **Lake Arrowhead** (27m-43km)
LAKE ARROWHEAD	► **Silverwood Lake** (20m-32km)
SILVERWOOD LAKE	► **Riverside** (35m-56km)
RIVERSIDE	► **Chino** (21m-34km)
CHINO	► **Los Angeles** (38m-61km)

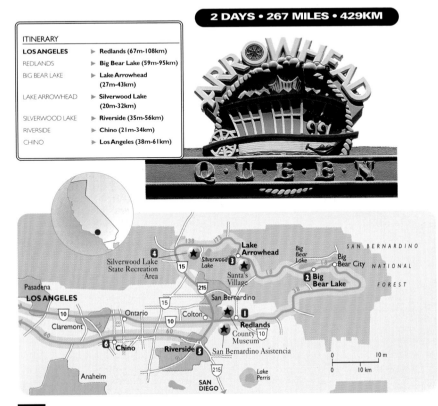

▶ *Leave Los Angeles on I-10. Just before Redlands, the San Bernardino County Museum at 2024 Orange Tree Lane gives a good overview of how the Inland Empire has grown from cattle ranching and citrus farming days to the present dormitory developments. Directly across the freeway to the south, at 26930 Barton Road, is a branch of the Mission San Gabriel called San Bernardino Asistencia, which re-creates early 19th-century life in its two-room museum. Continue into Redlands.*

❶ Redlands

The town was once the center of California's citrus industry and a few orange groves can still be seen around the town. The wealthy families that were attracted here by the warm climate and strong agricultural economy built many elaborate Victorian mansions and, fortu-

nately, many of them have been carefully restored. It is worth a detour to visit Kimberley Crest House and Gardens at 1325 Prospect Street. The French château-style mansion was built in 1897 with formal Mediterranean gardens extending down the hillside below the house. Several other fine examples of Victorian architecture can be seen in the town, but most are not open to the public.

▶ *Leave Redlands driving north on Orange Street and turn right onto **Hwy 38**. Follow the winding mountain road for several miles until it joins **Hwy 18** just before the town of Big Bear Lake. Turn left and follow **Hwy 18** into town.*

❷ Big Bear Lake

Big Bear is a winter ski resort, 7,000 feet (2,133m) up in the San Bernardino mountains. The lake extends for 7 miles (11km) and when the snow has melted it is a playground for all kinds of water sports. The air up here is clean and crisp and the addition

Kimberley Crest House, a 19th-century mansion at Redlands

SCENIC ROUTES

The Rim of the World Highway past Big Bear Lake and Lake Arrowhead is a 40-mile (64km) scenic drive that wanders through the 5,000- to 7,000-foot (1,524 to 2,133m) crest of the San Bernardino mountains, passing several quaint communities and resort areas. High forests often prevent the sweeping views that may be expected from up here, but the surprise of a view snatched from an unexpected clearing is part of the charm of the drive.

of rugged mountain scenery makes this a great escape from the Los Angeles metropolis. The town of Big Bear Lake has the feel of the European alps, with wooden chalets tucked away in the forests, surrounded by piles of newly chopped logs for the winter. Every October a

Bavarian-style festival adds to this ambience.

▶ *Continue west on Hwy 18, the Rim of the World Scenic Byway, to Hwy 173 and turn north to Lake Arrowhead.*

❸ Lake Arrowhead

This is the most picturesque area in the region. The town is almost too perfect, with exclusive resorts, fine shopping and good restaurants. Lake Arrowhead was man-made and developed as a hide-away for the rich and famous of Los Angeles, and their expensive homes can be seen around the lake shores. A 60-passenger paddlewheeler, the *Arrowhead Queen*, gives visitors a more intimate view of the lake.

FOR CHILDREN

On Hwy 18, between Lake Arrowhead and Running Springs, is Santa's Village. This North Pole children's theme park has pony rides, a puppet theatre, a petting zoo and other attractions. In spite of its winter theme, the park is open for seven days a week during the summer.

▶ *Continue north on Hwy 173 to Silverwood Lake.*

❹ Silverwood Lake State Recreation Area

This 976-acre (395-hectare) man-made lake has been completely undeveloped apart from a small marina and the recreation area. There are 13 miles (21km) of trails around the lake and good fishing and swimming.

▶ *Continue west on Hwy 138 to I-15 south. Turn off I-15 onto I-215 into San Bernardino. There is little of interest here except for the Route 66 Museum, which pays homage to this famous transcontinental highway that passed through the town. Continue south on I-215 to Riverside.*

Left: Big Bear Lake, a fine ski resort

BACK TO NATURE

The unspoiled shores and trails of Silverwood Lake are the best place to see over 130 species of birds and maybe spot bobcats, coyotes and ring-tailed cats that range in the forests. This is one of the less visited areas of the San Bernardino Mountains and is the closest you can get to a feeling of true wilderness.

---

❺ Riverside

The most interesting attraction here is a hotel. The Mission Inn dates back to the 1880s and is, in fact, a Spanish-style palace that sprawls across a whole city block and has entertained eight U.S. presidents. Riverside gave birth to the navel orange in the 1870s and on the south side of town is the California Citrus State Historic Park, which comprises several acres of orange groves with exhibits on their history and cultivation. The Riverside Municipal Museum at 3720 Orange Street also traces the history of citrus-growing in the region and is housed in a 1912 post office building. The unusual Museum of Photography at 3824 Main Street has excellent temporary exhibits.

▶ *From Riverside take Hwy 60 west to Chino.*

❻ Chino

This town is devoted to flight. At the Planes of Fame Air Museum there is a collection of aircraft from 1896 through to World War II, many flyable, and exhibits of military aviation memorabilia.

▶ *Return to Hwy 60 west and return into Los Angeles or take Hwy 71 north to I-10 west, which is considerably faster.*

An appropriate entrance to the Citrus State Historic Park

THE SOUTHWEST

San Diego is only 120 miles (193km) south of Los Angeles and is the second biggest city in the state, but it manages to retain a small town atmosphere. This is the birthplace of California. Portuguese explorer Juan Rodriguez Cabrillo claimed the area for Spain as early as 1542, but it was Father Junipero Serra who established the first permanent settlement when he built Mission San Diego de Alcala here in 1769. It became the first of a 21-mission chain that would extend as far as Sonoma north of San Francisco.

The early explorers were probably attracted by the mild climate and the enormous natural harbor. With an average temperature of 70° F (21° C). and average annual rainfall less than 10 inches (250mm), the climate is almost perfect and it is a wonderland for sportsmen. Throughout the region there is year-round golf, tennis, surfing, diving, fishing and sailing. The natural deep sea harbor is home to the 11th Naval District of the U.S., which is one of the largest fleets of fighting ships in the world.

It was not until 1848 that the city came under United States rule and there is still a strong Spanish influence, with the Mexican border and Tijuana only minutes away. Much of San Diego today has a distinctly Mexican feel and Spanish is widely spoken around town. It's a 40-minute ride on the San Diego Trolley to San Ysidro, within walking distance of the border to Tijuana (don't forget to take your passport).

Perhaps the most glorious feature of the region is the 70-mile (112km)-long strip of golden beaches, enticing coves and dramatic cliffs. Each of the more than 30 beaches has its own personality and devotees, whether you are looking for surfing, volleyball, scuba-diving or just getting a tan.

San Diego is much more than just a city. It is a vast county that includes the biggest state park in the country outside Alaska. Anza-Borrego, 90 miles (145km) northeast of San Diego, is one of the great desert areas of the state: during the spring, thousands of visitors descend on the park to witness the beauty of the desert in bloom. A range of mountains separates Anza-Borrego from the coast.

Mount Palomar Observatory

Up in the clean, clear air of these coastal mountains you can visit Mount Palomar, one of the world's great astronomical telescopes. The northern part of the county, around Temecula, has the most southerly concentration of vineyards of California's booming wine industry.

Tour 4

This tour offers a wide range of southern California's attractions, from the fascinating wildlife, protected in reserves along the stunning coast to the historic mission district and old wooden homes of San Juan Capistrano, and taking in the very modern amusements of the beach resorts. These include Newport Beach, with its fishing boats and glorious sands, the shoppers' paradise of Fashion Island and the sublime Laguna Beach, where watersports, art galleries and hotels manage not to disturb the local dolphins and whales.

Tour 5

One of the beauties of the City of San Diego is that most of the interesting attractions are in a relatively compact area, and the driving time between them is minimal. The tour starts in Balboa Park, where there is one of the most interesting concentrations of museums in the nation. Also here is the world famous San Diego Zoo, the finest of its kind. The route continues to the cradle of San Diego, the Mission de San Diego Alcala and on to experience the early Mexican days at Old Town San Diego. Next is the delightful, chic coastal town of La Jolla, returning past Sea World and the Cabrillo National Monument. A short ride back into town past the Maritime Museum and Seaport Village ends in the Gaslamp Quarter and the adjoining Horton Plaza complex, where it is easy to find a wide choice of places to unwind after a day's sightseeing.

Tour 6

Head inland from San Diego towards Anza-Borrego and take the Sunrise National Scenic Highway through Mount Laguna and Cuyamaca State Park to the old gold town of Julian, now famous for its apple pies. It is only 60 miles (96km) inland from San Diego, but it is like stepping back in time. Travel north past Mission Santa Ysabel to Palomar Mountain State Park and climb steep, winding roads to the world-famous Mount Palomar Observatory. Continue to the Mission San Antonio de Pala and Mission San Luis Rey de Francia before returning to the coast and the quaint town of Carlsbad. A short drive inland takes you to the San Diego Wild Animal Park, near Escondido, which is the last stop before returning south to San Diego.

The Lily Pond, Balboa Park, San Diego

Orange County
Beaches

This tour is an introduction to authentic southern California beach life, taking in bird sanctuaries and wildlife reserves, the hottest surfing spots, harbor cruises, theatrical entertainment and art festivals – with the added option of simply spending a day at the beach obtaining that highly prized Californian tan. For those who love the ocean, this is an ideal trip. **3 DAYS • 75 MILES • 120KM**

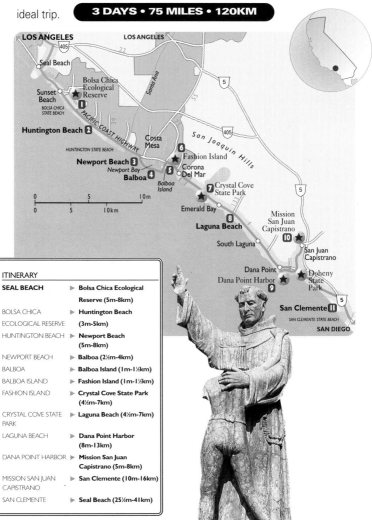

ITINERARY

SEAL BEACH	▶ **Bolsa Chica Ecological Reserve (5m-8km)**
BOLSA CHICA ECOLOGICAL RESERVE	▶ **Huntington Beach (3m-5km)**
HUNTINGTON BEACH	▶ **Newport Beach (5m-8km)**
NEWPORT BEACH	▶ **Balboa (2½m-4km)**
BALBOA	▶ **Balboa Island (1m-1½km)**
BALBOA ISLAND	▶ **Fashion Island (1m-1½km)**
FASHION ISLAND	▶ **Crystal Cove State Park (4½m-7km)**
CRYSTAL COVE STATE PARK	▶ **Laguna Beach (4½m-7km)**
LAGUNA BEACH	▶ **Dana Point Harbor (8m-13km)**
DANA POINT HARBOR	▶ **Mission San Juan Capistrano (5m-8km)**
MISSION SAN JUAN CAPISTRANO	▶ **San Clemente (10m-16km)**
SAN CLEMENTE	▶ **Seal Beach (25½m-41km)**

i *Tourist information Center, Hollywood Chamber of Commerce, 7018 Hollywood Boulevard*

▶ *Take I-405 south from Los Angeles and exit at Seal Beach Boulevard. Turn right and proceed west to the ocean; at Pacific Coast Highway, turn left and go south to Huntington Beach. The Bolsa Chica Ecological Reserve is on the approach to Huntington Beach along Pacific Coast Highway.*

❶ Bolsa Chica Ecological Reserve

This is a 'must-see' for anyone interested in rare birds, some of which are endangered. Its 300 acres (121 hectares) include a 1.5-mile (2km) loop trail that crosses inland over Inner Bolsa Bay on a boardwalk, then continues to the Bolsa Chica Cliffs, with good views of wildlife in Outer Bolsa Bay. Bird species that can be spotted include

Left: a statue at San Juan Capistrano recalls Father Junipero Serra's work

heron and egrets, the endangered Californian least terns (as well as other varieties of terns), the highly endangered Belding's savannah sparrows, which nest only in pickleweed, indigenous to this reserve, the light-footed clapper rail and black-bellied plovers. If that isn't enough, there is also an abundance of sea life, such as stingrays, smooth-hound sharks and schools of anchovies and topsmelt – all plainly visible. Parking and entrance are free and tours are self-guided.

▶ *Continue 3 miles (5km) further south along Pacific Coast Highway to Main Street.*

❷ Huntington Beach

A stroll down California's largest concrete municipal pier, rebuilt in 1992, gives a first-hand look at serious surfing. On any given day, hundreds of surfers can be seen in the waters here, stalking the perfect wave. The 8.5 miles (14km) of uninterrupted beach that comprise the Huntington Beach area include a paved path

The ultimate rooms with a view, overlooking Balboa's sweeping bay

through the sand for bicycling, roller-blading, jogging or just beautiful sunset strolls. Main Street begins opposite the pier, heading inland, and has taken on a refurbished look, with new buildings housing outdoor cafés, shops and movie theaters.

Further inland along Main Street, at 411 Olive Street, is the International Surfing Museum, where one wall is entirely devoted to surf music, and homage is paid to such artists as Dick Dale and The Beach Boys. Another exhibit describes the early days of the surfing craze, in Hawaii.

i *Visitors Bureau, 2nd Floor Suite 2A, 101 Main Street, Huntington Beach, California 92648*

▶ *Take Pacific Coast Highway south to Newport Beach exit, on Newport Boulevard – Balboa Peninsula/Lido Bay Bridge. Turn right and follow signs to Newport Pier.*

3 Newport Beach

Newport Pier deserves a quick visit for its tradition of "Newport Dorymen": for 75 years these fishermen have risen with the sun to fish the waters off Newport Beach, catching rock cod, bonito, sea bass, halibut and calico bass. A walk down the pier gives a good view of the Balboa Peninsula, to the south, and the white-sand beaches of Newport. It's worth trying the well-known Crab Cooker restaurant, across the street from the pier, for a fresh fish lunch or dinner.

▶ *Continue south along Newport Boulevard, which becomes Balboa Boulevard, and on into Balboa.*

4 Balboa

Since 1936 Balboa has been a Newport Beach institution. The Balboa Fun Zone provides hours of entertainment, with an amusement park for children complete with merry-go-round, arcades, bumper cars and a ferris wheel, which has a panoramic view of Newport Bay. The Pavilion Queen, moored at the Balboa Pavilion, is a Mississippi-style cruise boat that crosses the harbor every hour on the hour during summer. Also moored at the pavilion is The Catalina Flyer, a 500-passenger catamaran which ferries people over to Catalina Island, 26 miles (42km) off the Newport Coast. Here snorkeling, diving, golf, camping and tours around the island are all available, and buffalo, wild boar, deer and bald eagles roam freely. Avalon, Catalina's town, has great restaurants, nightlife, shopping and lodging.

▶ *Southern California's only ferry, which takes only three cars at a time, travels from Balboa to Balboa Island; it is reached by heading up Agate Street to Park Avenue and turning right to Marine Avenue.*

5 Balboa Island

This small haven in the middle of Newport Bay provides excellent views of the bay and the area's opulent waterfront homes. Marine Avenue is lined with beachwear shops and a wide variety of eateries, including the famous Balboa Bar and Banana Bar.

▶ *Take Marine Avenue across the Balboa Island Bridge and up the hill to Pacific Coast Highway; turn right, continue to Newport Center Drive and turn left to Fashion Island.*

6 Fashion Island

Shopping enthusiasts can have a field day exploring Fashion Island's 200-plus stores and restaurants. Open-air concerts are given in the main courtyard of Farmers' Market every Wednesday in July and August from 6 to 8pm, featuring artists from all over the world. The famous Hard Rock Café is a landmark, with its 30-foot (9m) neon guitar.

▶ *Take Newport Center Drive back to Pacific Coast Highway and turn left to Crystal Cove State Park, approximately 4 miles (6km) along on the right.*

7 Crystal Cove State Park

Set on rugged cliffs some 200 feet (61m) above the ocean, this park has trails leading down to the deserted beaches, where white egrets, sparrow-tail hawks, rabbits, road-runners and occasional deer and bobcat can be seen. The park service maintains plantlife which is indigenous to this area and is well equipped with information boards. Try the only take-out food establishment in this area, the Orange Inn, for a great sandwich and a dateshake.

▶ *Leave the park on Pacific Coast Highway and turn right to Laguna Beach.*

8 Laguna Beach

Often referred to as the Pacific Riviera of Southern California, this resplendent seaside resort boasts rocky shoreline coves, small bays, pristine waters where

dolphins, sealions and whales swim, and protected tidepools – as well as first-rate hotels and opportunities for swimming, kayaking, diving and hiking in the surrounding wilderness parks. Laguna Beach is also an artists' colony, with hundreds of galleries to choose from and art festivals during the summer months, the two largest being the Sawdust Festival and the Festival of the Arts. During the annual Pageant of the Masters, famous works of art are recreated on stage using people in costumes and make-up.

As a contrast to all this activity, Laguna is blessed with immaculate beaches and coves. As many as 15 small bays make up an 8-mile (13km) stretch of the coastline – all clean and well-maintained, many containing fascinating tidepools, and some providing views of schools of dolphins swimming offshore.

ℹ *Visitors Bureau, 252 Broadway, Laguna Beach, California 92651*

▶ *Drive south on Pacific Coast Highway to Dana Point. Turn right on Golden Lantern and down to the Dana Point Harbor.*

9 Dana Point Harbor

Hundreds of pleasure craft are moored here, and a walk along the waterfront promenade passes a floating community where people live aboard their boats, before reaching the fishing fleets. A day of fishing off this stretch of

Turn left at Pacific Coast Highway. Take the right-hand road, hugging the coast, and proceed to San Clemente. Turn right on to Avenue Del Mar.

11 San Clemente

This seems like a very relaxed Spanish town, in its architecture and in its atmosphere. At San Clemente Pier, biking and walking paths lead along the beachfront and two fine seafood restaurants are great vantage points for views of the magnificent California sunset behind

Above: the deserted sands of Crystal Cove State Park
Right: Mission San Juan Capistrano

shoreline brings in bonito, sea bass, rock cod and an occasional yellow fin tuna, if the waters are warm. Boats also set out from late December to March to follow the whales during their migration, and an annual whale festival takes place in February and March.

Next to Dana Point Harbor is Doheny State Park, a center for camping and water sports, with a beautiful stretch of beach and a biking path.

▶ *Continue to Dana Point Harbor Drive, turn right and follow this road to a traffic signal. Cross the signal heading east; this road becomes Del Obispo. Proceed east (inland) to San Juan Capistrano and turn left to Mission San Juan Capistrano.*

10 Mission San Juan Capistrano

This was the seventh in the chain of 21 missions, founded in 1776 by Franciscans under the leadership of Father Junipero Serra. Its 10-acre (4-hectare) site has furnished rooms, restored to look as they did some 220 years ago, and a museum with artifacts from Spanish, Mexican and Native American periods. The mission is famous for St Joseph's Day, which marks the return of the swallows to nest. Self-guided tours are available.

Also within this area, on Los Rios Street between Del Obispo and Mission Street, is San Juan Capistrano Historic District, with Victorian homes, adobe structures and wooden cottages. The Amtrak rail station is actually a number of vintage trains connected to one another, and is the oldest depot in Southern California.

▶ *Return to Del Obispo and head west, back to the ocean.*

Catalina Island. Just south of this area is San Clemente State Beach and Park, where recreational vehicles and camping are permitted. Miles of undeveloped beaches can be enjoyed here, along with a magnificent rocky coastline.

▶ *Return to Pacific Coast Highway, heading north to Avenue Califia. Turn right to 5 Freeway. Signs indicate 5 Freeway north to Los Angeles.*

San  Diego

San Diego is one of America's most pleasant cities. The climate is idyllic, never too warm and never too cold, and although the city now has sprawling residential areas, the sites that are of most interest to visitors are in a fairly compact and accessible area. The problems of urban blight and inner-city social conflicts that affect other US cities are mercifully absent. San Diego can offer everything from world-class sailing to museums to the world's biggest zoo. All the city's attractions can be sampled in a day, but most deserve much more time than this itinerary will allow.

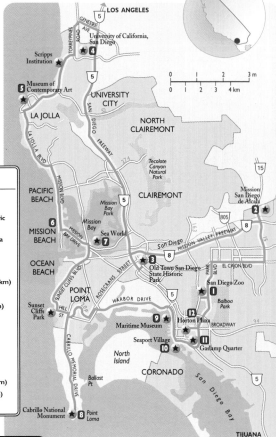

ITINERARY

BALBOA PARK	▶	**Mission San Diego de Alcala (8m–13km)**
MISSION SAN DIEGO DE ALCALA	▶	**Old Town State Historic Park (10m–16km)**
OLD TOWN STATE HISTORIC PARK	▶	**University of California (13m–21km)**
UNIVERSITY OF CALIFORNIA	▶	**La Jolla (6m–10km)**
LA JOLLA	▶	**Mission Beach (6m–10km)**
MISSION BEACH	▶	**Sea World (3m–5km)**
SEA WORLD	▶	**Point Loma (8m–13km)**
POINT LOMA	▶	**Maritime Museum (10m–16km)**
MARITIME MUSEUM	▶	**Seaport Village (½m–1km)**
SEAPORT VILLAGE	▶	**Gaslamp Quarter (1½m–2km)**
GASLAMP QUARTER	▶	**Horton Plaza (½m–1km)**
HORTON PLAZA	▶	**Balboa Park (2m–3km)**

1 DAY • 68½ MILES • 111KM

_i_ *San Diego International Visitor Information Center, 11 Horton Plaza, CA 92101*

▶ *Start in the parking lot at the San Diego Zoo in Balboa Park, located off Park Boulevard.*

❶ Balboa Park

Balboa Park is a destination in itself. It was set aside as public parkland in 1868, and many of the buildings were added during the 1915 Panama-California International Exposition and the 1935 California-Pacific International Exposition. The only way to see the park is to walk. From the zoo parking lot, walk south past the Spanish Village to El Prado, the main thoroughfare, where most of the museums are located. Time will not allow visits to the museums, but their architecture alone is worth the walk. Plan a separate day just for museum visits.

The San Diego Zoo is far too important and extensive to see on this driving tour. As perhaps the world's greatest zoo it should not, however, be disregarded. The zoo covers 128 acres (52 hectares) and houses over 3,900 animals from over 800 species. A major effort has been made to concentrate on endangered species and to develop breeding programs for these animals. The zoo is built across a steep canyon and for those unable to cope with the strenuous walking there is a 3-mile (5km) bus tour. Alternatively, an aerial tram called the Skyfari gives visitors a bird's-eye view above the tree-tops. Even if there isn't time to enter, the sounds of the zoo can clearly be heard as you walk down into Balboa Park.

Immediately on the left, after leaving the parking lot, you will see a collection of low, Spanish-style buildings. This is the Spanish Village, an arts and crafts complex housing the studios of 42 wood-carvers, potters, painters, sculptors, photographers, and silversmiths.

Continue to Balboa Plaza, which is at the end of El Prado. The Inez Grant Memorial Rose Garden will be behind you as you look down El Prado to the landmark California Tower. You can reach the garden across the footbridge, over Park Boulevard. Next to this all-American Rose Selection Display Garden is the Desert Garden, with a wide variety of succulents indigenous to the desert.

Walk down El Prado towards the California Tower, to the Lily Pond. During World War II this was used as a swimming pool for patients at the US naval hospital. The steel frame structure behind the pond is the Botanical Building, containing

The popular Cabrillo National Monument at Point Loma

over 500 species of tropical and sub-tropical plants. The framework for the building, which looks like a huge overturned basket, was made for a station belonging to the Santa Fe Railroad, but was purchased for the 1915 Exposition.

Continue down El Prado. Past the colonnades of the San Diego Art Institute, on the left, there is an enclosed courtyard called the Alcazar Garden. This was designed for the 1915 Panama-California Exposition and was modelled on the gardens of Alcazar in Seville, Spain, which were destroyed during the Spanish Civil War. To the left, after leaving the garden, the California Tower stands 200 feet (61m) above El Prado: it was built as the centerpiece for the 1915 Exposition. At its foot is the Museum of Man, with a fascinating collection of artifacts from the Pueblo Indians of the southwest and the ancient Aztec and Mayan settlements of Latin America.

Return up El Prado and turn right. On the left is the Japanese Friendship Garden, a traditional

Serenading snackers at the Bazaar del Mundo, Old Town San Diego

Japanese garden which has been adapted to the climate and topography of San Diego. It provides a perfect place for quiet contemplation. Next to the garden is the Spreckels Organ Pavilion, but unless you are in the park on a Sunday at 2pm, the world's biggest organ will be protected behind a 12-ton/tonne metal curtain.

The Aerospace Historical Center is at the end of the Pan-American Plaza, just past the Japanese Friendship Plaza. The whole history of aviation is covered in this circular building, from the Montgolfier brothers' hot-air balloon to the latest spacecraft. Every conceivable aspect of aviation is covered, including an extensive exhibit on the role of women in the field. Next door is the San Diego Automotive Museum, with a display of over 80 vehicles, including horseless carriages, exotic cars and future prototypes.

▶ *Return to the parking lot and drive north on Park Boulevard. Turn right on El Cajon Boulevard and drive to I-15 north. Exit on San Diego Mission Road.*

❷ Mission San Diego de Alcala

Considering the importance of Father Junipero Serra's first mission in California, Mission San Diego de Alcala is in a curiously suburban setting. The mission is virtually the only site of interest in the valley and is refreshingly uncommercial. The original mission was built in 1769, but it was moved a few years later because of disputes between the Spanish and the Indians. The second mission was burned down by the Indians in 1775, and the present mission was constructed in 1777. It was finally destroyed by an earthquake in 1803 and all that remains now is a church with a bell tower and a small museum set in beautiful gardens.

▶ *Return to I-15 south, turn west on I-8, continue along Mission Valley Freeway (I-8), and turn south on I-5. Turn off on Old Town Avenue, then turn left and left again on San Diego Avenue.*

❸ Old Town San Diego State Historic Park

Old Town is where San Diego began, as the first European settlement in California. The State of California bought six blocks of historic buildings in the 1960s to preserve the atmosphere of Mexican California with restored original buildings and costumed interpreters. The core of the park is a Mexican plaza, around which many of the old buildings are set. Although there are 16 historic structures, 10 of which house museums, the park feels much larger, mainly due to the presence of 33 craft and speciality shops and seven restaurants.

The commercial element of the town tends to be concentrated on the Bazaar del Mundo, a loud and garish shopping and restaurant complex immediately off the main plaza, that is supposedly an imitation Mexican street market. Fortunately, most of the visitors tend to congregate here, leaving the rest of the park

relatively quiet, and preserving the historic atmosphere of the area. The most interesting buildings are the old adobe structures, most of which surround the Plaza. Casa de Estudillo, at the Mason Street end of the Plaza, is the largest: this housed the 12-child family of the commander of the presidio.

▶ *Return to I-5 north and exit west on Genesee Avenue and south on Torrey Pines Road North.*

4 University of California at San Diego (UCSD)

The impressive campus of the state university stretches along Torrey Pines Road, with an eclectic collection of commissioned, site-specific modern sculpture on display in the public areas. Brochures are available at the UCSD information booths at the Torrey Pines Road North entrance. Most people, however, come here to visit the aquarium administered by the Scripps Institution. Opposite the Scripps Institution of Oceanography, turn up Expedition Way to a hillside location overlooking La Jolla

Shores Beach. Here you will find the new Stephen Birch Aquarium and Museum, featuring marine life from both the cold northern waters and the tropical oceans of the Pacific. There are also interactive exhibits and changing displays that explore the latest developments in oceanography.

▶ *Return south along Torrey Pines Road to downtown La Jolla.*

5 La Jolla

Both Prospect and Girard streets reflect the trendy, upscale

WALKING TOUR

Old Town San Diego State Historic Park gives an intimate view of early California and over the last 200 years Spanish, Mexican and American flags have flown above the town. The only way to see the park is on foot; self-guided walking tour maps are available from the Visitor Center at the Robinson-Rose House at the northwest end of the Plaza.

Beautiful blue sea and top-class facilities come together at La Jolla

atmosphere of the expensive residential enclave of San Diego. According to Indian legend, Jolla means 'cave' or 'hole'; not surprisingly, residents tend to prefer the Spanish translation of 'jewel'. They also think of their ritzy neighborhood of San Diego as a separate entity, and call it 'The Village'. Even the post office stamps bear the name La Jolla, although it is officially part of the city of San Diego. The area is not unlike an exclusive Mediterranean resort, with the same mix of expensive houses, exquisite boutiques, gourmet restaurants and grand hotels. The cliff-lined coast adds to this overall impression, and it is worth taking the time for a short walk along the coast in front of the grand Valencia Hotel.

At 700 Prospect Street is an interesting building designed by the renowned San Diego architect Irving Gill. It houses the La Jolla Museum of Contemporary Art specialising in the best modern art produced in California.

▶ *Drive south past the boutiques and art galleries of Girard Avenue and turn right onto Pearl Street. Follow Pearl to La Jolla Boulevard and turn left. Follow the coast to Mission Beach.*

6 Mission Beach

This is the perfect example of a southern California beach. It is usually humming with activity, from surfers to volley ball-players to roller-bladers, with far more flesh on view than clothing. The boardwalk is worthy of a short stroll, if only to enjoy a glimpse of the beach life. At its southern end is an amusement park complete with a roller coaster and an antique carousel.

Inland from the beach is Mission Bay, 4,600 acres (1,861 hectares) of water that form the world's largest municipal aquatic park. There are 27 miles (43km) of beaches, boat-launching ramps, picnic areas and playgrounds here, making up one of San Diego's major tourist attractions.

Riding along on the crest of a wave at Sea World

▶ *From Mission Bay take Mission Bay Drive to Sea World.*

7 Sea World

This is the marine equivalent of Disneyland – a fantasy land inhabited by all forms of marine life. Featured in this 135-acre (55-hectare) park are six major shows, alternately staged throughout the day at various stadiums and indoor auditoriums. Between shows, you can touch or view live animals at 20 educational exhibits and four aquariums. Sea World really deserves a whole day to do it justice; on this familiarisation tour it may be better just to note the location and return at leisure.

▶ *Drive south on Midway Drive and turn off on Sunset Cliffs Boulevard. Turn left onto Hill Street and right onto Catalina Boulevard, which becomes Cabrillo Memorial Drive.*

8 Point Loma

The drive from Mission Bay passes the dramatic sandstone bluffs of Sunset Cliffs Park. As well as a spectacular setting, it enjoys big waves, making it very popular with expert surfers. The drive continues down the peninsula that separates the San Diego Bay from the Pacific Ocean. On the way, the road passes through Fort Rosecrans National Cemetery, part of a U.S. Navy installation, where thousands of pristine white gravestones mark the resting place of San Diego's fallen troops. At the end of the road, at the very tip of Point Loma, is the Cabrillo National Monument, one of the smallest but most historic and most visited monuments in the country (it has more visitors than the Statue of Liberty). Cabrillo's statue, which was a gift from his Portugal homeland, faces Ballast Point, where the great navigator landed in 1542,

BACK TO NATURE

Point Loma is an ideal place to watch migrating birds between mid-December and mid-February each year. There is a glassed-in observatory at the Cabrillo National Monument, for protection against winter weather. Close by is one of the best tidepool areas in California. A nature trail leads down to the pools and passes an area with a unique plant community. There are daily ranger-led tours, and information can be obtained from the Visitor Center.

SCENIC ROUTES

The drive to Point Loma provides spectacular views of the San Diego skyline. Plan the drive for late afternoon, when the sun lights up the city.

becoming the first European to reach California. A nearby visitor center tells the story of Cabrillo's discovery of San Diego Bay and its subsequent history. On a high bluff overlooking the monument is the Point Loma lighthouse, that was used to guide ships into the Bay between 1855 and 1891. It is open to visitors.

The most impressive aspect of Point Loma is the spectacular view – it is worth the drive for this alone. On a clear day you can see from the mountains of Mexico all the way up to La Jolla, and from San Diego and its Bay all the way out to the Pacific Ocean.

▶ *Return along Cabrillo Memorial Drive and turn right on Canon Street and left on Rosecrans Street. Turn right again onto Harbor Drive.*

A golden city: San Diego's skyline basks in the California sun

Follow Harbor Drive until it reaches the downtown area and look for the Maritime Museum on the right, opposite Ash Street.

9 Maritime Museum

The drive towards town is particularly good at the end of the day, when the high-rise buildings are bathed in warm, late-afternoon sunlight. Photographers may want to stop by the harbor to capture this classic view of the city. San Diego is very definitely a seafaring town and, apart from the strong U.S. Navy presence, sailors from all over the world congregate in this massive harbor. Sailing is one of the most popular sports in town and it was the San Diego yacht Stars and Stripes that brought home the Americas Cup from Australia in 1987. Two nautical museums sit next to each other by the harbour. The Maritime Museum is the grand name given to three ships that are moored on the Embarcadero. The highlight of the group is the Star of India, a fully equipped three-mast merchant ship, built in 1863: the oldest iron-hulled ship still afloat in America. Also here is the San Francisco Bay ferry boat, Berkeley, which played a major role in evacuating victims of the 1906 earthquake, and a 1904 steam yacht, the Medea, which still makes occasional trips around the San Diego Bay. In an adjacent warehouse is the Americas Cup Museum, where the story is told of this great sailing event, capable of whipping up as much patriotic fervor as the Olympic Games. San Diego hosted the race in 1992.

▶ *Continue along the Embarcadero to Seaport Village.*

10 Seaport Village

This modern shopping and dining complex, only a few minutes' walk from the very heart of downtown San Diego, is intended to depict the harborside as it was a century ago. It is difficult to believe that it could have been so well manicured back then, but it does provide a very agreeable environment for shopping with pleasant, landscaped walks overlooking the harbor. In all, 14 acres (6 hectares) have been developed, with over 60 shops and 17 restaurants. Street performers are usually out entertaining visitors and although this is a totally tourist-orientated development there is a merciful absence of T-shirt shops and other barometers of tourist culture.

SPECIAL TO...

The best way to experience the San Diego Bay is on the ferry that runs between the dock at Broadway and Harbor Drive in San Diego and the Ferry Landing Market Place in Coronado. It leaves San Diego on the hour and Coronado on the half-hour, and the crossing takes 15 minutes. Coronado is a beach resort, where the main attraction is the grand old Hotel del Coronado, built in 1888 and featured in the hit film *Some Like It Hot*.

▶ *Take Harbor Drive to 6th Avenue and turn north. Turn right on Market Street and enter the Gaslamp Quarter.*

11 Gaslamp Quarter

The 16- block strip along 4th, 5th and 6th Avenues from Broadway to the Waterfront is one of America's largest national historic districts. In the 19th century this was San Diego's main street area, but by the turn of the century it had become a flourishing red-light district. It sits right in the heart of San Diego and, like many inner-city areas, it has suffered years of neglect. Fortunately, none of the

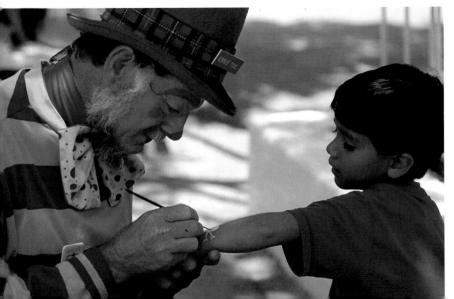

buildings were lost to make way for modern office blocks, and a concerted effort has been made to restore the district to its original glory, including its designation as a National Historic Distoric. Many of the buildings have been renovated but it has not entirely lost its seedy image: there is still a fair share of pawn shops and dilapidated buildings, but they now rub shoulders with trendy restaurants and antique shops. At this stage of the drive it will almost certainly be early evening – and what better place to be than this atmospheric Victorian neighborhood, filled with interesting restaurants and cafés. Hopefully there will still be enough light to see some of the fine examples of Victorian architecture that abound in the area.

More than 100 old Victorian buildings have been lovingly restored and a detailed map of the main points of interest is available from the William Heath Davis House, at 410 Island Avenue. This house also happens to be the area's oldest structure, a "salt box" home, shipped from New England to San Diego around Cape Horn in about 1850. Across the street, at 554 4th Avenue, a bakery has been in business on the site since 1875. Even when the second floor of the building was a notorious whore-house at the turn of the century, cakes and pies were still being baked downstairs. The area bordered San Diego's old Chinatown, and Wong's Nanking Café still retains the atmosphere of the period during which it was built, in 1913. Perhaps the most architecturally significant section of the quarter is on 5th Avenue, between E and F Streets. Most of the buildings here were erected during the latter part of the 19th century, and include the Marston Building, the Hubbell Building, the Nesmith-Greeley Building and the Louis Bank of Commerce, which

Left: clowning around to entertain a young Seaport Villager

many people regard as the most beautiful building in the quarter.

▶ *Take Broadway to G Street.*

🄓 **Horton Plaza**
This colorful, modern shopping plaza, that opened in 1985, is the centerpiece of the new down-

Modern architecture can be fun – as is evident at Horton Plaza

town San Diego area and is a textbook example of good design. The human scale and visually stimulating architecture combine with first-rate shops to make shopping here a totally satisfying experience. The Plaza is a multi-level, open-air, six block complex of bridges, piazzas, towers, sculpture and gardens inhabited by street performers and shoppers. There are 14 different architectural styles represented, from Renaissance to Post-modern. An efficient parking garage extends under the Plaza, alleviating the usual downtown parking problems. All this and parking too!

▶ *Take Broadway east to Park Boulevard north and drive back to Balboa Park.*

FOR CHILDREN

The San Diego Children's Museum, at 200 W. Island Avenue, at the corner of Front Street, is full of hands-on exhibits, from poetry-writing to wheelchair basketball. There is a strong emphasis on different cultures, and the Improv Theater provides costumes and a stage for youngsters to try out their thespian talents. The more traditional pursuits of painting and modelling are also offered.

THE MISSIONS

Long before the discovery of gold, California was transformed into a European colony, as zealous Catholic missionaries spread the Christian message. Baja California (Lower California, now part of Mexico) was well established by the Spanish, who were also anxious to settle Alta California (Upper California, the present-day state). It was a dramatic, wild and magnificently beautiful corner of North America, inhabited by over 300,000 native Indians belonging to 105 separate nations – a prize coveted by not only the Spanish but also the Russians and British. Spain put their faith in one man, Father Juniperro Serra, who was responsible for developing a chain of missions that became the backbone of the modern state.

In 1769, when he was 55, Serra travelled for six weeks, covering 750 miles (1,207km) by donkey, from Mexico to San Diego, to build his first mission. This would be the first of a series of missions that would eventually extend up the coast of California as far as Sonoma, north of San Francisco. Serra had to fight almost insurmountable obstacles in establishing the first community. Several previous expeditions had failed to achieve their goal and Serra's group was dogged by illness and Spanish bureaucracy, and almost ran out of supplies. Nevertheless, they struggled into San Diego in July 1769 to erect a large wooden cross and conduct Mass in front of a group of curious Indians. Junipero Serra had moved to Mexico from his birthplace in Majorca when he was 37. He was a small man with a pronounced limp, resulting from an injury in Mexico for which he refused to have treatment. At the time of his death in 1784 he had travelled thousands of miles and established a further nine missions in what were then the most remote outposts of California. The second in the chain, which he built in 1771, was the Mission San Carlos Borromeo in Carmel. This was Serra's favourite mission, and it remained his headquarters until his death (he is buried at the mission chapel). Everywhere you go in California today, you see Junipero Serra's name – on schools, on highways and on monuments. His role in establishing an unshakable Catholic base to religion in the state inevitably lead to his candidacy for sainthood, and he was beatified by the Vatican in 1988. The Junipero Serra Museum in San Diego sits high on a hill near Old Town, overlooking the site that is the birthplace of modern California. It was here, in 1769, that Serra built the first non-native settlement in California. The original mission was located here, too, but four years later it was moved to its present site for agricultural reasons. The museum documents the early history of the state and of the Indians, Spanish and Mexicans who made this area their home.

Following Junipero Serra's death his role was taken over by

Monument to faith: San Francisco de Asis (Mission Dolores)

Fermin Francisco de Lasuen who, like Serra, had moved to Mexico in his 30s. He established a further eight missions during his 18 years in the office of President of the Missions, and he was already 66 years old when he started the project. It was Lasuen who developed the style of architecture that has come to be known throughout California as the mission style: thick, adobe walls, with red-tile roofs and shaded courtyards, surrounded by arcades.

The missions were linked by El Camino Real – the King's Highway. Streets bearing the same name, following the original route, can be found in most of California's coastal towns today. Highway 101 closely follows this route. The missions were built as links in a chain that extended all the way from Mexico to the north of Alta California. Each link was one day;s journey from the next by horseback, and missionaries could theoretically reach the farthest outpost in Sonoma within 21 days of leaving Mexico. Many of the first missions were destroyed by fire, and a few by earthquake, but

Above: a tribute in stained glass to the work of the 18th-century mission-builders

Left: Mission San Diego de Alcala

all were rebuilt, some on their original sites and some in new, more practical locations. Most of the missions today are restorations of the original buildings, but some still have the original decorations painted by Indian converts. One of the most interesting of all the missions is La Purissima, north of Santa Barbara. Typically, the original buildings were destroyed by fire, and the mission was rebuilt on the present site in 1813. Even the rebuilt mission was long since destroyed, and the present buildings are reconstructions – but it has been so well done that this is now the most authentic-looking mission in the chain. Adding to its convincing physical appearance are the surrounding gardens and farmland, perfectly replicating the life of the period. All of the missions are open to the public and several of them also have adjoining museums that document the spread of Catholicism along El Camino Real.

LIST OF MISSIONS

San Diego de Alcala
San Luis Rey de Francia
San Juan Capistrano
San Gabriel Arcangel
San Fernando Rey de Espana
San Buenaventura
Santa Barbara
Santa Ines
La Purisima Concepcion
San Luis Obispo de Tolosa
San Miguel Arcangel
San Antonio de Padua

Nuestra Senora de la Soledad
San Carlos Borremeo de Carmelo
San Juan Bautista
Santa Cruz
Santa Clara de Asis
San Jose de Guadalupe
San Francisco de Asis (Mission Dolores)
San Rafael Arcangel
San Francisco de Solano

San Diego
County

San Diego County is surprisingly mountainous and the fresh mountain air provides relief from the surrounding hot deserts. Here is one of the States most beautiful wilderness parks, the most southern wineries, a safari park and even a world famous astronomical telescope. This is a far cry from the fast life of Los Angeles or even San Diego.

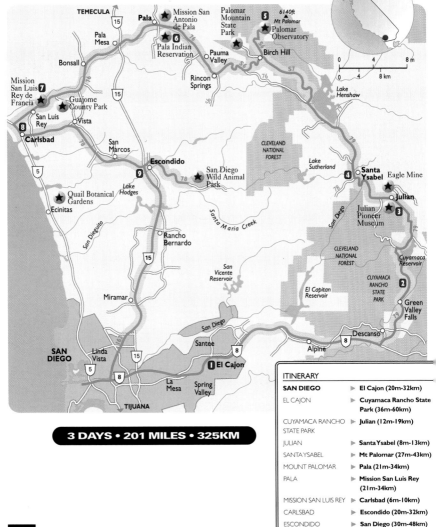

3 DAYS • 201 MILES • 325KM

ITINERARY

SAN DIEGO	▶ **El Cajon (20m-32km)**
EL CAJON	▶ **Cuyamaca Rancho State Park (36m-60km)**
CUYAMACA RANCHO STATE PARK	▶ **Julian (12m-19km)**
JULIAN	▶ **Santa Ysabel (8m-13km)**
SANTA YSABEL	▶ **Mt Palomar (27m-43km)**
MOUNT PALOMAR	▶ **Pala (21m-34km)**
PALA	▶ **Mission San Luis Rey (21m-34km)**
MISSION SAN LUIS REY	▶ **Carlsbad (6m-10km)**
CARLSBAD	▶ **Escondido (20m-32km)**
ESCONDIDO	▶ **San Diego (30m-48km)**

[i] *San Diego International Visitor Information Center, 11 Horton Plaza, CA 92101*

▶ *Leave San Diego on I-8, heading east.*

❶ El Cajon

This sprawling suburb of San Diego does not have a great deal to offer visitors, but the Heritage of the Americas Museum, on the campus of Cuyamaca College, at 2952 Jamacha Road, is worth a visit. This cultural and educational center is concerned with both the natural and human history of the Americas. Exhibits include fossils, seashells, minerals and meteorites, tribal tools, baskets, jewelery and a small art gallery. The best reason for visiting the museum, however, is the sweeping view of the campus and surrounding area from the hilltop. The Main Street of El Cajon has several good antique shops which are good for a browse.

▶ *Continue along I-8 to the turn off for Hwy 79 north at Descanso Junction. Continue north directly into Cuyamaca Rancho State Park.*

❷ Cuyamaca Rancho State Park

This 25,000-acre (10,117-hectare) park is only 40 miles (64km) away from San Diego, but feels much more remote. Peaks as high as 6,500 feet (1,981m) are covered in Ponderosa pines, firs, incense cedar and oaks, and at certain times of the year there are abundant wildflowers. Over 100 species of birds enjoy this habitat, as well as mountain lions, coyote, deer, fox and bobcats. The views from here extend from the Pacific in the west to the deserts of the east and south. The park was originally a gathering place for Indians, and during the Spanish occupation it was a ranch. Its name is the Spanish translation of an Indian word for 'the place where it rains'. A small museum at the visitor center has an exhibit illustrating the

Indians' resistance to 19th-century settlers' attempts at logging.

▶ *Continue north on Hwy 79 to Julian.*

❸ Julian

In 1870 a gold strike put this little mountain community on the map. In the years following, over 2,000 miners extracted more than $15 million in gold ore. The Washington Mine (at the end of Washington Street) was Julian's first hard rock mine; today it is a State Historic Park, open daily. The tunnels collapsed years ago but you can still see the assay office and blacksmith's shop. Follow the signs from C Street to the Eagle Mine, which still offers tours underground. This educational, if claustrophobic tour, can be enhanced by a visit to Miners Camp, at 2605 Washington Street, where you can practise hands-on gold-panning and learn even more about the Gold Rush days. Julian itself is a quaint, attractive town with many historic buildings along the Main Street, which still has wooden sidewalks. The Julian Hotel was built in 1887, the Julian Drug Store still has an old-fashioned soda fountain

serving sarsparilla, and an old brewery has been turned into the Pioneer Museum – almost too grandiose a term for this eclectic assortment of exhibits, which includes the first bathtub and the oldest pool table in town. It also houses a surprisingly good collection of lace. Today, Julian is known for its apples. Orchards surround the town and the apple pie shops are a big attraction. At the Julian Cider Mill, off Main Street, you can watch the production of cider and sample honey made from the mill's own beehives. Julian's proximity to San Diego makes it a popular weekend excursion.

FOR CHILDREN

Hop onto a horse-drawn wagon in front of Julian's drug store for a half-hour tour of the town and its country lanes. The tour is operated by Country Carriages and even adults will enjoy being transported back to this more relaxing mode of travel.

▶ *Drive 7 miles (11km) north on Hwy 79.*

❹ Santa Ysabel

Apart from a general store dating back to 1870, the main interest here is a branch of the mission in San Diego that is still used by the local Indians. The Mission Santa Ysabel was originally built in 1818, but the present white stucco structure is a 1924 recreation. There is a tiny one-room museum and a large Indian cemetery.

▶ *Continue north on Hwy 79 for over 11 miles (18km) and turn right onto Hwy 57. After another 11 miles (18km), turn right onto Hwy 56 and make a steep climb of over 4 miles (7km) to Mount Palomar Observatory.*

Julian's abundant apple crops come in handy for making apple pies

5 Mount Palomar

The 200-inch (5,080mm) reflecting Hale telescope at the Palomar Observatory is one of the biggest in the world, housed in a 13-story-high dome operated by the California Institute of Technology. A self-guided tour explains the working of this monstrous mirror and the telescope can be viewed from the visitors' gallery. The adjoining Greenway Museum has exhibits of photographs of celestial secrets taken through this mighty lens. There are three other domes that house 48-inch (1,219mm) Oschin and 18-inch (457mm) Schmidt-type telescopes and a 60-inch (1,524mm) reflecting telescope. The interior of the observatory has to be kept at constant night-time temperatures to prevent distortion of the mirror. It can feel quite chilly after entering from the heat of the day, and a sweater can be very useful. The observatory sits at the summit of 6,140-foot (1,872m) Mount Palomar. The air up here is fresh and clear and the scenic drive up through the chaparral and the rock-covered landscape is quite beautiful.

▶ *Return down* **Hwy 56** *and continue all the way down through almost 7 miles (11km) of hairpin bends back to* **Hwy 76**. *Stay on* **Hwy 76** *all the way into Pala.*

6 Pala

Mission San Antonio de Pala was built in 1815 as a branch of Mission San Luis Rey de Francia. It lies within the Pala Indian Reservation and is the only mission in California where the original chapel is still used primarily by Native Americans. The interior of the chapel is adorned with primitive Indian frescoes, complementing the rustic interior. Outside, the cemetery is filled with simple hand-made wooden crosses marking Indian graves. Tourmaline Queen Mountain, once teeming with miners, rears up behind the mission. To see displays of some of the world's finest tourmaline, that came from this mountain, visit Gems of Pala at 35940 Magee Road, which has both exhibits and retail displays.

▶ *Return to* **Hwy 76** *and continue west to San Luis Rey.*

California's largest mission, the Mission San Luis Rey de Francia

7 Mission San Luis Rey de Francia

On the right of the highway is the largest of the California missions, built in 1798 by Father Fermin de Lasuen as the 18th in the chain. The sanctuary interior has a wooden double-dome construction with high, beamed ceilings; Indians painted the original, colorful decorations. At

---

FOR HISTORY BUFFS

Three miles (5km) east of Mission San Luis Rey is the Guajome Adobe, one of the finest examples of domestic Spanish adobe architecture in California. Rancho Guajome was a mission-owned tract of land granted to Spanish-Mexican settlers for farming when Mexico gained independence from Spain in the 19th century. The 20-room Guajome Adobe now sits at the centre of the 569-acre (230-hectare) Guajome County Park.

one time it included almost 6 acres (2 hectares) of buildings and had 3,000 Indian neophytes. The mission has been beautifully restored and still operates as a seminary.

▶ *Drive west on **Hwy 76** and turn south on the San Diego Freeway (**I–5**). Take the Carlsbad exit, continue for one mile, the town is on the west side of the freeway.*

8 Carlsbad

Carlsbad became a spa town in the 19th century, drawing the crowds to its natural well and the apparently health-giving properties of its waters. A small museum at the Alt Karlsbad Haus Gift Shop records the history of this era, when Carlsbad was a prosperous resort. Although the spring disappeared years ago the town is still noted

---

BACK TO NATURE

Nine miles (14km) south of Carlsbad, near Encinitas, Quail Botanical Gardens has over 30 acres (12 hectares) of rare plants. A chaparral area serves as a bird refuge and provides a great opportunity to see many different species of birds from the garden's self-guided trails.

SPECIAL TO...

One of the more bizarre attractions in California is a few minutes' drive north of Escondido. Popular dance band leader Lawrence Welk liked the area so much that he built a resort around his mobile home, including a restaurant, a motel, a theater and a museum of Welk memorabilia. To many older Americans, who grew up on his television broadcasts, the Lawrence Welk Resort is something of a shrine. Take the Mountain Meadow Road exit off I-15 north; the resort is located at 8860 Lawrence Welk Drive.

---

for its spas, including the famous La Costa Hotel and Spa, frequented by the rich and famous. The cobblestone streets and quaint shops of the revitalised town center have once again made Carlsbad a popular destination.

▶ *Take **Hwy 78** east to Escondido.*

9 Escondido

In recent years Escondido has become the centre of California's most southerly wine-producing region. More than a dozen wineries have

sprung up in the surrounding area, and they are all open for tours and tasting. Ferrara Winery, at 1120 West 15th Street, is the oldest in the county, and has been designated a state historical site. However the reason most people come here is the San Diego Wild Animal Park. If you continue east through Escondido on Hwy 78 to San Pasqual Valley Road, the Park is clearly signposted. It began as a breeding facility for San Diego Zoo's large animals, and its 2,100 acres (850 hectares) are now home to over 2,500 animals from Africa and Asia, including elephants, rhinos, giraffes and zebras. The park has been landscaped to resemble the natural habitat of the animals and the experience is as close to actually being on safari as possible. A monorail makes a 50-minute circuit of the park and there is a marked walking tour. Wide expanses of land allow the animals to roam with considerable freedom, free from disturbance by their human observers. A good pair of binoculars can be an extremely useful accessory here.

▶ *Return to San Diego on **I-15** south.*

A photo opportunity grasped at San Diego Wild Animal Park

THE DESERTS

Within a couple of hours' drive from the urban concentration of Los Angeles, you can be in the middle of an arid wilderness. The deserts of southern California are one of the great natural features of the state – though at first appearance these barren tracts of land look bleak and inhospitable, and most people drive through with never a thought of stopping. What a mistake this is. The deserts are a fragile and fascinating environment, with their own austere beauty that unfolds slowly to the visitor. Wildlife abounds, but only patience will give rewards. Bighorn sheep can still be seen in some of the more remote areas, and there are wild burros, sidewinder snakes, kit foxes and a host of cacti and other plants adapted to the harsh, dry conditions. The hand of man has unfortunately left an indelible scar on the desert. Wherever development has occurred it seems that little care has been taken to harmonise with or protect the landscape. Old mining operations lie in ruins, trailer homes are surrounded by abandoned cars and machinery, rusting tin cans and empty bottles litter the sides of highways. Fortunately, though, the fragility of the desert has not escaped attention, and with the passing of the California Desert Protection Act in 1994 most of the state's deserts are now protected wildlife sanctuaries. No one should leave without experiencing this desolate grandeur.

There are two distinct desert areas. The Mojave is high desert, ranging in elevation from 3,000 to 5,000 feet (914 to 1,524m). At a much lower elevation are the northern extension of the Sonora Desert, most of it within Anza-Borrego Desert State Park, and the southern extension of the Colorado Desert, culminating in Death Valley National Park. From May to October the temperatures can reach infernally high levels, especially in Death Valley, where some of the highest temperatures on earth have been recorded. Death Valley is a popular winter vacation destination and during November hundreds of recreational vehicles descend on the valley to take advantage of the pleasant climate. In the high desert, winter usually brings snow and the temperatures can be extremely low. In both areas, early spring is the best time to visit, when the desert floor suddenly comes alive with a carpet of flowers.

Over 1,000 years ago the Agua Caliente Indians were attracted to the shady palm oases and fresh water springs of the desert. Today the clean air and a dry, sunny climate have attracted world class health spas, resorts for tennis and golf, and some of the most exclusive housing in America. Palm Springs, Palm Desert and Rancho Mirage are an extension of Hollywood, in terms of both their residents and the extravagant lifestyle that is offered.

The whole desert is punctuated with old mining operations. Gold, silver and borax were at one time profitably mined throughout the high desert region, but as the mineral deposits ran out and the mines closed, towns were abandoned, leaving a legacy of ghost towns scattered along the desert highways. Today, where irrigation is possible with water diverted from the Colorado River, agriculture has become a thriving industry and valleys full of date palms and other produce extend down to the Mexican border.

The venerable bristlecone pines

Tour 7

Palm Springs is only a short drive from Los Angeles and it became an extension of Hollywood during the 1930s. Since those early days, even more exclusive resorts have been built and the tour continues through the fashionable desert communities of Rancho Mirage and Palm Desert to Coachella and the date palm groves that lead down to the surreal, artificial Salton Sea. A spectacular drive takes you through the desert of Anza-Borrego Desert State Park.

During the spring this huge area, the largest state park in the contiguous United States, is a riotous explosion of color, as thousands upon thousands of desert plants burst into flower. The tour continues north through the desert, returning to Los Angeles via the alpine community of Idyllwild, sitting a mile (1.6km) high in the San Jacinto mountains.

Tour 8

Passing through Palm Springs Desert Resorts, the road travels east to Joshua Tree National Park, where the Mojave and Colorado deserts meet and dramatic Joshua trees are set against chaotic boulder formations. This is the southern limit of the Joshua tree but the giant, distorted yuccas can be seen throughout the high desert. The tour travels through the Mojave Desert across to Needles on the Arizona border, then back east across the northern boundary of the desert to Barstow and San Bernadino County.

Tour 9

This tour provides an outstanding introduction to two of California's major deserts. After leaving Los Angeles, it crosses the high Mojave Desert to Owens Valley, before climbing over the Panamint Mountains and dropping into Death Valley and the lowest point in the western hemisphere.

From the lowest point the tour returns to Highway 395 and at Lone Pine there are spectacular views of Mount Whitney, the highest peak in the continental US outside Alaska. Continue up to the White Mountains to see the world's oldest living plants, *Pinus longaeva*, the ancient bristlecone pines.

Palm Springs, Salton Sea &
Anza-Borrego

This tour shows the extremes of desert life, from the manicured golf courses of Palm Springs and Palm Desert to the barren mountains of Anza-Borrego. Glittering resorts line the Coachella Valley, while endless pristine deserts await exploration. This region gets unbearably hot in the summer, but in winter and spring the blue skies and warm days are ideal.

ITINERARY		
LOS ANGELES	▶	**Ontario (38m-61km)**
ONTARIO	▶	**Desert Hot Springs (11m-18km)**
DESERT HOT SPRINGS	▶	**Palm Springs (14m-22km)**
PALM SPRINGS	▶	**Rancho Mirage (13m-21km)**
RANCHO MIRAGE	▶	**Palm Desert (3m-5km)**
PALM DESERT	▶	**Indio (11m-18km)**
INDIO	▶	**Salton City (36m-58km)**
SALTON CITY	▶	**Anza-Borrego (27m-44km)**
ANZA-BORREGO	▶	**Los Angeles (195m-314km)**

3 DAYS • 348 MILES • 560KM

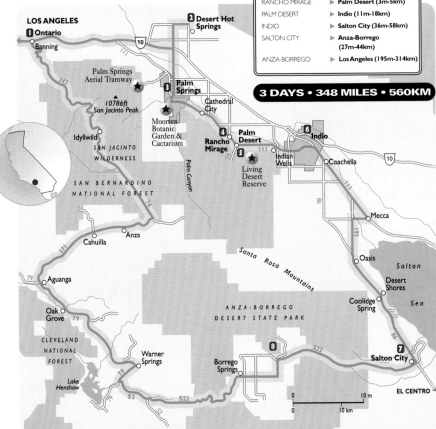

ℹ️ *Tourist information Center, Hollywood Chamber of Commerce, 7018 Hollywood Boulevard*

▶ *Leave Los Angeles on I-10.*

❶ Ontario

This otherwise uninteresting suburb of Los Angeles has an international airport and is an important gateway to the desert regions. Once a thriving agricultural community, its only remaining vestige of this era is the Garber Olive House at 315 East 4th Street. Established in 1894, this olive-processing facility conducts tours and tastings, but is at its most active during the harvest, from October to December.

▶ *Continue east on I-10 take the Desert Hot Springs exit.*

❷ Desert Hot Springs

As the name suggests, this resort exists because of the springs – and they are hot. The water comes out of the ground at a searing 207°F (84°C) and have to be cooled for therapeutic purposes. Two Bunch Palms is perhaps the most famous spa in town because of its dubious past as a hideaway for Al Capone. The desert has always attracted its share of eccentrics: one of the first settlers in Desert Hot Springs was a prospector named Cabot Yerxa. He arrived in the valley in 1913 with a bottle of water and bag of food and proceeded to build a pueblo loosely based on Indian architecture. His adobe home eventually had 35 rooms with 150 windows made from odd-shaped pieces of glass. It is now Cabot's Old Indian Pueblo Museum and visitors can look at the intriguing collection Cabot gathered together, including an 8-foot (2m)-tall grizzly bear and a 20-ton/tonne carving from a giant sequoia tree that fills the four-story home. The museum is located at 76-616 East Desert View Avenue.

Flowers of the wilderness: the Living Desert park at Palm Desert

▶ *Return towards I-10 but continue across the freeway to Palm Springs.*

❸ Palm Springs

Palm Springs became the favorite Hollywood celebrity vacation during the 1930s, and it is easy to see why. First there is the balmy winter weather, when the temperature rarely exceeds 85°F (29°C) nor drops below 55°F (13°C). Then there is the natural mineral spring that has helped to make this the country's most famous resort. Many celebrities established homes here, including Bob Hope, Frank Sinatra and Liberace, and this brush with glamour still accounts for much of the resort's popularity. Golf courses abound – in fact, if you don't play, there is little else to do apart from sunbathe. The city is certainly pleasant, but it has the feel of a commuter suburb, rather than a major resort. Most of the action takes place along Palm Canyon Drive. This is the main thoroughfare where, at peak times, there can be bumper-to-bumper

traffic. All the major shops are here, along with restaurants and the Palm Springs Follies. The Village Green Heritage Center sits incongruously in the midst of a modern shopping development at 221 South Palm Canyon Drive. It is about the only historic site in town – and the entire history of the town is covered in three buildings. The McCallum Adobe is the oldest building, once the home of the city founder. Built in 1884, it houses an exhibit of tools, books and clothes from the early years of the town, and has a display of photographs of Hollywood stars associated with Palm Springs. The railroad tie-house, next door, was built by pioneer

Cornelia White in 1893, and was originally part of the city's first hotel. Ruddy's General Store Museum is the third building, which recreates a typical 1930s general store. Close to here is the Desert Fashion Plaza, an upscale shopping mall with designer boutiques and department stores. Behind it, on Museum Drive, is the Palm Springs Desert Museum. In a town that appears to be devoid of any culture, this is one of the country's best regional art museums. Even the modern red rock building, that seems to be part of the desert itself, is standing in exceptionally interesting landscaped sculpture gardens. The museum is widely acclaimed for its superb collection of modern art and a strong collection of the fine art of the American West. In

RECOMMENDED WALK

An area of Palm Springs called the Old Movie Colony will provide a glimpse at some of the homes owned by the great names of show business. Kirk Douglas still lives here, although most of the other stars have long since left. You can see where Elvis Presley spent his honeymoon, the house where Liberace spent his last days, the winter homes of Douglas Fairbanks and Mary Pickford, Clark Gable and Liz Taylor. All of them are set beside easily walked streets, and a location map is available from the Palm Springs Visitor Center at 2781 North Palm Canyon Drive.

One of the Agua Caliente Indians who own most of Palm Springs

addition, there are good natural science exhibits on the surrounding environment and Indian culture.

Way down South Palm Canyon Drive, the Moorten's Botanical Garden has displays of desert plants from all over the world. Over 3,000 varieties of plants grow among 4 acres (2 hectares) of petrified trees and dinosaur fossils. The garden is often filled with birds, and lizards are everywhere.

Visitors are often surprised to hear that most of Palm Springs is owned by the Agua Caliente Indians, from whom businesses rent land on 99-year leases. Their tribal lands are 5 miles (8km) south of Palm Canyon Drive, at the Agua Caliente Indian Reservation. This vast, scenic area is filled with canyons tucked into the mountains, and it abounds with hiking trails – but it is best to experience the canyons by car. Palm Canyon is the most accessible, and a parking lot at Hermit's Bench gives great views of the stands of 1,500 hundred-year-old Washington Palms that line the canyon for 7 miles (11km). A steep trail drops down into the canyon for the adventurous. Beyond Palm Canyon, Andreas Canyon has a shady grove of sycamores and cottonwoods, and there is an impressive grove of California fan palms close by.

On the northern edge of Palm Springs, at Chino Canyon, the Palm Springs Aerial Tramway takes passengers from 2,600 feet (792m) to 10,800 feet (3,292m) in less than 18 minutes. Mount San Jacinto is one of the sheerest mountains in North America and the Tramway is the largest single-span, double-reversible aerial tramway in the world. On clear days the views from the top are awe-inspiring, and during the winter it is not unusual for travelers to leave the warm desert valley and be surrounded by snow within minutes. At the top is an observation deck and a restaurant serving lunch and dinner. There are over 50 miles (80km) of trails into the San Jacinto Wilderness State Park.

► *From Palm Springs, continue along* **Hwy 111** *to Rancho Mirage.*

4 Rancho Mirage
Golf courses and high-walled estates dominate this wealthy bedroom community. The wife of President Ford gave her name to the country's most well known drug treatment clinic, based here. Don't expect to see any celebrities going to the Betty Ford Clinic, however: it is very discreet, and impossible to approach without an appointment. The streets are named after film stars and directions tend to be along the lines of 'go down Bob Hope, cross Frank Sinatra and turn right on Jack

Benny'. There is nothing to stop for in Rancho Mirage – but take a drive through some of the streets to witness Californian excess.

► *Continue on* **Hwy 111**.

5 Palm Desert
This is a mirror of Rancho Mirage, with the addition of one of the most expensive shopping streets in the world. El Paseo is the desert equivalent of Rodeo Drive in Beverly Hills.

The golf courses here are very highly rated and musical events are produced at the Bob Hope Cultural Center. The Living Desert is the highlight of this town – if you don't like shopping, that is. The 1,200-acre (485-hectare) wildlife and botanical park features rare plants and animals from deserts around the world. Among the animals are Mexican wolves, bighorn sheep, mountain lions, gazelles and

---

SCENIC ROUTES

Route 74 from Palm Desert leads up into the Santa Rosa mountains. The tree-lined highway climbs high above the Coachella Valley, giving tremendous views of the desert communities.

Arabian oryx. The whole park is beautifully designed, and so cleverly laid out that the animals could easily be in the wild.

► *Continue along the Coachella Valley on* **Hwy 111** *to Indio.*

6 Indio
The blue-collar environment of Indio is in stark contrast to the ritzy estates of Palm Springs and its neighbors. This is the start of the Coachella Valley's agricultural region. Early this century, sophisticated irrigation systems

transformed this arid desert into a major agricultural centre producing grapefruit, cotton, alfalfa, vegetables and dates. Indio is surrounded by palm trees and is the self-proclaimed "Date Capital of the World." All the way along Highway 111, orderly rows of date palms alternate with roadside stands, often with elaborate Moorish façades, selling date products. The big event of the year in Indio is the National Date Festival, held in mid-February every year. It started in 1921 and the traditions include an Arabian Nights pageant and ostrich and camel races. Apart from dates, Coachella Valley has a Museum and Cultural Center at 82616 Miles Avenue, housed in the 1920s adobe home and office of a local doctor. Exhibits include Cahuilla Indian artifacts, old farm and household equipment and a blacksmith's shop. Of more specific interest is a large relief map showing the development of the desert's water system, and dioramas explaining the date-growing industry.

► *Continue south, at Mecca turn west on* **Hwy 195** *and then south on* **Hwy 195** *to* **Hwy 86**; *then go south through Oasis to Salton City.*

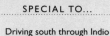

SPECIAL TO...

Driving south through Indio and the date palm groves, roadside stands abound selling dates and the local specialty: date shakes. These date milkshakes taste better than they may sound, and give plenty of energy to fuel your continuing journey through the hot, desert valleys.

A sheet of salty water at the Salton Sea National Wildlife Refuge

7 Salton City

One of the most surreal places in California is the town of Salton City, on the shores of the Salton Sea. Planned as the next Palm Springs, it never attracted the numbers expected, so its carefully laid-out streets lead nowhere and there are more vacant lots than houses, giving the town a strange, deserted look. The marina, with its adjoining hotel, submerged in the rising waters of the lake, add to the feeling of desolation. In fact there is a significant population, many of whom developed their land before the dream evaporated (and with summer temperatures often exceeding 100°F (38°C), evaporation is an all too common occurrence).

The 35-mile (56km)-long Salton Sea, one of the biggest salt-water lakes in the world, appeared by accident in 1905. Canals directing waters from the Colorado River to the Imperial Valley breached their banks

BACK TO NATURE

The Salton Sea is the most southerly stop on the Pacific flyway. At its southern tip, the Salton Sea National Wildlife Refuge has attracted 371 different bird species, including stilts, green-winged teal and the endangered Yuma clapper rail. One third of all North America's white pelicans winter here and during the autumn the skies are full of Canada and snow geese. A 2-mile (3km) nature trail follows the shore of the lake and a lookout tower provides a perfect vantage point. To reach the refuge headquarters turn west on Sinclair Road and drive for just over 4 miles (6km).

during an exceptionally severe winter. Billions of gallons of water flooded into this once dry desert and were trapped 235 feet (72m) below sea level, with no natural outlet. The sea has become increasingly saline over

the years, and is now more salty than the Pacific Ocean – but it still manages to support fish and other wildlife. It is an important winter recreation area for sports such as fishing, boating and water-skiing.

▶ *Turn west on* ***route S22*** *into Anza-Borrego Desert State Park. Continue into Borrego Springs.*

8 Anza-Borrego Desert State Park

A thousand square miles (2,590 sq km) of desert make this the biggest state park in the contiguous United States. An extension of Mexico's Sonora Desert, it was named after Juan Bautista de Anza, who first pioneered a route through these inhospitable surroundings in 1774. Borrego is the Spanish word for sheep, and the rare desert bighorn sheep can still be seen in some of the more remote areas of the park. The landscape is stark, but during the spring Anza-Borrego bursts into bloom as colourful wildflowers carpet the desert

floor. Special wildflower maps can be picked up at the Visitor Center at Borrego Palm Canyon, 3 miles (5km) west of Borrego Springs.

▶ *From Borrego Springs take* **route S22** *west. Turn north on* **Hwy 79** *then take* **Hwy 371** *east to* **Hwy 74** *north. Turn north onto* **Hwy 243** *and climb the wonderfully scenic but steep road to Idyllwild, sitting high on the western edge of the San Jacinto Wilderness Area. This charming, alpine community is a sharp contrast to the desert areas that surround the San Jacinto mountains. Continue north on* **Hwy 243** *and join* **I-10** *west at Banning to return to Los Angeles.*

Right: wildflowers bring a flash of spring color to the desert at Anza-Borrego Desert State Park
Below: the harsher landscape of Anza-Borrego's "southern badlands"

Mojave
Desert

This tour gives a thorough introduction to California's vast Mojave Desert, from the distinctive Joshua trees to the banks of the Colorado River and the border with Arizona. It returns through historic gold- and silver-mining country, before heading back to Los Angeles.

3 DAYS • 635 MILES • 1022KM

[Map with the following labels:]

Calico Ghost Town
Calico Early Man Archaeological Site
LAS VEGAS
MOJAVE NATIONAL PRESERVE
ARIZONA
Barstow
Daggett
Newberry Springs
Ludlow
Goffs
Fenner
Needles
Victorville
Havasu National Wildlife Refuge
Bristol Lake
Cajon Junction
SAN BERNARDINO NATIONAL FOREST
San Bernardino
Redlands
Joshua Tree
Twentynine Palms
Cadiz Lake
Danby Lake
Vidal Junction
Ontario
Beaumont
5185ft Keys View
Rice
LOS ANGELES
Riverside
Banning
Palm Springs
Palm Desert
Indio
JOSHUA TREE NATIONAL PARK
General Patton Museum
PHOENIX
Visitor Center
Chiriaco Summit

ITINERARY	
LOS ANGELES	▶ **Palm Springs** (107m-172km)
PALM SPRINGS	▶ **Indio** (24m-39km)
INDIO	▶ **Chiriaco Summit** (30m-48km)
CHIRIACO SUMMIT	▶ **Joshua Tree National Park** (12m-19km)
JOSHUA TREE NATIONAL PARK	▶ **Twentynine Palms** (70m-113km)
TWENTYNINE PALMS	▶ **Needles** (144m-232km)
NEEDLES	▶ **Daggett** (113m-182km)
DAGGETT	▶ **Calico** (7m-11km)
CALICO	▶ **Barstow** (11m-18km)
BARSTOW	▶ **Los Angeles** (117m-188km)

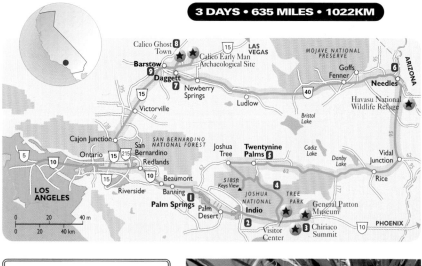

Part of Indio's massive date crop

ℹ️ *Tourist information Center, Hollywood Chamber of Commerce, 7018 Hollywood Boulevard*

▶ *Take I-10 out of Los Angeles to Redlands and continue to Palm Springs. Take Hwy 111 into the Coachella Valley.*

❶ Palm Springs

(see pages 49–51)

Both the Palm Springs Desert Museum and the Moorten's Botanical Garden give a good introduction to desert natural history, with displays of over 3,000 different desert plants at the gardens and more general natural science exhibits at the museum. Combine this with a visit to the Living Desert, just outside Palm Desert, where there are 1,200 acres (485 hectares) of habitat for desert animals from throughout the world, and 6 miles (10km) of trails to introduce visitors to desert life.

▶ *Continue on Hwy 111 to Indio.*

❷ Indio

(see page 51)

The 200,000 date palms surrounding this town yield 40 million pounds (18 million kg) of dates a year. Several date growers have exhibits, but one of the best is at Shield's Date Gardens on Hwy 111, just before entering town. Not only can you feast on blackdate ice cream and date

shakes but their slide show The Romance and Sex Life of the Date will tell you everything you ever needed to know about this desert fruit.

▶ *Leave Indio on I-10 and continue for 30 miles (48km) to the Chiriaco Summit exit.*

❸ Chiriaco Summit

General Patton Museum stands just off the freeway, on the site that was General George S. Patton's Desert Training Center during the early 1940s. The museum concentrates on

Joshua trees and rock-climbers at Joshua Tree National Park

displays of memorabilia from World War II, but other eras of American military history are also covered, and include displays of tanks and heavy artillery. A video of General Patton's life and career provides a structure to the exhibits. A relief map indicates the site of the 11 desert training camps and, more importantly, shows the development of Southern California's water system, so vital to the area.

▶ *Return west along I-10 to the Cottonwood Springs Road exit.*

❹ Joshua Tree National Park

About 7 miles (11km) north of the freeway is the southern entrance to Joshua Tree National Park. The small visitor center at Cottonwood Springs has a very basic display relating to the park, but there are maps and guide books available there. Covering 870 square miles (2,253 sq km) in all, the park's elevations range from 1,000 to 6,000 feet (305 to 1,829m), making it pleasant at almost any time of year. It rarely reaches the unbearable temperatures of the lower desert areas. The Joshua tree after which the park is named is a striking cactus-like plant that only grows on high ground between 3,000 and 5,000 feet (914 and 1,524m). It is actually a giant member of the lily family – older specimens are frequently over 40 feet (12m) tall – and got its name from the Mormon pioneers making their way across the desert. They also called it the "praying plant," because of its upstretched arms. Don't expect to see any of the trees near the southern entrance: it is far too low. The vegetation here consists of smoke trees, cottonwoods, spindly ocotillos and cholla cactus.

Drive north for about 20 miles (32km) to the Cholla Cactus Garden, an extensive area of opuntia, also called jumping cacti for the way they seem to leap to attach themselves to clothing. Directly across the road is an ocotilla patch. As the road continues north, the Joshua trees start to appear. At the first road junction, turn left onto Loop Road and drive through one of the most beautiful sections of the park. Joshua trees abound and the landscape consists of large, rounded granite boulders in an area aptly named Wonderland of Rocks. This is a popular rock-climbing area: climbers are often seen scaling the smooth boulders. Keys Road is the next turn left; follow it to the end to Keys View, where there are sweeping vistas stretching from the Salton Sea, 235 feet (72m) below sea level, to the San Gabriel Mountains, 10,000 feet (3,048m) above sea level. Return to Loop Road and continue north, past more bizarre rock formations, to leave the park at the town of Joshua Tree.

▶ *Turn right onto **Hwy 62** and drive 17 miles (27km) east to Twentynine Palms.*

5 Twentynine Palms
There are far more than 29 palms in this small desert community – but there is not much else. The main entrance to Joshua Tree National Park is here, and the Oasis Visitor Center has good displays providing an introduction to the flora, fauna and history of the park. At 6136 Adobe Road, the small Historical Society Museum has displays of mementos of the early days of mineral prospecting around Twentynine Palms, and explains the origins and growth of this desert settlement.

▶ *Continue east on **Hwy 62** to Vidal Junction and turn north onto **Hwy 95** and drive 45 miles (72km) to Needles.*

6 Needles
Sitting on the great Colorado River, which forms the boundary between California and Arizona, Needles was first settled in 1869 as a steamboat landing and supply station on the Old Emigrant Trail. The building of the Atchison, Topeka and Santa Fe Railroad in 1882 established the town, and there is a well preserved Harvey House train depot and hotel. The town was named for the needle-like peaks that can be seen across the river in Arizona. The river is its focal point, and is a major recreational facility. Good beaches line the water and there is boating, fishing and water skiing available. One of the most spectacular boating trips is through the Topock Gorge, where the I-40 crosses the river. The gorge is 15 miles (24km) long and the river winds through steep, colorful walled canyons that are impossible to approach by road. For those less interested in the natural world, the casinos of Laughlin, Nevada are just 15 miles (24km) up the road. Surrounding Needles are several

---

BACK TO NATURE

About 11 miles (18km) south of Needles on I-40 is the Havasu National Wildlife Refuge. This is a big attraction to fishermen, for the striped bass and trout that swim there, and it is also good for bird-watching during the winter months.

---

mountain groups: Turtle, Whipple, Spirit and Hackberry, all attracting rock hounds looking for fossils, petrified wood and semi-precious stones.

FOR HISTORY BUFFS

Across in Arizona, only 20 miles (32km) from Needles, London Bridge spans Lake Havasu. It was moved here from London, stone by stone, in 1971. At one end is a marina; at the other, the London Bridge Resort and English Village – complete with Tudor-style shops!

SCENIC ROUTES

Take the Goffs exit north off I-40 just outside Needles, and drive to Mid Hills campground, where Wildhorse Canyon Road makes an 11-mile (18km) link with Hole-in-the-Wall campground. This was declared the country's first official Back Country Byway. The road passes through dramatic volcanic desert scenery scattered with several kinds of cactus, and during the spring, the desert floor is carpeted with wild flowers.

▶ *Drive west along **I-40** through dramatic desert scenery to Daggett.*

7 Daggett
On the south side of the road, as you drive through Daggett, a high tower something like a lighthouse can be seen glowing in the sun. This is Solar One Power Plant, an experimental solar energy plant with hundreds of mirrors directing the suns rays to a receptor at the top. The experiment has been spectacular but not too successful. However, if the Visitor Center is open it is worth taking a tour of the plant.

▶ *Return across **I-40** and drive north on Yermo Road, which*

becomes *Ghost Town Road*
after passing under I-15.
Continue to the end.

8 Calico Ghost Town

Calico was founded in 1881 after a particularly rich silver strike. At its peak, it had a population of over 4,000 people, with two hotels, a church, a schoolhouse and even a small Chinatown. Like many of these wooden boom towns, it was destroyed by fire – twice – and rebuilt each time. Over $13 million of silver was mined here, but when the price of silver plummeted in 1895 the town fell into ruin. In 1951, Walter Knott of Knott's Berry Farm recognised the tourist potential and restored the town. Knott's uncle had grub-staked for the original prospectors. Today, Calico Ghost Town is a contrived tourist attraction with strong commercial overtones, but it is close enough to the main road to merit a short visit. The tunnels of the high-yielding Maggie Mine can be explored, you can take a cable tram or a ride on the Calico-Odessa Railway; but the building on the main street form the core of Calico, and their shops always seem to be the main attraction.

For a more authentic and educational historic experience, visit the Calico Early Man Archaeological Site, reached along the I-15 east, taking the exit north on Minneola Road. The site was discovered by an amateur archaeologist in 1942; Dr. Louis Leakey began excavations here in 1964, and since then more than 12,000 stone tools have been found, dating back 200,000 years – making this one of the oldest prehistoric tool sites ever discovered in the West. The tools can be seen in the walls and floors of the excavated pits.

▶ *Return to I-15 west and*
continue to Barstow.

9 Barstow

Most people use Barstow as a rest stop on the drive from Los Angeles to Las Vegas. It was founded as a railroad town in 1886 and became an important mining centre. The Mojave River Valley Museum at 270 E Virginia Way chronicles the area's history and also has a good collection of desert minerals and archaeological finds from the Calico excavation site. More information on deserts is available at the California Desert Information Center, at 831 Barstow Road, with maps, exhibits and displays on most aspects of desert life. For many visitors the Factory Merchants Outlet Plaza, with 50 factory stores selling heavily discounted goods, 4 miles (6km) south on the Lenwood Road exit, is more than enough reason to stop here.

FOR CHILDREN

Returning to Los Angeles on I-15, the road passes Victorville, which is home to the log fort that is the Roy Rogers and Dale Evans Museum. Any lover of Westerns will find this treasure trove of cowboy memorabilia fascinating. Roy Rogers' faithful horse Trigger, now stuffed for eternity, presides over the collection.

▶ *Return to Los Angeles on I-15.*

A remnant of past glories: one of the survivors of Calico Ghost Town

Highest, Lowest
&
Oldest

4 DAYS • 873 MILES • 1404K

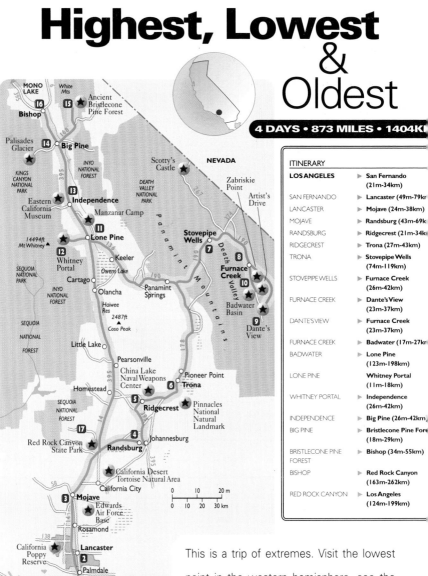

NEVADA

ITINERARY		
LOS ANGELES	►	**San Fernando (21m-34km)**
SAN FERNANDO	►	**Lancaster (49m-79kr**
LANCASTER	►	**Mojave (24m-38km)**
MOJAVE	►	**Randsburg (43m-69k**
RANDSBURG	►	**Ridgecrest (21m-34k**
RIDGECREST	►	**Trona (27m-43km)**
TRONA	►	**Stovepipe Wells (74m-119km)**
STOVEPIPE WELLS	►	**Furnace Creek (26m-42km)**
FURNACE CREEK	►	**Dante's View (23m-37km)**
DANTE'S VIEW	►	**Furnace Creek (23m-37km)**
FURNACE CREEK	►	**Badwater (17m-27kr**
BADWATER	►	**Lone Pine (123m-198km)**
LONE PINE		**Whitney Portal (11m-18km)**
WHITNEY PORTAL	►	**Independence (26m-42km)**
INDEPENDENCE	►	**Big Pine (26m-42km**
BIG PINE	►	**Bristlecone Pine Fore (18m-29km)**
BRISTLECONE PINE FOREST	►	**Bishop (34m-55km)**
BISHOP	►	**Red Rock Canyon (163m-262km)**
RED ROCK CANYON	►	**Los Angeles (124m-199km)**

This is a trip of extremes. Visit the lowest point in the western hemisphere, see the highest mountain in the continental United States and walk among the oldest living things on earth. The trip can be completed in four days, but as it covers some of California's most exceptional scenic sites, many people will prefer to take longer.

i *Tourist Information Center,*
Hollywood Chamber of Commerce,
7018 Hollywood Boulevard

▶ *Leave Los Angeles on **I-5** to*
the San Fernando Valley.

❶ San Fernando

The San Fernando Valley is
home to many of the world's
great film and television studios,
including the worlds biggest,
Universal Studios. Here you can
also find Disney, Warner Bros,
Burbank Studios, NBC Studios
and Columbia. Universal was
established in 1914 with the
philosophy that film-making is
an attraction in itself, and it has
grown to become one of the
major visitor attractions in
America (see page 21). NBC
Studios, in Burbank, is the only
national network television

The old gardens of the
mission, now called Brand Park,
have flowers and shrubs from
all the missions in the chain.
The museum theater is
damaged in the most recent
Northridge earthquake, but
when it reopens it will screen
several different films, including one on the history of the
mission and another on the life
of Father Junipero Serra (see
page 40). There is an Indian
craft room and an archive
center preserving historic documents of California's Catholic
heritage.

▶ *Return to **I-5** and exit onto*
***Hwy 14**, the Antelope Valley*
Freeway. Drive past
Palmdale, which is the gate-
way to the High Desert, and
continue to Lancaster.

Reserve and Interpretive Center
are on Lancaster Road, between
130th and 170th Streets.

▶ *Continue north on **Hwy 14** for*
20 miles (32km).

❸ Mojave

The town of Mojave sits in the
middle of the high desert from
which it was named. A typical
desert town, it has the wind-
blown, desolate feeling of a frontier community. Mojave still
bears traces of its own colorful
history as a mining community.
In the late 19th century, the
famous 20-mule team hauled
200 tons/tonnes of borax on each
trip from Death Valley, across
165 miles (265km) of inhospitable desert to Mojave. There
is a marker outside the Mojave
County Building to commemo-

studio to open its doors to the
public and allow them to witness
the behind-the-scenes life of
broadcasting. They also offer
tickets to many of the television
shows that are taped there.

Further north along the
valley, at Mission Hills, just to
the south of the expensive Los
Angeles suburb of San
Fernando, is the fourth mission
to be built in as many months.
Mission San Fernando Rey de
Espana was founded in 1797 but
was continually damaged by
earthquakes, the most recent
being in 1994.

❷ Lancaster

Lancaster was established in
1884, along the Southern
Pacific Railroad line. It grew up
on agriculture and mining but is
increasingly becoming a Los
Angeles bedroom community,
which gives a frightening idea
of just how big Los Angeles is.
Every spring, the hillsides of
Antelope Valley west of
Lancaster are ablaze with
orange, as hundreds of thousands of California poppies
burst into flower, providing one
of the state's great natural
sights. The California Poppy

Taking a break on the lonesome
drive across the Mojave Desert

rate the unloading site.
Just to the southeast of
Mojave is the Edwards Air Force
Base. This was where the first
astronauts did their training, and
is now the landing site for the
Space Shuttle. It is still the
primary location for experimental rocketry and jet aircraft test-
ing. On Memorial Day in May,
the base is open to the public,
and organises displays of some of
the latest, state-of-the-art military aircraft.

▶ *Continue north on* **Hwy 14** *for 19 miles (30km) and turn east onto the Redrock–Randsburg Road.*

④ Randsburg

This is still an active mining town, although many of the old gold- and silver-mines have been abandoned. At one time, the Yellow Aster Mine produced over $16 million worth of gold and over 3,000 prospectors set up camp here. It was so important that the Santa Fe Railway built a line to the camp in 1897. During the celebrations for the opening of the line, an explosion started a fire that destroyed several of the town's buildings. As often happened in the wooden gold rush towns, the rest of the buildings went up in flames a few years later. The town was rebuilt and the last significant traces of gold, silver and tungsten were mined in the 1920s. Randsburg is a ghost town that still has a spark of life: many of the old buildings have been restored along the main avenue, and now contain antique shops and a general store.

▶ *From Randsburg take* **Hwy 395** *north to China Lake Boulevard.*

⑤ Ridgecrest

Ridgecrest is the home of the China Lake Naval Weapons Center. At the Ridgecrest Maturango Museum there are displays relating to the cultural and natural history of the upper Mojave Desert, including an interesting section on ancient Indian petroglyphs. This is also a good place to pick up information on both the Mojave Desert and Death Valley areas.

▶ *From Ridgecrest take* **Hwy 178** *east to Trona.*

BACK TO NATURE

About 21 miles (34km) from Randsburg, on the Red Rock–Randsburg Road, is the California Desert Tortoise Natural Area. Turn south on Neuralia Road just before the junction with Hwy 14, follow the road to California City Boulevard and turn east to Randsburg-Mojave Road, a dirt road for about 2 miles (3km). A kiosk here gives information on California's state reptile. Tortoises are most active in the spring, when they can be seen munching on the desert wildflowers.

---

⑥ Trona

Trona is an ugly community, whose main economy is the Kerr McGee Chemical Plant – not the best reason for a visit! Two miles (3km) before the chemical plant there is a turnoff to the right: follow the dirt road to the "Y" and continue to the right until you reach the Trona Pinnacles, the most impressive tufa towers in America, with more than 500 magnificent Tioga Spires, some as high as 140 feet (43m). Their strange, other-worldly appearance has earned them a career as the background for many commercials and films, including Star Trek V. They formed in the waters of Owens Lake and, as the water receded, these gigantic calcified towers remained. Fortunately, they are sufficiently off the beaten track to avoid vandalism.

▶ *Continue north on* **Hwy 178** *to* **Hwy 190**, *turn east into Death Valley.*

⑦ Stovepipe Wells

Death Valley, whose very name is awe inspiring, was recently designated a National Park – and not before time; this is one of the truly great landscapes of

Left: windblown sand dunes near Stovepipe Wells in Death Valley

the world. Entering the valley across the Panamint Mountains gives a taste for what is to come. Totally arid, austere desert mountains plunge down to Stovepipe Wells, a dusty group of buildings including a general store, motel and campground. Just past Stovepipe Wells, on the left, is an extensive area of sand dunes. These are best visited in the cool of dawn, when overnight winds will have erased the footsteps of the previous day's visitors. During the middle of the day the dunes can be unbearably hot.

FOR HISTORY BUFFS

Scotty's Castle is by far the biggest visitor attraction in Death Valley. At the far north-ern end of the valley, just off Hwy 267, a flamboyant rogue and sometime prospector nick-named Death Valley Scotty per-suaded millionaire Albert Johnson to build an extravagant, Spanish-style man-sion in the desert. Scotty had originally lured Johnson out here with bogus tales of a gold mine. Johnson found that the climate suited his fragile health and forgave Scotty, and the two became lifelong friends. The 25-room house has a 50-foot (15m)-high living room, a music room with a 1,600-pipe organ, and even indoor waterfalls that acted as air-conditioners in the summer.

▶ *Continue east on **Hwy 190**. After a few miles a dirt road exits to the right. It heads into the flat, white salt pan on the valley floor and enters The Devil's Golf Course, an area of crystalline salt formations, pushed up from hundreds of feet underground and sitting in the midst of brine pools. The salt pan here is up to 5 feet (1.5m) thick and is as pure as table salt. **Hwy 190** turns south to Furnace Creek.*

8 Furnace Creek

The National Park headquarters are at the Furnace Creek Visitor Center, which has very good exhibits, plenty of literature on all aspects of the park and an 18-minute film on Death Valley. There are also evening programs and naturalist-led walks conducted from the center.

▶ *Leaving Furnace Creek, **Hwy 190** climbs 4 miles (6km) to Zabriskie Point, which gives the best panoramic views in the southern part of Death Valley. In the light of early morning and late afternoon it is particularly beautiful. For the ultimate view, continue for another 23 miles (37km), turning south off **Hwy 190** onto Dante's View Road.*

9 Dante's View

At the road's end, 5,478-foot (1,670m)-high Dante's View gives a 360° panorama of the Valley. Badwater lies one vertical mile (1.6km) below as you gaze out across the desolate land-scape. Take a sweater: it can get cool up here – 20° F (6°C) cooler than in the Valley.

▶ *Return to Furnace creek on **Hwy 190**. Just before entering town, take the minor road that exits to the south. Continue south past Artist's Drive to Badwater.*

SCENIC ROUTES

Just south of Furnace Creek, on Hwy 178, a dirt road branches off into the Black Mountains. Artist's Drive, as it is called, makes a 9-mile (14km) loop through some of the most barren but colorful landscape in the world.

RECOMMENDED WALK

The best walk in Death Valley is from Zabriskie Point, 4 miles (6km) east of Furnace Creek, down through the badlands, across the foot of Manly Beacon and on through the Golden Canyon. It shows the best Death Valley has to offer and it is downhill all the way! The 2.5-mile (4km) trail takes well under two hours, but you need to arrange a ride back to the parking lot at Zabriskie Point.

10 Badwater Basin

The main reason to visit Badwater is the novelty value of standing in the lowest place in the western hemisphere. This murky little pond lies 282 feet

Artist's Drive, where the landscape is marked by changing shades

The jagged peak of Whitney Portal, near Lone Pine

(86m) below sea level and is surrounded by hot, hostile desert. Fortunately, Badwater is just by the side of the road, and the effort involved in achieving this goal is minimal. It is more interesting to hike a few minutes out from Badwater into the salt flats, to experience the true desolation of the Valley.

▶ Return north to **Hwy 190** and follow it out of Death Valley until it becomes **Hwy 136**. Continue to **Hwy 395**.

11 Lone Pine
Sitting at the entrance to the Owens Valley, this small mountain community provides the doorstep to some of the most impressive scenery in the entire state. Drive west out of town on the Whitney Portal Road and you will arrive at the Alabama Hills. These huge, rounded boulders take on the bizarre appearance of human skulls and giant bowling balls in the early morning light. Their unique appearance has landed them many background roles in Western films and TV commercials.

▶ Continue on Whitney Portal Road to the end.

12 Whitney Portal
The highest peak in the United States outside Alaska is just 10 miles (16km) from here, but those miles are hard-earned. A very steep trail leads to the 14,494-foot (4,417m)-high summit of Mount Whitney. Most people spend a night on the mountain and only the fittest climbers should attempt it in one day. Even if you have no thoughts of physical exertion, the views of the High Sierra make Whitney Portal worth a visit. During the autumn, the trees turn intense shades of red and yellow, providing a vivid foreground for the snow-covered peaks.

▶ Return to **Hwy 395** and drive north for 16 miles (26km).

13 Independence
Excellent exhibits in the Eastern California Museum cover the history, geology and ecology of this region, and there is also a good section on the crafts of the Shoshone and Paiute Indian tribes. More recent history is covered with an exhibit on Manzanar Camp, where 10,000 Japanese-Americans were interned in 1941 following the outbreak of hostilities between the U.S. and Japan.

The climates here are extreme. The mountains receive over 48 inches (1,219mm) of snow a year, while the valley floor is semi-arid desert, with less than 6 inches (152mm) of rain a year.

▶ Continue on **Hwy 395** for 26 miles (42km).

14 Big Pine
Like most of the East Sierra towns, there is little here other than food, lodging and spectacular scenery. Just above town is the most southerly ice sheet in the United States: the Palisades Glacier, high in the Sierra Nevada.

▶ *Leave Big Pine on* **Hwy 168** *east which climbs steeply for 12 miles (19km) into the White Mountains.*

15 Ancient Bristlecone Pine Forest

First go to the Visitor Center at Schulman Grove for information on the trees that are the oldest living things on earth. Reaching ages in excess of 4,000 years, they grow only at extreme altitudes, at barely one inch (25mm) a year. The thin, cold air at almost 11,000 feet (3,352m) can be uncomfortable after such a rapid rise; do not attempt anything too strenuous. The best section of the forest is 11 miles (18km) of dirt road further on from Schulman Grove. Up at over 11,000 feet (3,352m) is a barren, rocky landscape, scattered with the gnarled, twisted

shapes of the bristlecones. The landscape is so evocative of the moon that NASA used this terrain to test their lunar rover.

▶ *Return to* **Hwy 395** *and drive north for 15 miles (24km).*

16 Bishop

Bishop is the major town in this eastern corridor of California and an important center for all manner of outdoor activities, from skiing and mountaineering to fishing in the crystal-clear mountain lakes. The town is filled with motels, restaurants, shops and outdoor-adventure outfitters. Also of interest, on a more cerebral level, is the Paiute Shoshone Cultural Center and Museum, which gives an excellent introduction to the lifestyles and handicrafts of the native population.

▶ *Return south on* **Hwy 395** *for 140 miles (225km).*

17 Red Rock Canyon State Park

This little-known state park is one of the great secrets of the desert. Red, brown and grey sandstone cliffs have eroded into shapes that used to serve as landmarks for freight wagons stopping at the canyon's springs. Red Rock Canyon is more than great scenery: there are Joshua trees, cholla cacti, golden eagles, desert tortoises and coyotes. A visitor center has information and a self-guided nature trail.

▶ *Hwy 395 forks east. Drive south on* **Hwy 14** *to Mojave and continue on* **Hwy 14** *back into Los Angeles.*

Ancient Bristlecone Pine Forest

THE HIGH SIERRA

The 450-mile (724km)-long range of Sierra Nevada ("snowy mountain" in Spanish) is California's most majestic feature. It averages between 60 and 80 miles (96 and 129m) in width, starting in the north near Mount Lassen and ending in the desert near the Tehachapi Mountains. Volcanic activity started its creation some 200 million years ago. Subsequent earthquake activity jolted the mountains into their dramatic peaks and valleys, which were further sculpted and polished by relentless glaciers over the last million years.

The High Sierra refers specifically to a 150-mile (241km)-long section of the Sierra Nevada, above the tree line from north of Yosemite Valley south to Cottonwood Pass – a section of high peaks, alpine meadows and icy lakes, which is certainly the most spectacular part of the chain; but in everyday usage, the term High Sierra includes the entire range, from Lake Tahoe to the desert. The range is home to the largest and deepest alpine lake in North America, the world's biggest trees, towering waterfalls, quaint old western towns and, of course, mountains. The mountains effectively divide the state – and they are big. Mount Whitney, at 14,494 feet (4,418m) above sea level, is the highest peak in the continental United States (outside Alaska), and is surrounded by sister peaks almost as high. Several mountain passes give access to the eastern slopes from the coastal region, and during the summer months these are magnificent, if somewhat tortuous drives. During the winter they are closed by deep deposits of snow, and the only reliable access across the Sierra is either via the Tehachapi Pass or via Lake Tahoe. In severe conditions even these roads can be closed for days at a time.

In the summer the Sierra Nevada provides every kind of outdoor recreation, including fishing, boating, mountain biking, white-water rafting, rock-climbing and hiking. Every type of accommodation is available, from luxury hotels to simple cabins, but during the height of the holiday season, in the more popular areas, even campsites have to be booked several weeks in advance.

Tour 10

When James Marshall found gold in the waters of the Sierra Nevada's western foothills he sparked off the 1849 Gold Rush that was to be instrumental in forming the California of today. This drive follows the trail of townships, linked by Highway 49, that reflect that era of rapid settlement and high hopes. From Chinese Camp, where thousands of Chinese miners lived harsh lives of discrimination and toil, it continues through a succession of historic gold towns, as well as visiting eerie underground caverns, Mark Twain's temporary cabin home, the ancient decorations of Indian Grinding Rock and even a stretch of wine-growing country, always returning to pick up the golden trail on its circuit from San Francisco.

Tour 11

Yosemite National Park is one of the most popular natural sights in America – and rightly so. This tour includes not only the highlights of the park but also other equally exceptional destinations, making this one of the best road journeys in North America. Leaving San Francisco, the route crosses the great agricultural Central Valley before starting its climb through the southern gold country and the Sierra foothills. It passes through the old gold town of Mariposa and continues into Yosemite Valley to reveal one of America's greatest iconographic landscapes.

After leaving the Valley, a visit to the Tuolomne Grove of giant sequoia trees requires only a short detour before heading over the wild, rocky

Opposite; plunging waterfalls at beautiful Yosemite National Park
Right: Placer County Courthouse, Auburn

landscape of Yosemite's high country. The drive then crosses the Sierra watershed and heads down to the surreal landscape of Mono Lake, before continuing north through the wild country of the eastern Sierra to perhaps the best preserved and biggest ghost town in America. Bodie never fails to fascinate visitors, with its authentic atmosphere and remote mountain location. The return to San Francisco crosses back over the High Sierra by the Sonora Pass, and once more traverses the Gold Country and Central Valley.

Tour 12

Lake Tahoe is the jewel of the northern Sierra Nevada. After leaving Sacramento this tour heads straight up into the mountains, and then down to this crystal-clear lake on the Nevada border.

An excursion to the less-than-natural wonders of the Nevada casinos on the lake's southern shore makes an interesting contrast to the surrounding mountain wilderness. The tour continues up the beautiful western shore of Lake Tahoe, past historic mansions and hidden coves, to Truckee, a town

straight out of the Wild West and close to the site of the last winter for many of the tragic Donner party. Only half of the 89-member group survived the harsh winter of 1846.

Once across Donner Summit, the Sierra watershed, the tour passes through two of the biggest and most developed Gold Country towns, Nevada City and Grass Valley, where, apart from charming streets lined with Victorian houses, there is one of the most interesting mine tours in California. Sacramento is a short drive back down the freeway.

Tour 13

Fresno lies at the heart of the Central Valley and, during the spring, the fruit orchards surrounding the town are ablaze with colour. The tour climbs up through the foothills east of Fresno to King's Canyon National Park. Here, there are giant sequoia trees and some of the most grand, wild mountain scenery in the Sierra. Unlike Yosemite, King's Canyon National Park does not attract massive crowds, so that this is a much more authentic wilderness experience.

Sequoia National Park is next to King's Canyon and the trees here are even bigger than those next door. The world's biggest tree grows here, and whole groves of giants have been flourishing for thousands of years. Leaving the High Sierra, the tour returns to the central valley and the old agricultural town of Hanford, with its rich Chinese heritage, and then on to Kingsburg, established in the 19th century by Swedish railroad workers on the Southern Pacific Railroad and even today looking more Swedish than American. Fresno is a short drive to the north.

The Gold Country

2 DAYS • 463 MILES • 745KM

California's history was transformed when James Marshall discovered gold in the Sacramento River and began the Gold Rush of 1849. This drive follows the southern section of Highway 49 for about 300 miles (483km) through Gold Country, where the average altitude is 2,000 feet (610m) and in summer, temperatures can be unbearably high. There are no hotels on the route but the area has charming bed and breakfast establishments and inns. At San Francisco, the Wells Fargo Museum (Montgomery Street) and the Bank of California (California Street), have memorabilia and gold specimens from the Gold Rush.

ⓘ San Francisco Convention and
Visitors Bureau, 201 Third Street,
Suite 900, CA 94103

▶ Leave San Francisco across the
Bay Bridge and take **I-580** to
I-205. Exit **I-205** on **Hwy 120**
at Manteca and drive for 49
miles (79km) to Chinese
Camp.

❶ Chinese Camp

The role of the Chinese in the
Gold Rush has been largely
obscured, although in 1851 one
in 10 of California's miners was
Chinese. Most of the Chinese
workers were indentured
servants, and a "foreigner tax"
prevented any of the Chinese
miners from making a significant
profit from their labors. Many of
them went on to build railroads,
before settling in San Francisco's
Chinatown. At one time over
5,000 Chinese lived in Chinese
Camp and it was the scene of a
violent war between two frater-
nal groups. Now, all is quiet:
Chinese Camp is deserted, with
only a post office and gas station
showing any sign of life. The
past is represented only by ruins
of the Wells Fargo building and a
19th-century store.

▶ Drive north on **Hwy 49** for 7
miles (11km).

❷ Jamestown

The first gold discovery in
Tuolumne County was made
here in 1848, and more gold was
taken from Woods Creek than
from any other stream of its size
in the state. Many of the original
false-front buildings are still
standing and extensive restoration and preservation has
resulted in a picture-perfect
main street from the Gold Rush
days. Commercialism has
inevitably crept in, with antique
shops, restaurants and gift shops,
but there is still a strong sense of
the past – to the extent that
Jamestown is frequently used as
a backdrop for film and television. Both High Noon and Butch
Cassidy and the Sundance Kid
were filmed here, as were the
television series Little House on

SPECIAL TO...

Melt-water from the High
Sierra fills the rivers flowing
through the foothills,
particularly in April and May.
Outdoor adventure enthusiasts
make the most of it, attempting
to navigate their rafts through
the ferocious white-water on
rivers such as the American,
Tuolumne and Stanislaus. A raft
full of people, hurtling through
the water, attempting to avoid
almost inevitable capsize, is a
common sight. A far safer and
drier pursuit is watching the
action from the river bank.

---

the Prairie and The Big Valley.
The Sierra Railway Company
began operating from
Jamestown in 1897, carrying
passengers and freight throughout the gold-mining area.
Railtown 1897 State Historic
Park preserves what is left of the
railroad, including a roundhouse
museum with a blacksmith's
shop, turntables, trains, rolling
stock and yard facilities. You can
watch the maintenance and
restoration of railroad equipment
and even ride a 19th-century
steam train to nearby gold
towns.

▶ Continue north on **Hwy 49** for
4 miles (6km).

❸ Sonora

Sonora is the capital of the
southern Gold Rush region and
the seat for Tuolumne County; it
is also one of the largest and
most beautiful towns on the
Mother Lode. This has always
been an important center and in
the old days it had a reputation
for lawlessness. Mexican miners,
from Sonora in Mexico, founded
the town, and its fine Victorian
houses are interspersed with
adobe buildings. Sonora soon
developed into one of the
wealthiest communities in the
Gold Country, and still retains its

Shooting the rapids on the fast-
flowing Stanislaus River

commercial importance. New
development has destroyed the
charm around the edge of the
town, but it is nevertheless very
well preserved and many of the
fine, old Victorian mansions are
still standing on Washington
Street. The other building of
note is the red-and-white St
James Episcopal Church, which
was built in 1859 and is perhaps
the most elegant structure in the
foothills. The Tuolumne County
Museum, at 158 W Bradford
Avenue, was originally a jail-
house, dating back to 1857. (It
now doubles as a tourist office.)
The cells are filled with exhibits
depicting the Gold Rush era,
with photographs, costumed

mannequins, gold specimens and antiques. The heavy equipment of gold mining, such as pelton wheels, stamp mills and arrastras, used in Sonora during the 19th century, can be seen in an outdoor display at Bradford Street Park.

▶ *Continue north on **Hwy 49** for 2 miles (3km).*

Below: Sonora, capital of the southern Gold Country, strung elegantly along its main street

RECOMMENDED WALK

One of the best preserved towns on the Mother Lode is Sonora. Known as The Queen of the Southern Mines, its history can be traced through its architecture. The Tuolumne County Museum, at 158 W Bradford Avenue, has a walking tour brochure that highlights about 20 points of interest in the heart of town.

❹ Columbia

Once known as the Gem of the Southern Mines, Columbia was one of the most important mining centers of the 1850s, with a population of over 15,000 and 50 saloons. In 20 years over $87 million in gold was extracted from the local placer mines. Twelve square blocks in the old business district have been painstakingly restored to their original 1860s appearance and designated a state historic park. Most of the town is closed to cars and the tree-lined main street is the preserve of pedestrians and stagecoaches, which transport visitors in an appropriately sedate fashion. Although there is a strong commercial element in the park, with shops, restaurants and even an operating hotel, the Gold Rush atmosphere has been perfectly captured, with costumed interpreters adding to the effect. The saloon at the end of town, still serving sarsparilla, could be a Hollywood film set; and you can still get a haircut at the state's oldest barber shop. Nowhere in the Mother Lode is there a more complete example of a 19th-century mining community. At the southern end of town, a grizzled old prospector gives

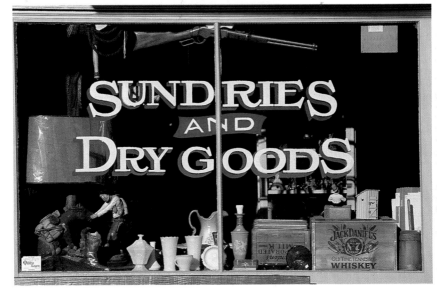

instruction in gold-panning, and most people leave with a few flakes of their own Sierra gold.

▶ *Take Parrots Ferry Road north out of Columbia and drive for 9 miles (14km).*

5 Moaning Cavern

The limestone in this area of the foothills is riddled with underground caverns. Moaning Cavern, to the south of Parrots Ferry Road, got its name from the sound that used to come from its entrance. A wooden staircase descends 65 feet (20m) and a steel spiral stair descends a further 100 feet (30m) into the cave. The staircases changed the acoustics of the cavern and stopped the moaning. Just to the north of Highway 4 are the even bigger and more impressive Mercer Caverns, discovered by miner Arthur Mercer in 1885. Visitors can now tour 10 different underground chambers with various extraordinary limestone and crystalline formations.

▶ *At **Hwy 4** drive north for 3 miles (5km) to Murphys.*

6 Murphys

Little has changed in this lively little town since it was established by two Irishmen back in 1848. In 1852, after the discovery of giant sequoia trees in what is now Calaveras Big Trees State Park, the rush of tourists through Murphys led to the building of Murphys Hotel in 1856, and the guest book is full of 19th-century celebrities such as Bret Harte, Count von Rothschild, Horatio Alger and Ulysses S Grant. The hotel still stands, among other historic buildings on the tree-lined Main Street. Across the street from the hotel, the Old Timers Museum displays Gold Rush memorabilia.

▶ *Return south on **Hwy 4** to Angels Camp.*

Left: a shop window reflects the 19th-century air of Columbia

7 Angels Camp

Writer Mark Twain lived in a cabin just outside Angels Camp for a few months during the 1860s and it was here that he wrote The Celebrated Jumping Frog of Calaveras County, the work that first propelled him to fame. Since 1928, the annual Jumping Frogs Jamboree has taken place every May, drawing contestants from far and wide for the significant prize money on offer. The highlight of this county fair is the frog jumping competition – now a more serious business than originally intended – owners take care of their frogs as if they were thoroughbred racehorses. Goliath frogs from Africa have recently caused controversy by consistently outjumping all the competition. The Angels Camp Museum at 735 South Main Street presents a static and predictable display of gold-mining equipment – a repetition of far better exhibits elsewhere along the Mother Lode.

▶ *Drive north on **Hwy 49** for 13 miles (21km).*

An eager contestant at the Angels Camp Jumping Frogs Jamboree

8 San Andreas

What was once just a few adobe buildings, erected by the original Mexican miners who settled here, has become a bustling, touristy little town. The Calaveras County Museum and Archives, one block east of Main Street, consists of three buildings: the IOOF Hall, the courthouse and jail. The infamous stagecoach bandit, Black Bart was held in this jail awaiting trial in the adjoining courthouse. In 1883 he was sentenced to six years in prison for 28 robberies. He served his time and then disappeared. In the museum is a full-size room display of a typical miner's cabin and a gold rush general store. Among the memorabilia is a black-edged invitation to a public hanging, signed by the sheriff. On a similarly somber note, the pioneer cemetery to the west of town provides a fascinating insight into the brief lives of the mining community. Even to this day, obituaries are posted on the Death Tree

Giant sequoias tower over the Calaveras Big Trees State Park

outside the old post office – because San Andreas has never had a daily newspaper.

▶ *Continue on* **Hwy 49** *for 7 miles (11km) to Mokelumne Hill and turn east on* **Hwy 26**. *Follow it across* **Hwy 88** *onto Volcano Pioneer Road to Volcano.*

🮆 Volcano

Once a town of 5,000, this old gold town, which sits in a crater-like depression, was famous for its dance halls and saloons. In fact, the town became a pioneer in many areas of California's cultural life. In 1845 California's first community theatre, the Volcano Thespian Society, was

BACK TO NATURE

The Calaveras Big Trees State Park lies on Highway 4, 25 miles (40km) east of Angels Camp at an altitude of 4,000 to 5,000 feet (1,219 to 1,524m). Forty miles (64km) of walking trails weave through two groves of giant sequoia trees – the largest living things on earth. One tree at Calaveras is 320 feet (97m) high; another is over 27 feet (8m) in diameter. When they were first discovered by a settler chasing a bear in 1852 they were thought to be the only examples of their kind. Subsequent press reports made these Calaveras trees a world-famous tourist destination.

built here. The Miner's Lending Library was the first public library in the state and the Volcano literary and debating society was also California's first. Two miles (3km) out of town, California's first observatory was built on what is now Observatory Hill. Some of the old town is preserved, but much of it disappeared in fires. During the 1850s, the McLaughlin family planted thousands of daffodils at a stagecoach stop on a hill about 3 miles (5km) north of town. Their descendants have continued the tradition and every spring Daffodil Hill still bursts into bloom, with over 300,000 daffodils covering 4 acres (2 hectares) of land on the private farm, and now attracting hundreds of visitors to view the lovely spectacle.

▶ *Drive for 2 miles (3km) along the Pine Grove-Volcano Road.*

10 Indian Grinding Rock State Historic Park

Using limestone bedrock as a natural mortar, Miwok Indians pulverized acorns and other seeds into meal, eventually grinding over 1,000 cavities in the rock. These flat expanses of pock-marked rock, together with hundreds of petroglyphs can be viewed from a self-guided trail, which also passes a re-created Indian village and ceremonial sweat house. The adjoining Chaw Se' Regional Indian Museum includes artifacts, exhibits and audio-visual programs.

▶ *From Pine Grove continue west on Hwy 88 for 12 miles (19km) to Jackson.*

some other communities, although it had its share of gambling halls and bordellos, which remained open until the 1950s. Even today there are card parlors on Main Street. The National Hotel at the foot of Main Street is yet another establishment that claims to be the oldest continually operating hotel in California, and on North Main Street the tiny St Sava Serbian Orthodox Church, tucked in between trees and tombstones, is, surprisingly, the mother church for the whole United States. Jackson is the Amador County seat, and the Amador County Museum at 225 Church Street is one of the best in the region, housed in an 1850s red-brick building on top of a hill and furnished with antiques. In the grounds is a working model of the Kennedy Mine,

flumes, then over two hills to a settling pond. To get a close view of the wheel, go down Jackson Gate Road at the north end of town to Tailing Wheels Park.

▶ *Continue north on Hwy 49 for 2 miles (3km).*

12 Sutter Creek

The picturesque Main Street of Sutter Creek is lined with dozens of buildings steeped in history. Most have been converted into antique and handicraft shops, and many of the fine Victorian mansions are now bed and breakfast inns. A self-guided walking tour brochure and city guide can be obtained from the City of Sutter Creek at 18 Main Street. The Historic Knight Foundry at 81 Eureka Street is the only

11 Jackson

Many of the buildings along the narrow streets of Jackson were destroyed in a great fire in 1862 and, although they were rebuilt, somehow the town has not retained quite the same historic character as many of the other towns along Highway 49. Jackson was never as wild as

which used to operate on the north edge of town. Both the Kennedy and Argonaut Mines were at one time the deepest mines in the world. They finally closed during World War II, but still standing are the headframes of some of the buildings and a huge tailing wheel, built in 1912 to carry mine tailings into

Victorian architecture still dominates Sutter Creek's Main Street

remaining water-powered foundry and machine shop in the country. The Knight & Co. Foundry was one of many developed on the Mother Lode when it was established in 1873. At one time they produced all types of mining equipment but they were particularly known for their water wheels. The foundry is still in operation and special ironwork for the restoration of the state capitol was produced here. Tours are offered allowing visitors to watch foundrymen use traditional methods for preparing molten iron.

▶ *Continue north on **Hwy 49** past the quaint brick and wood-frame buildings of Amador City to Plymouth and turn east onto Shenandoah Road.*

⓮ Shenandoah Valley

This region is of growing impor- ·tance as a wine-producing area. For 10 miles (16km) there are vineyards and wineries produc- ing some of the best zinfandel wines in California. Wine has been produced here since the gold rush days and the D'Agostini Winery, now called the Sobon Estate, was estab- lished 1856. The zinfandel grape is unique to California and flour- ishes in the heat of the Sierra foothills. Its spicy red wine is particularly prized when made from grapes off old vines and in Amador County several of the vineyards date back more than 100 years. The nickname Amador County was coined among serious winemakers because of the influx of people developing a second career in the wine business; but in recent years the Amador County wines have been able to hold their own in the best company. One of the best is Santino Winery next to Shenandoah Vineyards.

▶ *Return to **Hwy 49** and drive north for 22 miles (35km).*

⓯ Placerville

Placerville is a major stop on I-50 en route from Sacramento to South Lake Tahoe. Today the town looks much like any other town of its size, with shopping malls, motels and fast food restaurants lining the freeway frontage roads. Its modern appearance belies its notorious

past. Placerville was originally known as Old Dry Diggin's, and became so lawless that criminals were hanged in pairs. As a result the name was changed to Hangtown. A dummy dangling from the second story of the Hangman's Tree Bar at 905 Main Street is a grim reminder of these not too distant times. Placerville was always a prosper- ous town, strategically situated on the old Overland Trail, which is now I-50, and a surprising number of industrial leaders had their beginnings here. John Studebaker built wheelbarrows for miners before he turned his attention to cars; Leland Stanford, who founded Stanford University, ran a store close by in

FOR CHILDREN

From the ridge east of Placerville to near Camino is the old Pony Express route now known as Apple Hill. Every late summer and autumn, the orchards along the route sell apples straight from the tree, as well as many home-made apple confec- tions that never fail to delight young- sters. They can watch cider being made, eat a toffee apple and maybe even take a pony ride.

Cold Springs; Philip Armour, who developed a canned meat empire, ran a small butcher's shop in town, and railroad magnate Mark Hopkins had a shop on Main Street, bringing in groceries from

SPECIAL BLEND
FRESH CIDER

HANDMADE CANDY

Farm Pack
FRUIT BUTTER
and
PRESERVES

TAMALE PLATE

STOP HERE
4 the BEST
PIES
50 VARIETIES - BUT ALWAYS
OUT OF 44.

Wine produced in Amador County is now judged to be among the best you can get

Sacramento. The most interesting site is the old Gold Bug Mine, the nation's only city- owned gold mine, a mile (1.6km) from the N. Bedford exit off I- 50. The 60-acre (24- hectare) Bedford Park site used to have 250 active gold mines, but all that remains is Gold Bug and its well-lit tunnels.

▶ *Continue north on **Hwy 49** for 7 miles (11km).*

⑮ Marshall Gold Discovery State Historic Park

Coloma is perhaps the most historically significant town in the Gold Country. It was here that James Marshall discovered gold, at Sutter's Mill in January, 1848. Paradoxically, the town was one of the first to be abandoned, when richer deposits were found in other areas in the early 1850s. Within the space of five years the population exploded to 10,000 and then dwindled to the quiet village that it remains today. Most of Coloma now lies within the 265-acre Marshall Gold Discovery State Historic Park, and the centerpiece is a full-scale replica of Sutter's Mill on the banks of the American River. Thousands of visitors re-create the experience of the Fortyniners, trying their hand at gold-panning in the American River by the old mill. Even today those bright yellow flecks of metal continue to be washed down the river.

▶ *Continue north on* **Hwy 49** *for 18 miles (29km) to its junction with* **I-80**.

⑯ Auburn

Gold was discovered here in the spring of 1848, just a few months after the Coloma discovery. In fact, Frenchman Claude Chana, the discoverer, was a friend of James Marshall. Auburn is a major stop on the main road from Sacramento to North Lake Tahoe and, like Placerville to the south, it has developed way beyond its historic core and, some would say, has outgrown its rural charm. Fortunately, Old Town Auburn remains intact.

The landmark four-story, red-and-white fire station dates back to 1892 and inside it is California's first motorised fire engine. Close by is the state's oldest continuously used post office. The narrow streets of Auburn, with their false-front buildings are a magnet to antique-hunters looking for that elusive bargain. Old Town is dominated by the yellow, domed, neo-classical Placer County Courthouse, built in 1852 from local materials. The Placer County Central Museum, at 1273 High Street, has a walk-through model of a hard-rock mining tunnel as well as an interesting collection of quartz and gold specimens from the local mines.

▶ *Return to San Francisco via Sacramento on* **I-80**.

GOLD

James Marshall discovered gold in the millrace of a sawmill in Coloma on the morning of January 24 1848, and the course of California's history changed forever. Gold had always been the carrot dangling before the explorers of this frontier land: the Spanish looked in vain for El Dorado, the Golden City, during their occupation of the region; ironically, it was pure chance that finally led to its discovery.

Within a year, thousands of fortune-seekers were heading west and starting the migration to the Golden State that continues even today. News of the discovery spread rapidly throughout the world; towns mushroomed overnight, and the population of California exploded from 15,000 to 265,000 in a period of three years. From 1849, the boom year that lent its name to the prospectors, they would always be Fortyniners. Most of the adventurers were young men, but they were soon followed by ambitious women, some of whom helped establish the Barbery Coast's notoriously bawdy reputation.

The heart of the gold country was along the western slopes of the Sierra Nevada foothills. The Mother Lode, the rich vein of

gold that seemed to be inexhaustible, stretched from Nevada City in the north down to Mariposa near Yosemite Valley. A string of towns survives along what is now called Highway 49, many of which have changed little since the 19th century. False-front

The dirty work that leads to the reward. Above: a statue of a gold panner in Auburn; left: a display of shining gold nuggets

buildings line the streets and old mining equipment lies rusting in open fields.

Gold was extracted from the ground by several different methods. Many prospectors just used a simple gold-pan and patiently worked in the rivers flowing from the High Sierra, hoping to strike it rich. Few did, and many of those who did succeed lost it all gambling. Panning took considerable skill and more than a little luck. The attraction was that anyone could do it at very little expense, and thousands of people saw it as a way to rapid fortune. Latter-day Fortyniners can still try their hand at it at many sites along Highway 49. The perfect gold pan is made of steel, about 15 inches (380mm) in diameter and blackened by heat, so that the flecks of gold will be easier to see. Gravel from the stream bed is scooped up in the pan which, held in both hands, is rotated back and forth underwater to let the heavy particles of gold settle to the bottom. The dirty water is drained off and with consider-

A 19th-century illustration of gold prospectors in California

able luck there may be a few grains of gold left in the gravel in the bottom of the pan.

Hard-rock mining was a much more highly organised operation, with miners toiling underground to dig out the precious yellow nuggets. At its most sophisticated this became a huge industrial enterprise, and the Empire Mine in Grass Valley was one of the biggest, creating a vast network of tunnels under the town. This mine remained productive for over 100 years after the first discovery of the metal – and was one of the last to close. Close by, at the North Star Mine, there is a vast display of mining equipment from this era.

In the Malakoff Diggins State Park, 16 miles (26km) north of Nevada City, you can see an impressive example of the landscape erosion caused by hydraulic mining. Gold was literally washed out of the ground by the force of giant hoses that destroyed the landscape beyond recognition.

The boom period the gold rush lasted for little over a decade, but by then the development of the northern region of California had been well established. In 1849, over 90,000 miners passed through San Francisco, which overnight became a wild frontier city. This was the only way through which the miners could travel to get to the gold fields, and the legacy of this period lives on, although most of the old buildings were destroyed in the great 1906 earthquake. Many of the workers in the mines were Chinese; throughout the Gold Country traces of their past are still evident. When the gold ran out they settled in San Francisco and built the biggest Chinatown outside Asia. Sacramento also grew to be a major city, providing supplies for the gold fields only a few miles to the east.

As the deposits of gold ran low along the Mother Lode, new areas were explored. Gold was found as far north as Yreka, close

to the Oregon border, and as far south as the Mojave Desert. These fringe areas never produced the massive amounts that were found in the Sierra foothills but the old, abandoned mines can still be seen on a drive along the back country roads.

It is said that there is as much gold left in the ground in California as has been extracted. The problem is the expense of

A monument to James Marshall at Coloma, where he first found gold

mining it. Hundreds of weekend miners still go panning in the rivers and even some commercial mines have reopened. Many shops have California gold for sale and there is no shortage of museum exhibits, notably at the Oakland Museum and the Bank of California's Museum of Money in the American West.

Yosemite &
the High Sierra

3 DAYS • 568 MILES • 914KM

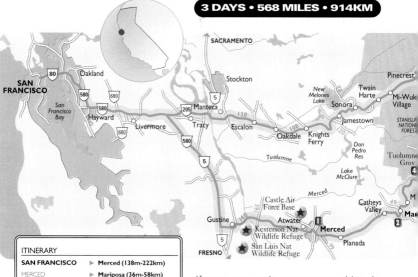

SACRAMENTO

Pinecrest

SAN FRANCISCO

Oakland

Stockton

New Melones Lake

Twain Harte

Mi-Wuk Village

Sonora

San Francisco Bay

Hayward

Manteca

Jamestown

STANISLA NATION FORES

Livermore

Tracy

Escalon

Oakdale

Knights Ferry

Don Pedro Res

Tuolumne Grov

Tuolumne

Lake McClure

Merced

Catheys Valley

M

Mar

Castle Air Force Base

Gustine

Atwater

Merced

Kesterson Nat Wildlife Refuge

FRESNO

San Luis Nat Wildlife Refuge

Planada

If you can only cover one drive in Northern California, it should be this one. Yosemite National Park is one of the nation's greatest natural treasures. Combined with the surreal landscape of Mono Lake and a visit to the perfectly preserved ghost town of Bodie, the drive includes some of the best that California has to offer. As a bonus, the route crosses the Central Valley, the agricultural heart of the nation. The journey involves two high passes, Tioga and Sonora. These are both closed by snow from November to at least April every year, so the drive is only feasible during the summer months.

ℹ️ *San Francisco Convention and Visitors Bureau, 201 Third Street, Suite 900, CA 94103*

▶ *Leave San Francisco across the Bay Bridge and take I-580 to I-5 south. Continue south for 29 miles (47km) to the Gustine exit and drive 38 miles (61km) east to Merced.*

❶ Merced
The Central Valley has a string of large towns that are virtually indistinguishable from each other. Many people drive from Los Angeles to the north past these towns without even blinking: they are sleepy, agricultural towns, where people rise early and go to bed early and, outside the fields, nothing much happens in between. Merced is, however, a convenient rest stop on the long drive from San Francisco to Yosemite.

▶ *Hwy 140 winds through Merced, combining with Hwy 99 for a short distance. Stay on Hwy 140 for another 48 miles (77km) to Mariposa.*

❷ Mariposa
The southern mines of the Gold Country never rivalled those of the north. Mariposa was a southern gold camp, and is one of the

The soaring rocks of Yosemite Valley, where most visitors stay

last towns along Highway 49. The boardwalks and false-front buildings immediately identify its lineage. At the north end of town is a two-story courthouse that has been in use continuously since 1854. The Mariposa County History Center, at Twelfth and Jessie Streets, has a group of reconstructed interiors, including a lady's boudoir, a sheriff's office and a miner's cabin. The California State Mining and Mineral Museum, 2 miles (3km) south of town, has a collection of over 20,000 gems and minerals, along with dioramas of mine interiors and a working model stamp mill.

▶ *Continue along Hwy 140 for 30 miles (48km), climbing through steep, pine-covered valleys and increasingly rugged mountain terrain.*

❸ Yosemite National Park
This must be America's favorite national park. Unfortunately, its popularity is reflected in the

numbers of people visiting. At certain peak times the park is actually closed because it has reached capacity. If at all possible, try to visit out of major holiday periods and during the week. Over 3 million people visit Yosemite every year and 70 percent of them arrive during the summer. Most, however, never venture out of the 7 square miles (18 sq km) of Yosemite Valley, which leaves 1,200 square miles (3,108 sq km) in splendid solitude. If you are planning to spend the night there, reservations must be made as early as possible. Rooms and even camp sites are often booked months ahead. However unpleasant the crowds may be, the park is always a rewarding visit. The road continues down into the heart of the valley, where everything is larger than life: granite cliffs towering 3,000 feet ((914m) into the air, waterfalls cascading down almost 2,500 feet (762m) - the second highest falls in the world. This is landscape on the grandest scale. Yosemite Village is the main centre of the valley, and the park headquarters and visitor center are located here, along with restaurants, a hotel and a post office. There are also a few shops, including the Ansel Adams Gallery, where the work of the great landscape photographer is available for purchase.

▶ *The road loops around the valley, passing most of the main landmarks, and 6 miles (10km) from Yosemite Village, Hwy 120 branches off to the right. Take this road up to Crane Flat and turn right, to reach a large parking area (on the left), where there are signs to Tuolumne Grove.*

4 Tuolumne Grove

A 1-mile (1.6km) hike down an easy trail leads to the Tuolumne Grove of giant sequoias, the

Winter lends its own special beauty to Yosemite National Park

most accessible grove in the park. The trees are not the biggest, and there are only 25 of them, but they are, nevertheless, an impressive sight.

▶ *Continue east on the Tioga Road, originally built by the Great Consolidated Silver Company in 1883 and dividing Yosemite National Park in two. The road passes through increasingly dramatic landscape, with polished granite slabs and massive, smooth, granite domes towering above the road.*

5 Olmsted Point
At marker T-24, 28 miles (45km) east of Crane Flat, Olmsted Point provides one of the most remarkable scenic outlooks in the park. There is a unique view of Half Dome and Cloud's Rest and, to the east, sweeping views of Tenaya Lake and the domes and peaks of Tuolumne Meadows. Spend a while here and watch the fat marmots and little golden-mantled ground squirrels come out of the rocks hoping for some crumbs from passing sightseers. Two miles (3km) down the road, Lake Tenaya looks inviting on a hot day. Be warned, though: the water is usually very cold. Sailboarding and windsurfing are allowed on the lake and there is usually a park ranger on hand to give information on regulations. The lake is in a wonderfully dramatic setting.

▶ *Continue east for 8 miles (13km) to Tuolumne Meadows.*

6 Tuolumne Meadows
This is Yosemite's high country. A beautiful sub-alpine meadow sits at 8,600 feet (2,621m), with the Tuolumne River winding through it at. At 2.5 miles (4km) long, it is the largest meadow of its kind in the Sierra Nevada, and is stunningly picturesque. This idyllic wilderness is only 55

miles (88km) by road from Yosemite Valley, but it is a world apart. It is almost a crime to pass through it without leaving the car – and, if time permits, there are numerous hiking trails. A ranger station just past the gas station and store can provide maps and information.

▶ *Continue east to the Tioga Pass, at an elevation of 9,945 feet (3,031m). East of Tioga, the road drops steeply through deep gorges, with views over the Eastern Sierra and Mono Lake. In Lee Vining a one-street town at the foot of the Tioga Road, the Mono Lake Committee Information Center has displays on the geology of the region and the ecology of Mono Lake.*

SCENIC ROUTES

A circuitous 30-mile (48km) drive out of Yosemite Valley follows Wawona Road to Wawona Tunnel, where a parking area provides the classic view of the valley from Bridalveil Falls to El Capitan. Continue through the tunnel and up to Glacier Point Road, and follow the road to the end for absolutely incredible views of the entire valley, including Half Dome and the 13,000-foot (3,962m) peaks of the High Sierra.

---

7 Mono Lake
Once known as the Dead Sea of California, the million-year-old Mono Lake is a large alkaline inland sea. Far from dead, however, Mono Lake is home during at least part of the year to over 300 bird species, including almost the entire breeding population of California gulls. Most striking are the lake's vast, surrounding salt flats and unusual formations of tufa – freeform pillars of calcium carbonate, originally created underwater where calcium-rich fresh spring water flowed into the salty lake. These 200- to 900-year-old bone-white spires

are now exposed to view, due to Los Angeles' thirst for new water sources. Since 1941, when Mono Lake's feeder streams were first tapped, the lake level has fallen more than 45 feet (14m), increasing the salinity and wreaking havoc with the wildlife populations. The best place to explore Mono Lake's tufa towers is the south tufa area, off Hwy 120: drive south from Lee Vining along Hwy 395 for 5 miles (8km) and turn east onto Hwy 120. Continue for another 5 miles (8km) past interesting volcanic formations, to a dirt road that leads down to the lake.

▶ *Return to Hwy 395 and drive north for 20 miles (32km) to Hwy 270. Turn right and a narrow road leading to Bodie is paved for all but the last 3 miles (5km).*

8 Bodie
The one-time gold-mining town of Bodie is California's largest ghost town, an evocative and ramshackle collection of wood-frame buildings, high in the Eastern Sierra. The 170 remaining buildings are preserved in a state of arrested decay: they will not be restored, but are not allowed to deteriorate further. Bodie was one of the wildest and most lawless town in the West, with a population of over 10,000. Visitors can take a self-guided walking tour and peer into the weathered homes, store and saloons that remain. Through the windows you can even see furnishings and personal belongings that were left when the town was finally abandoned.

▶ *Return to Hwy 395 and drive north through Bridgeport to Hwy 108. This road takes you west over the 9,624-foot (2,933m) Sonora Pass, traversing beautiful, high alpine scenery before descending to the gold country towns of Sonora and Jamestown (see pages 67–8). Take Hwy 120 west back to I-205 and then I-580 back to San Francisco.*

Lake Tahoe &
the Northern Gold
Country

This is San Francisco's mountain playground: during the summer, water sports, hiking and fishing are popular; in December skiing takes over. The tour is not recommended in winter, due to sudden and frequent storms. From Lake Tahoe, the drive returns through two of the most interesting towns of the northern Gold Country, before returning to Sacramento.

2 DAYS • 269 MILES • 433KM

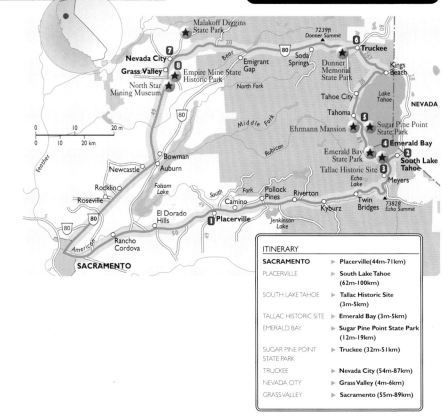

ITINERARY	
SACRAMENTO	► Placerville(44m-71km)
PLACERVILLE	► **South Lake Tahoe (62m-100km)**
SOUTH LAKE TAHOE	► **Tallac Historic Site (3m-5km)**
TALLAC HISTORIC SITE	► **Emerald Bay (3m-5km)**
EMERALD BAY	► **Sugar Pine Point State Park (12m-19km)**
SUGAR PINE POINT STATE PARK	► **Truckee (32m-51km)**
TRUCKEE	► **Nevada City (54m-87km)**
NEVADA CITY	► **Grass Valley (4m-6km)**
GRASS VALLEY	► **Sacramento (55m-89km)**

i Sacramento Visitor Information
Center, 1104 Front Street,
Sacramento, CA 95814

▶ *Leave Sacramento on I-50
east and drive 44 miles
(71km) to Placerville.*

❶ Placerville
(See page 72)
Once known as Hangtown, a
hotbed of crime, Placerville is
now a substantial and thriving
centre, where the Gold Rush era
is evoked in the underground
tunnels of the city-owned Gold
Bug Mine.

▶ *Continue east on I-50, climbing
to Echo Summit at 7,382 feet
(2,250m). During the winter
this section of the road is
frequently closed for several
hours at a time. Once over the
summit the road drops down
to Lake Tahoe, 6,225 feet
(1,897m) high, 22 miles
(35km) long and 1,645 feet
((501m) deep – the biggest
alpine lake in the nation, with
enough water to cover the
entire state to a depth of 14
inches (356mm). However
much snow and ice covers the
surrounding mountains, the*

*lake itself never freezes
because of its great depth. The
I-50 continues into the town of
South Lake Tahoe into the
most heavily populated part
of the lake.*

❷ South Lake Tahoe
For the next few miles, up to the
Nevada border, the road is a
continuous strip of motels, gas
stations, restaurants and shopping centers. Apart from rest
stops, the Historical Society
Museum, at 3058 State 50, is
worth visiting for an introduction
to the area's past and to pick up
maps and a guide to the lake's
historical landmarks. The other
reason for driving this section of
road is to experience the deca-
dent world of Nevada's casinos.
Within inches of the state
border, at Stateline, casinos
spring up like mushrooms: a
totally artificial world, incongruously set in the middle of a
wonderful natural landscape.

▶ *Return west along I-50 and
turn onto Hwy 89 and drive
north for 3 miles (5km).*

Heading for the slopes along
Heavenly Valley, South Lake Tahoe

❸ Tallac Historic Site
Nineteen historic summer
homes are spread over 74 acres
(30 hectares) on the shore of
Lake Tahoe, testifying to its past
as the playground for California's
rich and powerful. Several of the
houses have been fully restored,
including the 1884 Pope House,
brown-shingled Valhalia and
Lucky Baldwin's Baldwin
Estate, which houses the Tallac
Museum, where exhibits tell the
story of this élite retreat. There
are special events throughout
the summer, including Sunday
chamber music, a bluegrass festival in August and a weekend
jazz festival series in late
summer.

▶ *Hwy 89 winds north, climbing
through rugged, boulder-
strewn, pine forest scenery to
a point overlooking the lake
and specifically Emerald Bay.*

❹ Emerald Bay
This is perhaps the most
picturesque site on the lake. A
perfect cove, enclosed by pine
forests has the lake's only island,
Fannette. A 1-mile (1.6km) hike
down from the car park leads to a
38-room granite mansion called

The well-named Emerald Bay, and Lake Tahoe's only island, Fannette

Vikingsholm, which is considered to be the finest example of Scandinavian architecture in the western hemisphere. It was built for half a million dollars in 1928–9 and includes elements of everything from 11th-century castles to sod-roofed homes. An easier way to see Vikingsholm and its fjord-like bay is by boat – a very big boat, a stern-wheeler that departs from South Lake Tahoe.

After climbing back up to the car park, if you have any energy left, take a short walk up to Eagle Falls, directly across Hwy 89 from the vista point. The falls cascade over a series of granite steps with Emerald Bay glistening below.

Emerald Bay State Park sits on the lake shore and is contiguous with the D.L. Bliss State Park. Much of the shoreline does not have public access, but these parks provide for camping, fishing, swimming and boating. Lester Beach, at Bliss, is particularly popular, and fills up early on summer weekends.

▶ *Continue north on* **Hwy 89**.

5 Sugar Pine Point State Park

The rocky lake shore at Sugar Pine Point offers sunbathing and hiking, including a hike to its only operational lighthouse; but the Ehrmann Mansion is the main attraction. Built in 1903 by wealthy San Francisco banker, Isaias Hellman, the stone-and-wood baronial dwelling is the best example of the summer homes of the wealthy.

▶ *Continue north on* **Hwy 89** *to Tahoe City. Visit the Gatekeeper's Museum State Park, at 130 W Lake Boulevard, where the museum emphasises the area's native cultures and natural history. Continue north on* **route 28** *to Kings Beach and* **route 267** *to Truckee.*

6 Truckee

Truckee developed as a result of the transcontinental railroad, and the railroad is still dominant in the town's life, with a major line passing through the center of town. The false-front Main Street has a definite frontier-town feel: Charlie Chaplin chose this as the location for his classic film The Gold Rush. Apart from

tourists, little has changed since the Gold Rush days.

Two miles (3km) west of Truckee on I-80 is Donner Memorial State Park. It was here, in the winter of 1846, that 89 pioneers of the Donner Party were trapped by massive snow falls. Almost half the party died and a monument to them rests on a 22-foot (7m)-high stone base – the depth of the snow that dreadful winter. The Emigrant Trail Museum tells the story of the Donner Party, the construction of the railroad and the natural history of the region.

▶ *Drive west on* **I-80** *over Donner Summit at 7,239 feet (2,206m) and down through pine forests into the northern Gold Country. Turn off* **I-80** *onto* **Hwy 20** *and continue to Nevada City.*

7 Nevada City

Historically, Nevada City has been host to innovators and innovations. World-class soprano Emma Nevada and Andrew Hallidie, inventor of the cable-car, were both born here. Nevada City created new and radical mining techniques, including hydraulic mining, and social engineering had its part: U.S. Senator A.J. Sargent, a local resident, prepared legislation that led to American women's suffrage. Meetings held here ultimately established both the University of California and Pacific Gas & Electricity, the world's largest utility company. Nevada was once the third largest city in California and even today it is grand by Gold Country standards, though it keeps a small-town charm. There are gas lights in the streets and balconied stores; and in the autumn, the town blazes with sugar maples.

Nevada City's most unusual legacy is 16 miles (26km) out of town, on the North Bloomfield Road. The Malakoff Diggins State Historic Park is an oddly enchanting environmental horror, including a massive mine pit with colorful crags and spires, created by hydraulic mining in the 1870s. Malakoff also offers good hiking, camping and the Gold Rush ghost town of North Blumfield.

▶ Take **Hwy 49** south to Grass Valley.

8 Grass Valley

Like Nevada City, this is a big town, compared with the southern Gold Country settlements. The mines along this northern route were a far cry from the simple mining operations of the southern Mother Lode, where a gold pan and rocker were as sophisticated as it got. This was

RECOMMENDED WALK

Nevada City is one of the few Gold Rush towns that has an extensive historic core. A walking tour map that highlights the most interesting buildings, including the City Hall and art deco Courthouse, is available from The Nevada City Chamber of Commerce at 132 Main Street.

big industry: large corporations moved in and mined gold on a vast scale, leaving beneath Grass Valley over 367 miles (590km) of mining tunnels. On the edge of town, on East Empire Street, is the Empire Mine State Historic Park. This was the richest hard-rock mine in California, productive until 1956. It is thought that

there is four times as much gold still in the ground as was mined – but it is too expensive to dig it out. The mine stands in a 784-acre (317-hectare) estate, and many of the original buildings are still in perfect condition. Separated from the ugly mining operation by careful landscaping is Bourn Cottage, the elegant country seat of William Bourn, owner of the mine and one of the richest men in California.

Downtown Grass Valley's Cornish pasty shops are a legacy of the English miners who came over from Cornwall in the early 20th century.

▶ Take **Hwy 49** to Auburn and turn south onto **I-80** back to Sacramento.

One of downtown Nevada City's fine Victorian buildings

FOR HISTORY BUFFS

Grass Valley Museum, located in Mount St Mary's Convent, on South Church Street, gives a good introduction to the development of the gold-mining industry and at the North Star Mining Museum, at the end of Mill Street, there are displays of the machinery that created the labyrinth of tunnels under the town.

Deep Valleys
& Big Trees

2 DAYS • 219 MILES • 353KM   Yosemite always steals the spotlight from other High Sierra destinations, but the King's Canyon and Sequoia national parks, only a few miles further south, offer as much natural spectacle – without the crowds. This tour starts in the agricultural city of Fresno, in the Central Valley, and climbs up to these two pristine wilderness areas before returning to the valley. On the way back, it passes through the 19th-century railroad town of Hanford and Kingsburg, which still holds onto its Swedish routes. The journey tour is not possible during the winter, when snow closes the General's Highway, which connects King's Canyon and Sequoia national parks.

ITINERARY		
FRESNO	▶	**King's Canyon National Park (52m-84km)**
KING'S CANYON NATIONAL PARK	▶	**Giant Forest (29m-47km)**
GIANT FOREST	▶	**Crystal Cave (10m-16km)**
CRYSTAL CAVE	▶	**Hospital Rock (14m-23km)**
HOSPITAL ROCK	▶	**Visalia (43m-69km)**
VISALIA	▶	**Hanford (20m-32km)**
HANFORD	▶	**Kingsburg (29m-47km)**
KINGSBURG	▶	**Fresno (22m-35km)**

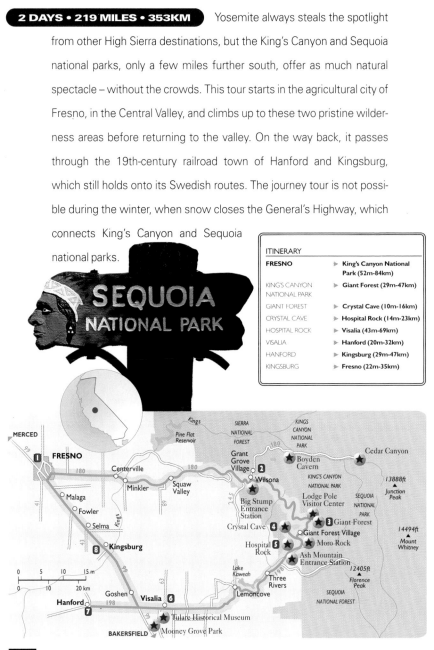

► *Start at Fresno.*

❶ Fresno

This is the gateway to the three Sierra Nevada national parks, and most visitors see it as little more than that. Fresno is a big, sprawling, agricultural center, established during the 19th century and now the eighth biggest city in California. There is more to see here than may at first be apparent. Fresno calls itself the Raisin Capital of the World and the Edwardian mansion of the father of the raisin industry, Theodore Kearney, is open for tours at weekends. It is set in spacious grounds 7 miles ((11km) west of town, at 7160 West Kearney Boulevard. Closer to town, Baldasare Forestiere spent 40 years digging out an underground home by hand at 5201 West Shaw Avenue, two blocks west of Hwy 99. The Forestiere Underground Gardens are open to the public, and there is a self-guided tour of the family's sky-lit living area and the 10-acre (4-hectare) maze of patios and passageways that were completed in 1946. The Fresno Metropolitan Museum of Art, History and Science features a large Asian art collection, as well as the Salzer collection of European and American still-life paintings. There is also a selection of Ansel Adams photographs of Yosemite.

Every spring, the fruit orchards surrounding Fresno burst into flower and the 67-mile (108km) Blossom Trail passes some of the more spectacular displays. Beehives are placed under the trees to produce honey from specific blossoms: as the blossoms peak, so do the bees – watch out! A map of the Blossom Trail is available from the Visitors Bureau.

i *Fresno City and County Convention and Visitors Bureau, 808 M Street*

FOR CHILDREN

Children can be amused for hours at 157-acre (63-hectare) Roeding Park, at 894 West Belmont Avenue in Fresno. Not only does it house Chaffee Zoological Gardens, with over 700 animals, including elephants and an Australian outback; it also boasts a Playland and a Storyland, with a fairytale theme featuring a castle.

► *Leave Fresno on* **Hwy 180** *east and drive for 49 miles (79km) through Centerville, before starting the climb up to King's Canyon and the Big Stump Entrance Station.*

The beautiful Blossom Trail in the fruit orchards around Fresno

❷ King's Canyon National Park

King's Canyon is split into two quite distinct areas. Tiny General Grant National Park was created in 1890 to protect the General Grant grove of sequoias. In 1940, it was incorporated into the King's Canyon National Park which includes the wild, mountainous country to the east.

Visitors enter King's Canyon through the Big Stump Entrance Station on Hwy 180; 3 miles (5km) further on is Grant Grove Village, the most developed area of the park. At the Grant Grove Visitor Center there is an exhibit on the logging history of

---

RECOMMENDED WALK

Most of the hikes in King's Canyon are serious undertakings, but one relatively easy way to get a feel for this magnificent wilderness is to follow the 1-mile (1.6km) walking trail through Zumwalt Meadow. Leaving from Cedar Grove, the trail crosses King's River by a suspension bridge, as it winds above and around Zumwalt Meadow.

Visitors to the Giant Forest are dwarfed by the mighty sequoia

sequoias, the wildlife and early Indian inhabitants of the region. Two groves of sequoias grow in this, the most accessible part of the park. The General Grant Tree is the third largest tree in the world – 267 feet (81m) tall, with a base circumference of 107 feet (32m), and it was alive during the Bronze Age, over 3,000 years ago. Close by is the Redwood Mountain Grove of smaller but, nevertheless, very impressive sequoias.

▶ *Turn onto the General's Highway. Follow this around to Sequoia National Park, which is contiguous with King's Canyon and does not involve passing another entrance station.*

❸ Giant Forest
Sequoia was the first national park in California and second in the nation after Yellowstone. It was established in 1890 to protect the groves of giant sequoia, which grow only in California; in fact, more grow here than in any other part of the state. Lodge Pole Visitor Center is the first stop, where there are good displays about sequoias and the geologic history of the park; 4 miles (6km) beyond it is the Giant Forest, home of the world's largest living thing: the General Sherman Tree, 275 feet (84m) high, 103 feet (31m) in circumference. The volume of the trunk alone is 52,500 cubic feet (1,485 cu m). The 2-mile (3km)-long Congress Trail begins near this mighty tree and goes past many other huge specimens. Booklets explaining the sites are available at the trail head.

Return to the General's Highway and turn left onto Crescent Meadow Road which passes the Auto Log, a massive fallen tree through which a tunnel has been made. Continue to Moro Rock. Steps lead 300 feet (91m) to the 6,000-foot (1,829m) summit of this massive

> ### SCENIC ROUTES
>
> Highway 180 continues down into King's Canyon leaving the national park soon after leaving Grant Grove Village and dropping 2,000 feet (609m) to the valley floor, in a spectacular, winding descent through impressive mountain scenery into the gorges of the King's River. On the deep valley floor, about 20 miles (32km) after Grant Grove, a road on the right is sign posted to marble-walled Boyden Cavern, where there are beautiful stalactite and stalagmite formations. Continue for 10 miles (16km) through the narrow gorge of the south fork of King's River to Cedar Canyon, the end of the road for vehicular traffic. Mountains rise 6,000 feet (1,829m) above the valley floor, which is the staging point for excursions into the back country, where there are over 700 miles (1,126km) of trails.

boulder, which gives sweeping views of the park and, smog permitting, the Central Valley.

▶ *Return to the General's Highway and drive 5 miles (8km) to the signed turnoff to the Crystal Cave.*

❹ Crystal Cave
A narrow, winding road descends 2,000 feet (609m) to the Marble Fork Kaweah River Bridge and then from the parking area, down a short, steep trail. Several chambers are open to the public, including the Organ Room, the Marble Hall and the Dome Room. The temperature inside is a constant 48°F (9°C), which can feel decidedly chilly after the hot Sierra sun.

▶ *Return to the General's Highway, which now becomes Hwy 198, and drive 6 miles (10km) to Hospital Rock.*

❺ Hospital Rock
This old village site of the Potwisha Indian tribe is marked by a large boulder covered in pictographs. A nearby rock has over 50 mortar holes, used by Indian women to grind acorns into flour.

▶ *Continue along Hwy 198 and leave Sequoia National Park by the Ash Mountain Entrance Station. The road descends to Visalia.*

❻ Visalia
Visalia is the oldest city between Stockton and Los Angeles, founded in 1852. It quickly became an important agricultural center, and the lavish homes that were built during this period can be seen on a self-guided walking tour through the historic district. Maps are available from the Chamber of Commerce, at 720 W Mineral King Avenue. For most visitors Visalia provides a convenient base for exploring the national parks, but there are a few sites of interest within easy reach. The Tulare Historical Museum, about 8 miles (13km) south of

Deep Valleys & Big Trees

town, traces the history of the area from the time when it was covered by one of the largest bodies of water west of the Mississippi. The museum is at 444 W Tulare Avenue, off Hwy 137, west of Hwy 99. Mooney Grove Park is 5 miles (8km) south of town, covering 155 acres (63 hectares), with a lake, valley oaks and date palms.

▶ *Return to Visalia and take* **Hwy 198** *west to Hanford along 11 miles (18km) of dead straight road.*

🔽 Hanford

Hanford is an atypical Central Valley town. It has charm, history, interesting architecture and even a nationally noted restaurant. Founded by the Southern Pacific Railroad in 1877, it was named after the popular paymaster, who paid the workers in gold. Courthouse Square is the core of historic

A hazy view of the Central Valley from the Giant Forest's Moro Rock

Hanford, built in the late 19th century and overlooking a picturesque town square that has been lovingly restored and now houses boutiques, gift shops and a restaurant. Close by are other architectural gems, including a fine art deco cinema and The Superior Dairy, an old-fashioned ice cream parlor in business for over 60 years. Hanford once claimed one of the largest Chinese communities in California: 800 Chinese families were brought by railroad at the turn of the century. All that is left now is China Alley, a few blocks east of downtown. The 1893 Taoist Temple still stands here, and can be toured by request, and next door is the Imperial Dynasty Restaurant, operated by the Wing family for more than a century and serving some of the best – and most expensive – Chinese cuisine in California.

▶ *Return east on* **Hwy 198** *and take* **Hwy 99** *north to Kingsburg.*

A Swedish coffee pot sits above the railroad station in Kingsburg

🔽 Kingsburg

Kingsburg was established in 1875 as a railroad town and its Swedish immigrant population earned it the name Swedish Village. Many buildings are half-timbered, with steep, wood-shingled roofs and dormer windows.

▶ *Return to Fresno on* **Hwy 99** *north.*

CENTRAL VALLEY

The Central Valley of California is one of the most productive agricultural regions of the world. Peach trees, apricots, walnuts, oranges, cotton and acres of vineyards stretch as far as the eye can see. The rich soil of the valley supports a myriad of crops that are watered by the rivers, lakes and reservoirs generated by the snow melt in the High Sierra to the east.

Before agriculture, gold was the valley's fortune. During the 19th century the area provided access to the Mother Lode, which ran up its eastern flank. Sacramento became the major supply centre to the mines and rapidly developed into a prosperous city. As the Gold Rush petered out, agriculture took hold, and within a few years the revenues from agricultural produce were rivalling those from the dwindling supplies of gold.

The 18,000-square-mile (46,620 sq km) valley extends for almost 500 miles (804km) from Chico, north of Sacramento, the state capital, to Bakersfield in the south. It has never been a tourist destination – and that is much of the area's charm. Along the valley are old agricultural towns with colorful pasts; some have a rich legacy of Chinese culture, established in the 19th century, when Chinese laborers came to work on railroads and in the fields. Mexicans have had a more recent influence. In the south, around Bakersfield, oil has eclipsed agriculture as the dominant industry and nodding oil donkeys sit amid fields of cotton on the valley floor. But the greatest interest is in the towns and cities, and the wildlife that flocks here on major migratory flight paths across North America.

Sacramento is the biggest, fastest-growing and most important city in the valley. This is the seat of the state government, a thriving shipping port and a major processing centre. With a population of over 370,000, Sacramento manages to retain a small-town atmosphere. Beautifully maintained Victorian houses are set on tree-lined avenues, and the State Capitol is surrounded by a well-tended park.

The other important cities in the valley are Modesto, Fresno and Bakersfield, quiet, working communities with little of interest to the visitor. The best of the Central Valley can be sampled by taking some of the tours in this book – but don't just rush through: slow down and experience the true California.

Tour 14

After leaving San Francisco across the Golden Gate Bridge, – where you can enjoy stunning views of the city from across the bay – this tour travels down through the chic, waterfront town of Sausalito, which has more of a Mediterranean than an American air, and then skirts around the northern edge of enormous San Francisco Bay, past the naval shipyards of Vallejo to the railroad museum at Suisun City.

The Sacramento Delta is a complex labyrinth of waterways, ideally explored by houseboat, Narrow country roads pass along the levees (raised embankments) through old towns such as Walnut Grove and Locke, built in around 1915 by members of a Chinese association who were working in the area. It remains a Chinese community to this day. A winding country road meanders past these towns before reaching Sacramento, the state capital. On the return journey, the route passes Davis, home of U.C. Davis, the state's foremost University for veterinary science and the Air Museum at Fairfield Air Force Base, before continuing past Benicia, a sleepy backwater that once knew headier days as the state capital. Across the water, in Martinez, is the home of the great environmentalist John Muir, and close by is the now forgotten town of Port Costa, suspended in time on the edge of the delta. The return to San Francisco takes you across the Richmond-San Rafael Bridge and back again to the Golden Gate Bridge.

Tour 15

This tour starts, appropriately enough, at Sutter's Fort, the first settlement in Sacramento, dating back to 1839. Next to the fort is the State Indian Museum. Wide, tree-lined avenues lead down past the elegant, Victorian Governor's Mansion, which was most recently used by President Ronald Reagan. A short distance away from the Governor's Mansion is the impressive State Capitol building, which has been faithfully restored to its original splendor.

Continue past the Crocker Art Museum, which has the distinguished claim of being the first art museum in the west, and houses an impressive collection of Californian art, and carry on to Old Sacramento, an area that covers 28 acres (11 hectares) and is made up of fully restored Gold Rush era buildings, set by the Sacramento River. Railroad enthusiasts are sure to appreciate the California State Railroad Museum, which is the crowning glory of Old Sacramento, and is generally considered to be one of the finest rail museums in the whole world.

Just across the Sacramento River you can visit another museum with international claims. The most complete collection of Ford cars in the world is on display at the Towe Ford Museum.

Opposite page: a tranquil scene on the Sacramento Delta waterways, near Walnut Grove
Right: the carefully restored State Capitol Building, the center of California's government

Sacramento
Delta

The two major rivers of Northern California, the Sacramento and the San Joaquin, flow together near Sacramento, creating a delta region of bridges, waterways and mists. Sam Goldwyn thought the Sacramento Delta looked more like the Mississippi than the real thing, and filmed *Huckleberry Finn* there. This drive passes through the heart of the delta, stopping at several waterfront towns, in an area of California that's escaped the modern world.

2 DAYS • 233 MILES • 369KM

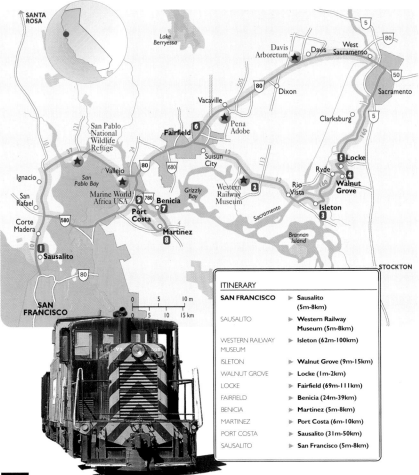

ITINERARY

i *San Francisco Visitor Information Center, Benjamin Swig Pavilion, Hallidie Plaza, Market and Powell streets, CA 94101*

▶ *Leave San Francisco via Lombard Street, past a seemingly endless strip of motels, and join Hwy 101 en route for the Golden Gate Bridge. (North-bound traffic is toll-free.) Cross the bridge and stop briefly at Vista Point, on the north side, which, on a clear day, gives sweeping views of San Francisco and other Bay Area cities. Take the Alexander Avenue exit immediately after leaving Vista Point.*

Houseboats leashed to the garden gates at Sausalito

town's popularity does create parking problems, and the meter wardens are particularly vigilant, even at weekends. Follow

FOR CHILDREN

The Bay Area Discovery Museum nestles below the Golden Gate Bridge at the former army garrison of Fort Baker in Sausalito. It is one of the best hands-on children's museums in the country, with exhibits ranging from an interactive computer room to a maze of optical illusions to a Port of San Francisco activity center, complete with fishing boat and fish market.

Hwy 37, which follows the edge of San Pablo Bay, giving sweeping views across the marshes of the north bay. After passing Marine World Africa USA, turn on to I-80 north and drive to the Hwy 12 exit to Suisun City. Take Hwy 12 east past Suisun City to the Western Railway Museum, which is located just outside Rio Vista.

❷ Western Railway Museum

Although its address is Suisun City, the museum is quite far out of town; its collection of over 100 streetcars and railroad cars, owned by the Bay Area Electric Railroad Association, is spread out over 25 acres (10 hectares). There are examples of trains

❶ Sausalito

Wind down Alexander Avenue to the Mediterranean-like waterfront of Sausalito. This is perhaps the most attractive town around the San Francisco Bay, with steep streets tumbling down to the harbor, which is packed with sailing boats and has fabulous views across the water to San Francisco. The

Bridgeway through town and turn right on to Marinship Way to visit a working scale model of the San Francisco Bay which, although it is at one-thousandth scale, still covers 1.5 acres (0.6 hectares).

▶ *Return to Bridgeway, turn right and join Hwy 101 north. Continue north and exit on*

from around the country, including a New York 'L' train and even a Blackpool tram from England. At weekends during the summer there are rides on old electric trolleys and a 12-mile (19km) round trip behind a vintage diesel engine.

▶ *Continue east on Hwy 12 through Rio Vista. Once across*

*the Sacramento River, turn north on **Hwy 160**, which winds up through the marshlands of the delta.*

SPECIAL TO...

East Brother Light Station sits on an island in the San Pablo Bay, just off Point Richmond. The old beacon, built in 1873 and in operation for almost 100 years, is still a working lighthouse, but it doubles as one of the most unique bed and breakfast inns in the state, with four rooms decorated with period furnishings.

3 Isleton

At one time, 90 per cent of the world's canned asparagus came from this little delta town, which billed itself as the 'Asparagus Capital of the World'. Sixty years on it is a shadow of its former self. The old tin-sided buildings remain, and can still evoke an atmosphere of the days when a flourishing Chinatown jostled for room with the gambling dens and brothels along Main Street. Most buildings stand vacant, but the Quong Wo Sing Company store still survives, having been owned by the same family for four generations.

▶ *Continue north along **Hwy 160** to Walnut Grove.*

4 Walnut Grove

Sleepy little Walnut Grove is the only town south of Red Bluff to occupy both banks of the Sacramento River. Once it was a lair for riverboat bandits, but it is now an agricultural community that fills up at weekends with people boating on the delta. The charming stores and houses date back to 1915, when the town was rebuilt after a fire.

▶ *Cross the river just north of town. Locke is below the levee.*

5 Locke

Members of a Chinese association that worked on the levees, railroads and farms in the surrounding area built this rustic community in 1915, soon after the Chinatown in neighbouring Walnut Grove had burned to the ground. At its height, over 2,000 people lived there, but today little more than the Main Street survives, with fewer than 100 residents. Listed in the National Register of Historic Places as the only rural community in America built and occupied by the Chinese, the town is overflowing with atmosphere. Chinese families still occupy the old buildings lining the boardwalks along Main Street, and the Dai Loy Museum, a former gambling house that closed in 1950, displays old gaming paraphernalia and games such as fantan and Flying Bull. Close by is Al's Place, a bar and restaurant called Al the Wop's in less sensitive times, which is usually crammed with locals: an essential part of any Locke experience.

▶ *Continue north on **Hwy 160**, winding along beside the Sacramento River through the delta countryside to Sacramento. Join **I-50** west to **I-80** and turn south. Drive past the university town of Davis to the Fairfield exit.*

6 Fairfield

Fairfield is an air force town, as well as being home to the Anheuser-Busch Fairfield Brewery, at 3101 Busch Drive, which offers one-hour guided tours of the brewing facility.

▶ *From Fairfield, take **I-80** south to **I-780** and follow it to the Benicia exit.*

7 Benicia

It is difficult to understand how this quiet delta town could ever have had delusions of grandeur. In 1847, when it was founded, the city fathers envisaged Benicia as the capital of California – and it did, indeed, hold that position in 1854; but its exalted status only lasted for 13 months. The Benicia Capitol still stands, a refined, brick building operated as a State Historic Park, with a restored interior, down to the candles on every desk of the senate chamber. During its period as capital, Benicia did achieve an impressive number of firsts for the state: the first public school, the first law school, the first chamber of commerce, the first railroad ferry in the West and the first steamboat built by Americans in California. One of

A unique Chinese community still thrives in the delta town of Locke

Above and left: the exterior and interior of the Benicia Capitol, legacy of a brief, distinguished past

the town's more bizarre historic attractions is the Camel Barn Museum, scene of a brief experiment using camels to transport military supplies across the Southwest in the 1860s.

▶ *Return to I-780 and turn south on to I-680 and exit on to Hwy 4 west. Exit at Martinez.*

8 Martinez
Scotsman John Muir has attained almost mythical status among American environmentalists. He did more for the preservation of California's wilderness than any of his contemporaries, as co-founder of the Sierra Club, founder of five national parks and the U.S. Forest Service, and

an indefatigable writer. From 1890 until his death in 1914 he lived with his wife in the elegant 1882 Victorian farmhouse, 4202 Alhambra Avenue, that is now the John Muir National Historic Site. Muir did most of his conservation writing while he lived here and the restored study, Muir's "scribble den," is littered with notes, manuscripts and editions of his books. The 17-room house has been restored to its original appearance and in the grounds is the Martinez Adobe, built by Don Vincente Martinez in 1844 as part of the old Rancho Las Juntas.

▶ *From Martinez take McEwen Road to Port Costa.*

9 Port Costa
Port Costa sits opposite Benicia, on the left bank of the Carquinez Strait, where fresh

water from the rivers meets the salt water of the Bay. Early this century this was a major grain-shopping port but now, like so much of the delta, it has become a sleepy backwater at the end of a country lane. Old buildings are being taken over by artists and antique shops, but the charm of the town relies heavily on the almost total lack of gentrification. On the corner of Erskine Street and Canyon Lake Drive is Muriel's Doll House, a museum housing the antique and handmade dolls that were collected by Muriel Whitmore for "loving and sharing."

▶ *Leave Port Costa on the Crockett Road, which follows the Carquinez Straits. At I-80 turn south and exit on Cutting Boulevard, which leads to the San Rafael Bridge. Cross the bridge and return to San Francisco on Hwy 101 south across the Golden Gate Bridge. Immediately before crossing the bridge a road exits to the Marin Headlands. Several parking areas give fine views of both the bridge and the city of San Francisco.*

Sacramento

3 HOURS

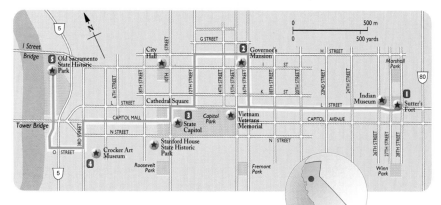

Since 1854 Sacramento has been California's

capital, fighting off challenges by Benicia, San Jose

and Monterey. The discovery of gold first gave the city its prominence,

but agriculture soon became the industrial base for the economy. More

recently, military installations and the aero-space industry have

contributed to its importance. In 1963 a deepwater channel to the San

Francisco Bay was completed, making Sacramento a major inland port.

All that apart, it is a very pleasant place, and although the city is primar-

ily the state's administrative center, it has many important visitor attrac-

tions. This walking tour starts

appropriately at Sacramento's first settle-

ment, at Sutter's Fort, and continues to

the 19th-century Governor's Mansion, the

State Capitol and the Crocker Art

Museum. It ends in Old Sacramento, four

blocks of restored Gold Rush era buildings

that now house shops, restaurants and

several interesting museums.

ⓘ *Sacramento Visitor Information Center, 2nd and K Street, Sacramento, CA 95814*

▶ *Start at 27th and L Streets.*

❶ Sutter's Fort

Captain John Sutter, an immigrant from Switzerland, established California's first inland settlement at the confluence of the American and Sacramento rivers, where the Mexican government had given him a 50,000-acre (20,235-hectare) land grant in 1839. An adobe fort was the first building erected; now restored, it stands among residential streets – a far cry from the pioneer days. At weekends, costumed interpreters add to the atmosphere. The California State

---

SPECIAL TO...

The Central Valley is a major almond-growing region and at 1701 C Street you can visit the Blue Diamond Almond Packing Plant and see how the nuts are sorted, cracked, sliced, halved and roasted. This is the largest almond-packaging plant in the world – and the tours are free.

Looming over Capitol Park: the 19th-century State Capitol

Indian Museum is in the grounds of Sutter's Fort and depicts California's Indian cultures, with displays of baskets, clothing, jewellery and art.

▶ *Walk down L Street to 15th and the black granite panels of the California Vietnam Veterans Memorial, engraved with 5,822 names of the state's dead and missing, in Capitol Park. Return one block to 16th Street, turn left and continue to H Street.*

2 Governor's Mansion

Ronald Reagan was the last governor of California to live in this 19th-century mansion, now open to the public. Furnishings and personal items of the state's former governors are displayed in this splendid Victorian mansion, which is filled with antiques. Some of the more interesting items include a 1902 Steinway piano and persian carpets bought by Mrs Earl Warren in 1943. The gardens contain plants dating back to 1877.

▶ *Walk down H Street and turn left on 12th Street. This goes through the heart of downtown Sacramento. Turn right on L Street then left on 10th Street into Capitol Park.*

3 State Capitol

A 210-foot (64m)-high dome on top of this grandiose neo-classical government architecture towers over Capitol Park. The dramatic, white building was erected between 1860 and 1874, and modelled after the nation's

A glimpse of the glorious Gold Rush days at Old Sacramento

Capitol in Washington D.C.. Since then it has undergone extensive renovation, and there are free tours of the main building and seven historic museum rooms which re-create the early days of the California legislature.

▶ *Leave on Capitol Mall and walk down the Mall to 3rd Street, not forgetting to look back for a great view of the State Capitol. Turn left on 3rd Street and continue to O Street and the Crocker Art Museum.*

4 Crocker Art Museum

This is the oldest public art

FOR HISTORY BUFFS

Virtually every car that Ford manufactured between 1903 and 1953 is on display at the Towe Ford Museum of Automotive History of California at 2200 Front Street, close to Old Sacramento. A vast warehouse is crammed with the world's largest collection of Ford vehicles.

---

museum in the West and it contains an extensive display of art, both fine and applied, from Northern California and Europe, that has been increasing since its foundation in 1873. Once the mansion of Edwin Crocker, the building dwarfs the collection with hand-carved walls, repoussé ceilings, parquet floors and the grandest of grand ballrooms.

▶ *Walk down O Street to the Sacramento River, turn right and continue to Old Sacramento.*

5 Old Sacramento State Historic Park

This 28-acre (11-hectare) national historic landmark has over 100 restored buildings, complete with wooden sidewalks, giving a remarkably good idea of how Sacramento must have looked during the height of the Gold Rush.

The B.F. Hastings Museum, at J and 2nd Streets, is a good place to start. It was once the western terminus of the Pony Express, and is now a museum with exhibits on that legendary delivery service.

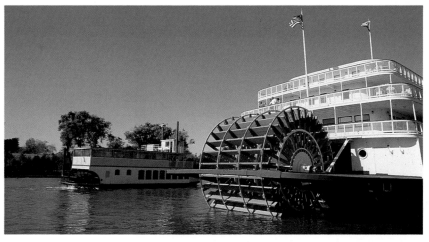

Above: replicas of the old paddle-wheelers ply the waters of the Sacramento River and relive the days when they were a common-place sight

Right: shining machinery from the age of steam, displayed in the splendid California State Railroad Museum

The Eagle Theater, built in 1849, is the oldest in California, and still stages Gold Rush-era shows. The showplace of the development is the California State Railroad Museum one block to the north, the largest museum of its kind in the world. In the three-story glass-and-steel structure are no fewer than 27 restored locomotives and more than 40 interpretive exhibits that set out to recapture the romance of steam. On summer weekends, you can take a 6-mile (10km) train ride on a historic locomotive from the museum's Central Pacific Depot.

In the 19th century, hundreds of paddlewheel riverboats used to ply the Sacramento River and one of the best examples, the *Delta King*, is permanently docked along Old Sacramento's waterfront. Cruises are offered on the riverboats.

▶ *Take a cruise along the river on one of the replica paddle-wheelers, or return along L Street to Sutter's Fort.*

THE SAN FRANCISCO BAY AREA

San Francisco is everyone's favorite city. With its cable cars, Golden Gate Bridge and sophisticated European ambience, it rarely fails to meet the expectations of millions of visitors. It has an intimate scale rarely found in American cities due, in part, to its geography: built on a series of hills on a peninsula, it covers only 46 square miles (119 sq km) and has a population of less than 800,000.

The climate is wonderful: it rarely gets too hot and almost never freezes. Most of the time, the air is clean and sparkling, but it does get cold, particularly in the summer, when the famous sea fogs roll in from the Pacific. The only people wearing shorts at this time of year are tourists!

Within two years of James Marshall discovering gold in the Sierra Nevada mountains in 1849, San Francisco grew from a population of 900 to 25,000. Forty years later it was over 300,000. This cosmopolitan community, drawn by the lure of gold, set the city's future pattern as one of the most international cities imaginable, with a Chinatown bigger than many towns in China, large Japanese, Filipino and Vietnamese communities, a Spanish-speaking Mission District that provides a home for families from Mexico and Central America, and a very strong Italian presence in North Beach. Even a French neighborhood has evolved in the downtown area, with Parisian-style bistros, cafés and bookstores. Along with this ethnic diversity comes a tolerance that has embraced the Beatniks of the '50s, the flower children of the '60s and now the largest gay population in the United States.

San Francisco is the jewel in the crown of the Bay Area, which has a population of over 6 million, making it the fourth largest metropolitan area in the US. From the Wine Country in the north to the beaches and redwood forests in the south, all in one of the most exquisite natural settings on earth, this region is exceptional. It is also the perfect base for visits to great natural attractions of Northern California, including Yosemite Valley, the giant coastal redwoods on the North Coast and the thermal wonders of Lassen Volcanic National Park.

Tour 16

If you only have one day to see San Francisco, take this drive, which passes virtually every major site in the city. The route is well signposted and easy to follow, but though the journey can easily be completed in one day, not much time will be available for visiting sites. There is so much to see along the way that this drive should be considered a sampler, to search out the more interesting places for a return visit at leisure.

Tour 17

Although San Francisco dates back only to the mid-19th century, its colorful past has created a wealth of historically interesting sites. Walking here is always a pleasure, and there is no shortage of charming rest stops on the way through diverse cultural neighborhoods. The tour passes through the biggest Chinatown outside of Asia, North Beach, relics of the 1906 earthquake, haunts of the gold miners of 1849 and a glimpse of the world of Dashiel Hammet and Sam Spade.

Tour 18

San Francisco is a city of hills, and a network of steps connects many of the major thoroughfares. This is one of the few American cities where the pedestrian can feel at home, and the steps of San Francisco represent the ultimate walk in the city. Rarely visited by tourists, they meander through residential districts, falling steeply between flower-covered gardens and giving a glimpse into the real San Francisco, that can only be experienced on foot.

Tour 19

No visit to Northern California would be complete with experiencing the world-famous vineyards of Napa Valley and the Wine Country. The drive from the metropolitan area to the closest vineyards takes little more than an hour, but it is well worth continuing north to Calistoga and over to the vineyards of Sonoma for a taste of the real thing.

Although a day trip will give you a pretty good feel for the area, it really deserves more time, and has more than enough attractions to keep even the most jaded visitor happily occupied. The route is scattered with bed and breakfast inns and fine restaurants – leaving no excuse for returning to the city too quickly.

Tour 20

The excursion to Monterey begins with a scenic introduction to Northern California's rugged coast line. Highway One hugs the coast as it passes through Half Moon Bay on its way to Santa Cruz, passing through mixed agricultural and natural landscapes. From Santa Cruz, the road makes its way through more agricultural land before eventually arriving at Monterey Bay.

San Francisco Peninsula has become one of the richest areas in America, mainly due to the phenomenal growth of the hi-tech industry, and the return journey up the east side of the peninsula is a dramatic contrast to the rugged Pacific coast. This is the home of Hewlett Packard, Apple Computers, Stanford University and a whole host of other household names in the computer industry.

The browsers' delight: City Lights bookstore, in North Beach, was the U.S.'s first paperback book shop

Left: looking down Montgomery Street, the Wall Street of the West. The city's first banking street boasts several historic skyscrapers

Forty-Nine-Mile Drive

1 DAY • 49 MILES • 79 KM

The best that San Francisco has to offer is covered by this well-signposted drive through the city, passing virtually every major site in the city. It is best to plan the drive to avoid the congested downtown area during rush hours, and to spend more of your time at the sites farthest away from town. Look for the '49-Mile Drive' blue-and-white seagull signs.

i San Francisco Visitor Information
Center, Benjamin Swig Pavilion,
Hallidie Plaza, Market and Powell
streets, CA 94101

▶ Start in Union Square, which is
the center of the hotel and
shopping district. Take Post
Street to Grant Avenue, turn
left and drive through the
Chinatown Gate to California
Street.

❶ Chinatown

The junction of California and
Grant is the heart of the biggest
Chinatown outside Asia. Old St
Mary's Church (see page 111) is
on the right – be sure to look out
for cable cars: this is on the cable
car line, and they always have
right of way.

RECOMMENDED WALK

San Francisco's Chinatown has
not changed very much over
the past 100 years. Its streets
are not designed to take
present-day traffic and the
congestion can be dreadful.
The only way to see this area is
on foot. An underground car
park on Kearny Street, at Clay
has an elevator that delivers
you right into Portsmouth
Square, the social center of
Chinatown, which is the ideal
place to start an exploration
of the neighbourhood.
Visit when it is most lively, in
the middle of the day.

▶ Continue up California Street
to Nob Hill, pass between the
Mark Hopkins Hotel on the
left and the Fairmont on the
right. Continue past the Flood
Mansion (see page 109) and
turn right in front of Grace
Cathedral (see page 109)
onto Taylor Street. Turn right on
Washington Street and
continue to Kearny Street.
There is an underground car
park here; the elevators exit

Two features of Fisherman's Wharf
Left: a clam chowder chef displays
his catch
Right: boats line the wharf

right in the square. Turn left on
Kearny and left again onto
Columbus, and continue
through North Beach (see
page 110) to Grant Avenue.
Turn right and continue as far
as Lombard Street. Turn left
onto Lombard Street: straight
ahead are the hairpin bends
of The Crookedest Street in the
World. Turn right on Powell
Street and follow it to Jefferson
Street. Turn left and follow
Jefferson through Fisherman's
Wharf.

❷ Fisherman's Wharf

Locals dismiss Fisherman's
Wharf as one big tourist trap, but
if you can overlook the amusement arcade museums and the
plethora of T-shirt and sea-shell
jewellery shops, there are still a
few authentic corners. A small
fishing fleet still operates out of
the harbor at the foot of Jones
Street. Their catch is sold to
local restaurants, and at the junction of Jefferson and Taylor
streets, old Italian families still
operate crab stands, selling
freshly cooked Dungeness crab
and sourdough bread. Pier 45 is
still a working wharf and gives a
feeling of what this area was like
before the T-shirts arrived. Pier
39 is a different story: this old
steamship wharf is now a two-
level shopping and restaurant
complex. The street performers
here provide some of the best
free entertainment in town, and
the views from the end of the
pier are some of the best in the
bay. Underwater World is the
latest attraction, where a
700,000-gallon (3 million-litre)
saltwater aquarium lets visitors

see the marine life from below the water through a large, acrylic tunnel. At the far end of Jefferson, The Cannery is a multi-story shopping complex built in an old Del Monte Corporation fruit-and-vegetable canning factory. Across the street, as it opens out into Aquatic Park, is the Hyde Street Pier, which is part of the National Maritime Museum. Seven historic ships are anchored here, including the *Eureka*, an 1890 ferryboat; the *Balclutha*, a Scottish merchant ship built in 1886 that rounded Cape Horn no fewer than 17 times carrying coal, wine and hardware from Europe; and a three-masted schooner, *C A Thayer*, that carried timber down the California coast.

working, and even sample the goods. Opposite Ghirardelli Square, the National Maritime Museum has a display of model ships, photographs and various nautical memorabilia.

▶ *Turn up Polk Street and right onto Bay Street. Continue to Laguna Street, turn right and Fort Mason is straight ahead.*

❹ Fort Mason
This collection of old warehouses and wharves is now home to over 50 non-profit organisations, including Greenpeace, and three small museums: the Mexican Museum, the Museo Italio-Americano, and the San Francisco Craft and Folk Art Museum. The SS *Jeremiah*

O'Brien, preserved as the National Liberty Ship Memorial, is also moored here. It is the last survivor of 2,751 Liberty Ships, launched during World War II. Amazingly, it took only 57 days to build.

▶ *Continue along Marina Boulevard, past Marina Green, where kite-flyers and joggers outnumber pedestrians. The Marina District was badly affected by the Loma Prieta earthquake in 1989, although little evidence of the disastrous fires is visible today. At the end of Marina Boulevard, turn left onto Baker Street.*

Home, sweet home: Ghirardelli Square was a chocolate firm's base

▶ *Turn left on Hyde and right onto Beach.*

❸ Ghirardelli Square
At the junction of Larkin and Beach is one of San Francisco's most attractive shopping and restaurant developments. Ghirardelli Square was originally the home of Ghirardelli chocolate, which is still highly regarded as one of the best in the U.S.. You can still see the antique chocolate machines

Sole survivor of the Panama-Pacific Exposition: the Palace of Fine Arts

5 Palace of Fine Arts

In 1915 the Panama-Pacific Exposition extended all the way across what is now known as the Marina District. Today there is only one remnant: the Palace of Fine Arts. The building was designed by eminent San Francisco architect Bernard Maybeck. Originally a stucco construction, it deteriorated so severely that in the 1960s the building was completely rebuilt in concrete. Set by a small lake, that is permanent home to several families of swans and geese, the Palace houses an auditorium and the Exploratorium, a children's science museum.

FOR CHILDREN

The Exploratorium, at the Palace of Fine Arts, is a hands-on museum for children of all ages, with over 600 exhibits. The prestigious Scientific American magazine has rated it as 'the best science museum in the world.'

▶ Return to Marina Boulevard and enter the Presidio on Lincoln Boulevard.

6 The Presidio

Established by the Spanish in 1776 and taken over by the US in 1846, these 1,440 acres (583 hectares) of wooded hills were an army base until 1995, when the army handed over the Presidio to the National Park Service. This landscaped corner of San Francisco is now part of the Golden Gate National Recreation Area. Still here is the Presidio Army Museum, protected by antique cannon and housing a collection of military uniforms and weapons. One of the more unusual sights at the Presido is an extensive pet cemetery, with headstones eulogizing the dear departed furry friends of the soldiers.

▶ Continue on Lincoln Boulevard and turn right to follow Long Avenue to the end.

7 Fort Point

The only brick fort to be built west of the Mississippi nestles under the girders of the Golden Gate Bridge. It was completed in 1861 to deter incursions into the San Francisco Bay, but is now so dwarfed by the bridge that it looks like a pretty futile deterrent. In its day, however, the fort was an impressive building. Rooms off the courtyard are filled with exhibits covering many aspects of U.S. military history, and costumed interpreters are on hand to answer questions.

▶ Return to Lincoln Boulevard and turn right. Continue through the beautiful tree-filled landscape of the Presidio and make a quick detour to Baker Beach. From here there are wonderful views of the Golden Gate Bridge and Marin Headlands. Lincoln Boulevard passes through the exclusive residential neighborhood of Seacliff and becomes El Camino del Mar. Follow this through Lincoln Park to the Palace of the Legion of Honor.

8 California Palace of the Legion of Honor

This newly remodelled museum is not only one of the most attractive in the city; it also houses one of the most interesting collections of art, and has the most commanding views, from its location above Land's End in Lincoln Park. The collection was started by Alma Sprekels, whose husband Adolph was a

The Cliff House, latest in a line of majestic buildings set on this spot

sugar magnate. She met Rodin on a visit to Paris and developed a lasting interest in his work, which now forms the core of the collection. Styled after the Palais de la Légion d'Honneur in Paris, the building was donated to the city by the Sprekels family in 1924. The collection has expanded from its original focus of French art and now covers an eclectic range of work, from medieval to contemporary paintings. Included in the collection is the Achenbach Foundation for Graphic Arts, which holds 100,000 prints and 3,000 drawings ranging from Albrecht Dürer to Georgia O'Keeffe.

▶ *Leave the museum down Legion of Honor Drive. Turn right onto Geary Boulevard and, after 39th Avenue, fork right onto Point Lobos Avenue.*

9 The Cliff House
On this far western point of San Francisco, jutting out into the Pacific, the Cliff House sits majestically, overlooking the crashing ocean waves. The original Cliff House was built in 1858 and became a favorite society restaurant, hosting dinners for no fewer than three U.S. presidents.

It was bought in 1881 by philanthropist Adolph Sutro, who laid a railway line to make the restaurant accessible to the ordinary people of San Francisco. A fire destroyed the building in 1894, but Sutro rebuilt it as an eight-story concoction with fancy spires that earned it the name French-Château-on-a-Rock. Next door were the Sutro Baths, a remarkable salt-water bath house that spread over 3 acres (1 hectare). Both the Cliff House and the Baths survived the 1906 earthquake and fire, but the Cliff House burned to the ground the following year. The Sutro Baths survived until yet another fire destroyed them in 1966 – the ruins can still be seen from the latest and considerably less grand incarnation of the Cliff House, which houses shops and a restaurant, with great views of Seal Rock and its colony of California sealions.

▶ *Continue down the Great Highway along the coast to Sloat Boulevard.*

10 San Francisco Zoological Gardens
Recent renovation has returned this zoo to its position as one of the top six in the nation. Most of the cages have been replaced with natural habitat enclosures,

using psychological barriers to separate man and beast. The zoo was developed in an area of sand dunes close to the Pacific Ocean and, during the summer, fog can blanket the area, making this a decidedly chilly excursion. Its collection of over 1,000 animals and birds includes snow leopards, white tigers, pygmy hippos and an excellent gorilla habitat. A new Primate Discovery Center has 16 endangered species of monkey and a nocturnal gallery. Within the zoo is a separate Children's Zoo, where all the animals can be petted and fed.

▶ *Continue south and join Skyline Boulevard, turning off onto John Muir Drive. Drive around Lake Merced, turning north onto Lake Merced Boulevard. Continue around to Sunset Boulevard and drive north through this residential district into Golden Gate Park.*

11 Golden Gate Park
The 1,017 acres (411 hectares) of parkland that stretch all the way across the western half of San Francisco are the work of 19th-century horticulturalist John McLaren, who turned an expanse of rolling sand dunes into one of the great urban parks of the world. This is a major

recreation area for the local population, with a boating lake, a lake for model boats, rhododendron dells, a casting pond for fishermen, and even a buffalo paddock and working windmill. At weekends John F. Kennedy Drive, the main road through the park, is closed to vehicles and opened to jugglers, roller skaters, skateboarders and anyone else who needs open space and an enthusiastic audience. Follow the 49-Mile Drive signs and, after making a circuit of Stowe Lake, you will enter the Music Concourse, where most of the park's attractions are based. The Asian Art Museum houses the collection of the former International Olympic Committee president Avery

BACK TO NATURE

The Strybing Arboretum, in Golden Gate Park, is a 70-acre (28-hectare) park within a park, containing over 6,000 species of bushes and trees. There is a Cape Province Garden with South African plants, a New World Cloud Forest, and imaginative ideas such as a Biblical Garden, where only plants mentioned in the Bible grow. All the plants are labelled, and the avid horticulturalist should find plenty to occupy a long visit.

The Japanese Tea Garden on Stowe Lake, Golden Gate Park

the California Academy of Sciences, the oldest scientific institution in the West, and a natural history museum with dioramas of African and North American wildlife and an excellent exhibit on evolution. The Steinhart Aquarium has a three-story fish roundabout, and the Morrison Planetarium presents astronomy during the day and laser rock at night.

▶ *Leave Golden Gate Park on Stanyan Street and drive south to Parnassus Street. Turn right and continue to 7th Avenue, turn left and continue onto Laguna Honda. Follow Laguna Honda past the hospital to Woodside and round to Twin Peaks Boulevard.*

Brundage; nearly 12,000 Asian works of art spanning 6,000 years make it the largest collection in the U.S.. It adjoins the M.H. de Young Memorial Museum, whose 40 well-lit galleries house the most eclectic collection imaginable. There is a good ethnographic exhibit, displaying folk art from around the world; displays of period furniture, glassware and silver, and over

6,000 tribal rugs from Central Asia. There are also paintings from major European and American schools up to the turn of the century. Next to these museums is the Japanese Tea Garden, laid out in traditional style with curved bridges, waterfalls, stone lanterns, a pagoda and, of course, Japanese tea served by kimono-clad women. Directly across the concourse is

⓬ Twin Peaks

The television and radio antennae crowning Twin Peaks, visible from all over the city, are surrounded by a 65-acre (26-hectare) park, and the 910-foot (277m)-high summit gives some of the best views of San Francisco and the Bay Area. The views at night are magical – but this is not the safest place to be in the dark.

San Francisco spreads out beneath the winding road to Twin Peaks

▶ *Drive down Twin Peaks Boulevard and turn right on 17th and left on Roosevelt. Continue down to 14th Street and turn right onto Dolores. Drive four blocks to Mission Dolores.*

⑬ Mission Dolores

Completed in 1791, this was the sixth of the 21 missions to be established by Father Junipero Serra. The adobe walls are 4 feet (1m) thick, and the roof timbers are lashed together with rawhide strips. It is so solidly built that the 1906 earthquake had no effect on the building, and it is now the oldest in the city. The price of construction was high: as many as 5,000 native Indians building the mission died from diseases caught from the Europeans. They are buried in a mass grave in the adjoining cemetery. The mission lies in the shadow of the Basilica built next to it in 1913.

▶ *Continue down past the palm trees lining Dolores Street through the edge of the Mission District. Turn left onto Army Street and drive east under the **Hwy 101** freeway to Indiana Street. Turn left and drive onto **I-280** freeway. Take this to the end, to the Brannan Street exit. Brannan Street crosses the revitalised SoMa (South of Market) district, site of the Moscone Center and the Museum of Modern Art.*

Continue along Brannan to the Embarcadero, given a facelift after the Embarcadero Freeway had be demolished following the Loma Prieta earthquake. Follow the Embarcadero round to the Ferry Building.

⑭ Ferry Building

Neither the 1906 nor the 1989 earthquake could shake this symbol of old San Francisco. It was built in 1903 and the 235-foot (72m)-tall clock tower has become a well-loved fixture. It once saw 50 million people a year – mainly commuters from across the bay – but with the completion of the Golden Gate and Bay Bridges the ferry services gradually went into decline. A resurgence in ferry use has occurred in response to impossible commuter traffic and you can once again travel in style from the San Francisco Ferry Building to the docks in Marin County and Oakland.

continue to Market Street. Turn right and drive down Market to Fifth Street.

16 Old U.S. Mint

The restored rooms of this imposing Greek Revival Federal building, which opened in 1874, display the original furnishings of the Mint, and one very secure room has a pyramid of gold bars worth $5 million on display. Other rooms have less valuable but equally interesting displays of Western art, pioneer gold coins, a vault and a re-created miners cabin.

▶ Return to Market and drive down to McAllister Street. Turn right and pass the buildings of the Civic Center, including the impressive City Hall. Take McAllister to Van Ness; turn right and then left on Geary Boulevard to Gough Street.

17 St Mary's Cathedral

This modern, white marble edifice is a remarkable architectural feat. The enor-mous roof was built without columns, so that views of San Francisco can be seen from all four sides. Stained-glass windows curve down and reflect on to the 7,000 free-hanging polished aluminium rods of the baldachin. The original cathedral was destroyed by fire in 1962.

▶ Continue down Geary Boulevard to Webster Street. On the right is an ugly, modern development: the Japanese equivalent of Chinatown.

18 Japantown

Unfortunately, Japantown has none of the color and atmosphere of its Chinese counterpart. Nihonmachi Mall, on Buchanan Street, is the most pleasant corner. Pass under a torii gate to a cobblestone pathway that meanders past fountains: on either side of the path are delightful little shops, selling every-thing from shojii screens to antique kimonos.

▶ Return to Union Square on Post Street.

15 Embarcadero Center

Directly across from the Ferry Building is a series of high, monolithic office buildings that dominate the skyline. The Embarcadero Center houses a three-level shopping mall, offices and a couple of major hotels. This is the center of the business district and parking around here is usually impossi-ble, but the Center has an exten-sive underground parking lot and (with a modest purchase at one of the Center's shops) the park-ing fee is nominal.

▶ Continue on the Embarcadero and turn left onto Broadway and left again onto Battery Street. Drive through the historic Jackson Square district (see page 110) and

The Ferry Building clock tower

TOUR
17

Historic
San Francisco

Although the city is new by European, or even East Coast standards, a lot has been compressed into a short time. The 1906 earthquake had a major impact on the downtown area, and this walk takes a look at the few buildings of note that withstood it, and the development that followed the devastating fire. Two major ethnic areas, Chinatown and North Beach, are also explored. Some of the route coincides with cable car lines – a fun alternative to walking. Cafés are part of the city's life and there are plenty along this route.

4 HOURS

ⓘ *San Francisco Visitor Information Center, Benjamin Swig Pavilion, Hallidie Plaza, Market and Powell streets*

▶ *From Market Street walk up Powell Street for two blocks, following the cable car line, to Union Square.*

❶ Union Square

This has long been considered the center of the city. The grand St Francis Hotel overlooks the square, and the hotel lobby is a celebrated place for meeting people. Many of the most prestigious department stores surround the square, along with high-fashion boutiques and art galleries. (The landscaped square itself attracts a clientele that is unlikely to be welcomed in any of the surrounding outlets.) Overlooking all this activity is a statue of Victory on top of a 97-foot (29m) granite column, erected in 1903, that miraculously withstood the 1906 earthquake. The underground, multi-level car park beneath the square was the first of its kind, built in the early 1940s.

▶ *Continue up Powell, across Sutter Street, which is known for its exquisite fashion boutiques, art galleries and antique shops, and up a steep hill to California Street. Turn left and walk up two more steep blocks to Huntington Park.*

❷ Nob Hill

Several great hotels sit up here presiding over the city. This has always been the best address in town, and many prominent 19th-century businessmen lived here. All but one of their mansions were destroyed in the 1906 earthquake. The brown, ominous-looking Flood Mansion remains, occupied by the exclusive, all-male Pacific Union Club. The other businessmen have had their names adopted by the hotels: Stanford Court, The Huntington, Mark Hopkins.

Overlooking the square is the great, neo-gothic Grace

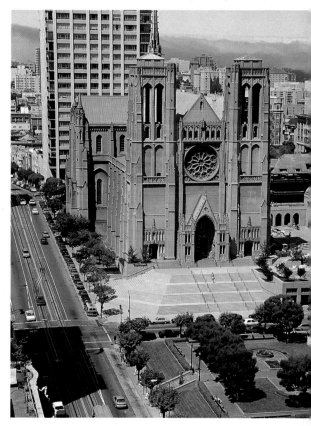

Cathedral, the third largest Episcopal cathedral in the country. Construction was started in 1910, but it was not until 1964 that the cathedral was dedicated. The main entrance doors are replicas of the Ghiberti Doors of Paradise, originally cast for the Cathedral Baptistery in Florence. Inside, the morning sun casts a spectacular palette of color across the cathedral, as it passes through the many stained-glass windows. The east rose window was created from over 3,800 pieces of glass.

▶ *Walk down Taylor to Washington Street, past expensive apartment blocks. Turn right onto Washington Street and left at Mason.*

❸ Cable Car Barn

This building on the corner of Mason and Washington is the

Grace Cathedral is a striking landmark among the city's office blocks

heart of San Francisco's legendary cable car system, housing the main control center. You can see the actual cables running at precisely 9.5mph (15kph) over 14-foot (4m) pulleys called 'sheaves'. There is a good exhibit of old photographs, drawings and models , and some of the original cars built in 1873 by Andrew Hallidie.

▶ *Continue walking down Washington Street and turn right onto Stockton Street.*

❹ Chinatown

Stockton Street is the true heart of the biggest Chinatown outside Asia. Walk one block to Clay Street; on the left corner, above the main post office, is the

1857 Kong Chow Temple, a typical example of the mixed-use buildings in this neighborhood. Continue around the corner on Clay and enter narrow Waverly Place, on the left. Half way down on the left, on the top floor of number 125, is the oldest temple in San Francisco: the Tien Hou, built in 1852. The temple is open to the public – but it's a long flight of stairs! Continue down Waverly Place, turn left onto Washington, right onto Stockton Street and continue to Columbus. This section of Chinatown is the most authentic: most people in the street are Chinese, English is the

Old St Mary's Church, built by Chinese laborers in Chinatown

second language, and the shops sell all manner of food stuffs from fresh fish to exotic fruit and vegetables.

▶ *At Columbus, turn left and walk for two blocks through North Beach.*

5 North Beach

This is still a distinctly Italian neighborhood, in spite of encroachment by Chinatown. In the 1950s it was the bohemian center of San Francisco, when Jack Kerouac and other Beat Generation poets would congregate in the Italian coffee bars. Columbus Avenue is the main street through North Beach, and coffee bars remain an important cultural gathering place. Continue walking to Washington Square, where old men sit on benches conversing in Italian, overlooked by the twin spires of Ss Peter and Paul Church, that took 15 years to build from 1922. Turn right on Filbert Street and walk up to Grant Avenue, then turn right and walk back towards Chinatown. Grant Avenue was the first street in the 1834 Spanish settlement called Yerba Buena. It was named Dupont Street until the 1906 earthquake destroyed it, by which time it had earned itself such a notorious reputation for debauchery that the rebuilt version was named Grant, in an effort to conceal its scandalous past. Along this section, Grant is full of small shops and coffee bars such as the splendidly Italian Café Trieste, on the corner of Vallejo Street.

▶ *Continue walking down Grant and across Broadway to Pacific. Turn left on Pacific and walk across Montgomery Street to the Jackson Square district.*

6 Jackson Square

Jackson Square is actually a few blocks of 1850s brick buildings, saved from the ravaging fires following the 1906 quake by a 1-mile (1.6km)-long hose bringing water from Fisherman's Wharf. In 1971 it became the city's first designated Historic District, and today the buildings house exclusive antique furniture, law firms and advertising agencies. To get a feel for the area, walk down to Sansome Street, exploring some of the narrow alley ways that give the area its character.

▶ *Return to Montgomery Street.*

7 Financial District

Montgomery Street is the Wall Street of the West. This deep canyon of office and bank buildings extends for several blocks. At 600 Montgomery is one of San Francisco's great landmarks: the Transamerica Pyramid, built in 1972, with a distinctive 853-foot (260m) profile that is now as much part of the city as the Golden Gate Bridge. There is an observation deck on the 27th floor (half-way up), but it only gives a limited view, directly north from the Pyramid.

▶ *One block past the Transamerica Pyramid is Commercial Street.*

8 Pacific Heritage Museum

The old Bank of Canton building, at 608 Commercial Street, houses the Pacific Heritage Museum, which explores the links between the countries on the Pacific Rim with a series of changing exhibits. This was also the site of the city's first US Branch Mint which, in 1875, was replaced with a new U.S. Subtreasury. The brick walled vault contains an exhibit of coins, bullion bags and other memorabilia, all of which attest to the fortune in gold that started coming down from the Sierra foothills.

▶ *Return to Clay Street, turn left and cross Kearny to Portsmouth Square.*

9 Portsmouth Square

It is difficult to believe that this was once San Francisco's waterfront. Water is no longer in sight, and the square is now a social centre for Chinese men who come here to gamble or practice tai chi. Walk up one block to Grant Avenue and turn left. This section of Chinatown caters more to tourists, with shops selling cheap toys from Hong Kong, oriental jewellery and other knick-knacks.

▶ *Follow Grant Avenue to the corner of California Street.*

10 Old St Mary's Church

At the corner of California Street is Old St Mary's Church, which has been a Chinatown landmark since 1854. It was built mainly by Chinese laborers, using granite from China and brick from New England which had been shipped around Cape Horn. This was the first Catholic church in the city, which, at the time, served a predominantly Irish population. An inscription on the tower beneath the clock has the message: "Son, observe the time and fly from evil" – which was reputedly directed at the many brothels that stood across the street during the Gold Rush days.

▶ *Continue along Grant, and through the Chinatown Gate. Grant suddenly changes to an up-scale shopping street. Continue to Maiden Lane and turn right.*

11 Maiden Lane

This attractive alley was once a notorious collection of bordellos. The earthquake and fire solved that particular problem, and in its present incarnation, designer boutiques sit next to pavement cafés. During the day, Maiden Lane is a pedestrianised area and makes a welcome relief from the traffic of Chinatown and Union Square. Look for number 140, the Circle Gallery, which was designed by Frank Lloyd Wright in 1948 as a prototype of the Guggenheim Museum in New York.

▶ *Turn left on Stockton Street and walk past Union Square down to Market Street. Turn right on Market and walk one block to Hallidie Plaza.*

Soaring between conventional high-rises and traditional San Francisco architecture, the Transamerica Pyramid is an instantly recognisable city feature

Steps of
San Francisco

There's no better way to see San Francisco than to wander up and down the steps of the two most prominent hills, catching spectacular glimpses of the city and bay between the homes and gardens clinging onto steep slopes. There are several places along the way to stop and rest, includ-ing many of North Beaches' Italian coffee houses. Parking is notoriously difficult, but on Vallejo Street, close to Powell, there is a public garage that almost always has space available at a moderate cost. Otherwise, public transport and taxis run to the junction of Broadway and Columbus.

2 HOURS

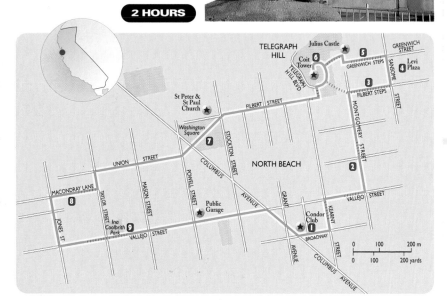

ℹ *San Francisco Visitor Information Center, Benjamin Swig Pavilion, Hallidie Plaza, Market and Powell streets, CA 94101*

▶ *From the public garage, turn left on Vallejo, turn right on Columbus and walk down to Broadway.*

❶ Condor Club
This once infamous club was the heart of the sleazy adult entertainment center of the city. A small plaque on the wall recognises it as the first topless (and bottomless) club in America. It is now an Italian restaurant.

▶ *Turn left down Broadway, past the remnants of the sex industry, and turn left again up Kearny Street. These are the first steps: the street seems to rise almost vertically. At Vallejo Street, turn right and descend down flower-strewn steps to Montgomery Street.*

❷ Montgomery Street
This is the Wall Street of the West as it passes through the Financial District, but up here it is a hillside vantage point with bird's-eye views of the Bay Bridge through the gaps between buildings, until it becomes too steep to continue. A staircase links the street to its upper section. Look back towards the Financial District for dramatic views of the Transamerica Pyramid.

▶ *Continue until the street divides and take the right fork to Filbert Street.*

❸ Filbert Steps
The Filbert steps are the most beautiful in the city, descending very steeply past charming cottages, with gardens overflowing with flowers, in a very intimate neighborhood. Breathtaking views over the bay can be enjoyed here.

▶ *The Filbert steps end at Levi Plaza.*

Above left: Coit Tower

❹ Levi Plaza
A new landscaped office and shopping complex has been developed here by the Levi Strauss company, of jeans fame attracting people from the surrounding advertising agencies to relax in the sun and eat their bag lunches. There are several good restaurants close at hand.

▶ *Continue left down Sansome Street to Greenwich Steps.*

❺ Greenwich Steps
All the altitude lost has now to be regained, and the Greenwich steps climb through charming residential buildings to Coit Tower. At Montgomery Street turn right to reach the pink

Julius Castle, a well-known restaurant.

▶ *Continue up the steps on the left to the tower.*

❻ Coit Tower
This San Francisco landmark was built in 1934 with money bequeathed by Lily Coit to beautify the city. Lily was crazy about fire-fighters and the tower is said to represent a fire hose. There are sweeping views of San Francisco Bay from the parking lot and an elevator goes to the top of the tower for an even

Viewing the city from the restful vantage point of Ina Coolbrith Park, on Russian Hill

higher viewpoint. More interesting are the WPA murals decorating the inside of the tower, which were part of the 1930s Federal Arts Project, covering nearly 4,000 sq ft of wall space.

▶ *Descend Telegraph Hill to the steps on Filbert Street, that start by a tiny green and yellow house at number 115. Continue down to Washington Square.*

7 Washington Square

Chinatown is steadily encroaching on the old Italian neighbourhood of North Beach, but Washington Square and its surroundings manage to hold on to the area's Italian heritage. It is surrounded by coffee shops and Italian restaurants; Mario's Bohemian Cigar Store, on the corner of Union and Columbus, is perhaps the most authentic North Beach coffee house left. Unfortunately, the landscaped square has become a refuge for homeless people (who often appear more threatening than they really are). St Peter and St Paul Church, dominating the square, was the first Italian parish church in America.

FOR HISTORY BUFFS

North Beach Museum, at 1435 Stockton Street, on the second floor of the Eureka Bank, documents the history of both North Beach and Chinatown in an exhibit of old photographs. Particularly interesting are the photographs of the bohemian period of North Beach, when the Beat poets made their mark on the world.

▶ *Cross the Square diagonally to Union Street. Continue right on Union and turn left on Taylor. A short way up Taylor, on the right, is a wooden stairway. This is the start of Macondray Lane.*

8 Macondray Lane

Steep wooden steps give way to a cobbled lane that winds past old San Francisco mews-type houses, lovingly and expensively restored. This is one of the most delightful residential areas of the city. Macondray lane was immortalized as Barbary Lane in Armistead Maupin's "Tales of the City" series.

▶ *At Jones, turn left and left again on Vallejo.*

9 Ina Coolbrith Park

Walk up to tiny Ina Coolbrith Park, which cascades down the hillside. A small, grassy area here accommodates not much more than a dozen sun bathers. Once again, the views over the Bay and the Financial District are magnificent.

SPECIAL TO...

Walk along Leavenworth Street to Lombard Street and look up at The Crookedest Street in the World. This section of Lombard was far too steep for vehicles to climb, so in the 1920s a series of eight extreme hairpin bends was constructed to overcome the 27° slope.

▶ *Continue down the steps, past a riot of colorful blooms, and return to the public garage on Vallejo.*

The leafy verges and cobblestones of exclusive Macondray Lane

Wine Country

2/3 DAYS • 184 MILES • 295KM

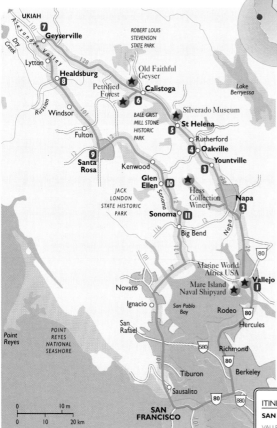

The grape harvest gets underway in Alexander Valley, Geyserville

Some of the world's greatest wines are produced in two valleys a one hour drive north of San Francisco. This tour visits the most interesting sites in the Napa and Sonoma wine areas. The elements that help create great wine – the right soil, warm days and cool nights – also create very pleasant countryside.

ℹ️ *San Francisco Visitor Information Center, Benjamin Swig Pavilion, Hallidie Plaza, Market and Powell streets, CA 94101*

▶ *Leave San Francisco across the Bay Bridge and take I-80 north. The buildings of UC Berkeley can be seen from the freeway. Continue north on I-80 over the Carquinez toll bridge to the Columbus Parkway exit. Turn west onto Marine World Parkway.*

❶ Vallejo

Founded at the junction of the Carquinez Straits and the Napa River by General Mariano Vallejo in 1851, Vallejo served as the state capital from 1851 to 1853. For over 100 years, Vallejo has been synonymous with the Mare Island Naval Shipyard, which was established in 1854. Over the years more than 520 ships have been built here, including USS *Saginaw*, the first US warship in the Pacific, and the 1920 battleship *California*, the largest naval craft built on the West Coast. The Vallejo Naval and Historical Museum, in the old Vallejo City Hall building at 734 Marin Street, has exhibits on the history of Mare Island, with relics, model ships and murals.

Today, most people go to Vallejo to visit Marine World Africa USA, a 160-acre (65-hectare) wildlife park and oceanarium. Killer whales, dolphins, sealions and tigers are all the stars of their own shows, and a range of interactive attractions includes Butterfly World, a tropical area filled with free-flying butterflies; Elephant Encounter, and Lorikeet Aviary, where the brightly colored birds sometimes interact rather too closely with the visitors. A clear, underwater tunnel passes through the Shark Experience, giving a fascinatingly intimate view of their world, and the latest exhibit features the Pacific Walrus. There is also an outstanding playground that includes a crawl-through, life-size model blue whale.

▶ *Continue west on Marine World Parkway and turn north onto Hwy 29, then Hwy 12, which is followed through sprawling, unattractive development into Napa.*

❷ Napa

The town from which this world-famous valley gets its name is at first a disappointment: this is not the expected romantic image of the Wine Country (see pages 120–1). Napa is a blue-collar town that provides many of the service industries to the wineries – cooperages, agricultural equipment suppliers and other mundane industries without which the vineyards could not survive. Main roads through Napa miss the most interesting areas. A century ago, this was a bustling port; the Napa River was the main transportation route to the valley, and river cruises show the town from the best perspective. Close to the river is the historic downtown area, and Main Street has many fine, restored Victorian buildings.

SCENIC ROUTES

To avoid congestion on Highway 29 follow the alternative route along the Silverado Trail, that parallels Hwy 29 and passes through some of the most beautiful vineyards in the Napa Valley. It also passes some of the best wineries, such as Stag's Leap, Conn Creek and Clos du Val. Zinfandel Lane, at the northern end of the Silverado Trail, connects back to Highway 29, just to the south of St Helena.

▶ *Leave Napa on Trancas Street and drive west across Hwy 29 to Redwood Road. Continue for 8 miles (13km), climbing Mount Veeder to the Hess Collection Winery, one of the more remote wineries in the valley, but well worth the drive, for its location, for the*

collection of contemporary art housed in its multi-level gallery, and for the self-guided tour of the winery. Drive back down to **Hwy 29** and turn north and exit at Yountville. Try to avoid **Hwy 29** on weekends, when the traffic can be impossible.

❸ Yountville

George Yount, the first white settler in the valley, is buried in the Pioneer Cemetery, off Jackson Street, near the land on which he planted the valley's first vines in the 1850s. Yountville has grown to be an important town with many very fine restaurants, Vintage 1870, a shopping complex housed in an old red-brick winery and a number of antique shops. Despite appearances to the contrary, Yountville is a large center and an important source of affordable housing for people working in the valley. Domaine Chandon is the American outpost of the French champagne house Moët et Chandon. It offers one of the best tours, demonstrating the production of sparkling wine; there is also a small museum and one of the area's outstanding restaurants. For a taste of old Napa, visit Trefethen Vineyards, reached via Oak Knoll Avenue, just south of town. The redwood winery was built over a century ago and sits splendidly in the midst of the vineyards.

SPECIAL TO...

The most peaceful and unusual way to see the Napa Valley is from a hot-air balloon. Several companies offer flights, which generally last for about an hour and go wherever the wind takes them. They always leave in the very early morning, when the air is cool, and float over the vineyards as the first rays of sun strike the vines.

▶ *Continue north for 3 miles (5km) to Oakville.*

A bird's-eye view of the Napa Valley vineyards, by hot-air balloon

taken by expensive boutiques and galleries. Two blocks west of Main Street, the modern St Helena Public Library houses the definitive collection of literature of the Napa Valley Wine Library Association, and the Silverado Museum. Robert Louis Stevenson spent his honeymoon in a cabin on Mount St Helena and lived there during 1880-81. He wrote about the experience in *Silverado Squatters*. The museum has a large collection of over 8,000 items relating to Stevenson's life and first editions of his work.

Just north of town, on the west side of Highway 29, the ornate, Victorian Rhine House of Beringer Vineyards can be seen at the end of an imposing drive. Established in 1876, it is the oldest Napa Valley winery in continuous operation, and the mansion is now on the National Register of Historic Places. Half-hour tours of the winery end with a tasting at the mansion.

A few minutes further north is three-story, stone Greystone building, built in 1888 and until recently owned by the Christian Brothers. Once a winery, it now houses the West Coast facility for the Culinary Institute of America. Directly across the road is the Charles Krug Winery, built in 1861; tours of the property look at both old and new wine making-techniques.

▶ Continue north on **Hwy 29** to the sign for the Bale Grist Mill State Historic Park. Dr Edward Bale, a London surgeon, built a small flour mill, powered by a 20-foot (6m) waterwheel on Mill Creek in 1846. The wheel and mill have been restored and can be reached from the parking lot. Continue north to Dunaweal Lane, where a cable car transports visitors up to Coca Cola's Sterling Vineyards. Across the road is one of the newest wineries, housing a vast art collection. Continue north on **Hwy 29** to Calistoga.

❹ Oakville
North of Oakville is one of the most celebrated areas of vineyards in California. The soil of the Rutherford Bench produces some of the finest Cabernet Sauvignon grapes in the world and, not surprisingly, some of the greatest wineries are to be found here. Oakville is little more than a cluster of houses and the Oakville Grocery, that rivals any big city grocery with its wide range of gourmet produce. Opposite the grocery is arguably the most significant winery in America. Robert Mondavi changed the face of wine-making when he opened it, raising the level of viticulture to new heights. His innovative methods have influenced a generation of wine-producers. In the 1980s he established a partnership with the late Baron Rothschild, of Mouton Rothschild fame, to produce Opus One, a new breed of premium American wine. The tour of the Mondavi Winery gives one of the best overviews

of the state-of-the-art wine-making process in the valley.

Traveling on towards Rutherford, St Supery offers one of the most educational tours available. Their wines may not be the equal of the finest in the region, but they have a modern winery designed specifically to allow visitors to see and understand the whole production system. The most interesting exhibit is a contraption that reproduces the distinctive "nose" of different varieties of wine.

▶ Continue along **Hwy 29** to St Helena.

❺ St Helena
To many, this is the heart of the Napa Valley. St Helena is an attractive, small town that has been at the center of the wine business for over a century. The 1890s look of Main Street is carefully maintained, although some residents are concerned that the small-town shops serving local needs are being over-

6 Calistoga

Although only a few miles north of St Helena, Calistoga has a much more down-home feel. The town was founded on a thermal stream in 1859 by Sam Brannan, who intended to make it a resort spa. Brannan's cottage still stands on Washington Street, next to the Sharpsteen Museum, and is furnished in period antiques. His dream came true, and Calistoga has become a popular spa destination, with hot springs appearing all over town. If you want a mud bath, a herbal wrap or just a plunge in a mineral pool, someone, somewhere in town will provide exactly what you need.

Just to the northwest of town, on Tubbs Lane, is Old Faithful of California, one of only a few geysers in the world that erupts at regular intervals. A nominal entrance fee gives access via a run-down group of buildings that shield a piece of wasteland, out of which the 100-foot (30m) jet of water shoots every 40 minutes.

About 5 miles (8km) farther west, at 4100 Petrified Forest Road, a short trail leads through the fossilised remains of the ancient redwoods that have become a California landmark. Volcanic ash from an eruption of Mount St Helena blanketed the area three million years ago, covering all the redwoods. Over the centuries, silica and other minerals from the ash infiltrated the trunks and gradually turned them to stone.

▶ *Return east along Petrified Forest Road and turn north onto* **Hwy 128**.

7 Geyserville

The tiny town of Geyserville, in the heart of Sonoma County's Alexander Valley, at the foot of Geyser Peak, is second only to Napa for the quality of grapes. Compared with the Napa towns, though, Geyserville has little interest for visitors. This is a wine-producing area, pure and simple. The striking architecture of Chateau Souverain appears across Highway 101, to the west of town; the winery offers chamber music and jazz concerts during the summer, but little else is offered to entertain visitors other than tours and tastings at the wineries.

▶ *Take* **Hwy 101** *south to Healdsburg.*

8 Healdsburg

St Helena must once have been like this. Healdsburg's town center is arranged around a charming, Spanish-style plaza, shaded by palms, redwoods and other trees – perfect for a summer picnic. Friendly little shops provide all you need for a delightful day out in the Wine Country. The extensive Sonoma County Wine Library includes the collection of the Vintners Club Library of San Francisco, and is housed in the new Healdsburg Regional Library at Center and Piper streets. At 221 Matheson Street, the Healdsburg Museum is dedicated to the preservation and exhibition of northern Sonoma County history. Housed in the old Carnegie Library, it has strong collections of Pomo Indian artifacts and every Christmas season there is a popular toy and doll exhibit. The town stands at the confluence of three major wine areas:

Alexander Valley, Dry Creek and Russian River. All three produce distinctly different wines. Over 50 wineries lie within the immediate vicinity of Healdsburg, most of them producing extremely good wines. Deciding which to visit is an enviable dilemma. Clos du Bois are in town, at 5 Fitch Street, in an uninspiring building; since 1974 their wines have given more than their share of inspiration. Just north of town, at 16275 Healdsburg Avenue, Simi Winery produce outstanding Cabernet Sauvignon and give tours of their state-of-the-art facilities. Pinot Noir lovers should head a few miles west to the Russian River area along Westside Road, where Davis Bynum and Rochioli produce very drinkable big, soft reds.

▶ *Drive south on* **Hwy 101** *for 14 miles (22km) to Santa Rosa.*

9 Santa Rosa

After a tour through all the small towns of the Wine Country, arriving in Santa Rosa is like reaching the big city: this is the biggest town in Sonoma County, with a population of well over 100,000. As one of the fastest-growing towns in Northern California, it has its share of shopping malls and suburban sprawl, and looks like any ordinary, modern city. What would have been the historic downtown area was destroyed by the 1906 earthquake, but an area called Railroad Square, west of Highway 101 between 3rd and 5th streets is part of a restored 1920s shopping district with gift and antique shops and cafés. One of the more unusual sites in town is the Church of the One Tree, at 492 Sonoma Avenue: a gothic-style church, complete with 70-foot (21m) steeple, built entirely from a single redwood felled near Guerneville in 1875. The church was immortalised by Robert L. Ripley in his long-

Old Faithful of California, near Calistoga, lets off steam again

Sonoma Plaza, where independence was declared in 1846

running *Believe It or Not!* comic strip, that became an American institution. Ripley hailed from Santa Rosa, and the church is now both the Ripley Memorial Museum and a State Historic Landmark. Across the street is the Luther Burbank Home and Memorial Gardens.

▶ *From Santa Rosa take College Avenue to Hwy 12 east. The urban sprawl of Santa Rosa soon gives way to the hills and wineries of the Sonoma Valley. Kenwood is the first settlement on the road south, and has one of the best restaurants in the area. Continue south on Hwy 12 for 3 miles (5km) to the exit to Glen Ellen on Arnold Drive.*

10 Glen Ellen

Glen Ellen is a quaint little village that grew up around a sawmill built up by General Vallejo in the 19th century. A narrow-gauge railway reached Glen Ellen in 1879 and San Franciscans came to visit the saloons and brothels that opened up around town. One of these visitors was writer Jack London, who decided to stay. His home, Beauty Ranch, is now the Jack London State Historic Park, an 800-acre (323-hectare) park reached from London Ranch Road, right in the center of Glen Ellen. London settled on his Glen Ellen Beauty Ranch permanently in 1909 and the white-frame cottage where he wrote many of his books has been restored, as has the log cabin he built in memory of his days in the Klondike. More interesting are the ruined remains of the Wolf House, which was to be the dream home of London and his wife, Charmian, until it mysteriously burned down, days before they were due to move in. The massive stone walls that remain give a good idea of the original grandeur of the house. London died at the early age of 40, soon after this disaster. His widow built the House of Happy Walls, now a museum dedicated to London's memory. London is buried close by, under a grove of oak trees.

On the left, returning down London Ranch Road, is Benziger Winery, whose steep, terraced vineyards were established by Julius Wegener. He had received the land as payment from General Vallejo for constructing his home in Sonoma. Mike Benziger came across the estate and persuaded his father Bruno, a master marketeer, to buy it. The winery soon became the second largest in Sonoma Valley, its Glen Ellen label wines representing good value and establishing an unassailable position in the marketplace. The family recently sold the label and now concentrate on their own Benziger wines. The winery offers tram tours of the property and a section of the vineyard has been set aside to demonstrate different viticultural techniques.

▶ *Return along Arnold Drive. Just before Hwy 12, turn left on Dunbar Road. A short way down, Shona Gardens, open only by appointment, has an extensive collection of sculpture in stone and metal by members of Zimbabwe's Shona people. Turn south on Hwy 12 to Sonoma.*

11 Sonoma

Sonoma was the birthplace of the California wine industry. Hungarian Count Agoston Haraszthy planted the first experimental vineyards, from which a vast wine industry developed at Buena Vista Winery. Daily tours and tastings are offered, as well as an historical presentation and an art gallery. The other major winery in this town is Sebastiani, which has the world's largest collection of carved wooden wine casks on display.

▶ *Leave Sonoma on Hwy 12 south; turn west on Hwy 121 and west again on Hwy 37. Take Hwy 101 south to San Francisco.*

RECOMMENDED TRIP

California Dreamin's Topless Tours gives sports car fans the chance to discover the best of northern California on scenic backroads and byways behind the wheel of a fine collection of two-seater convertibles, including a '96 Dodge Viper, a BMW Z3, and a classic '55 Porsche Spyder. Five-day tours, beginning and ending in San Francisco, take in the Monterey peninsula, the Napa Valley and the Gold Country. For details tel/fax: 510/284–5039.

WINE

When a Stag's Leap Wine Cellars' 1973 Cabernet Sauvignon won first place in a blind tasting in Paris, competing against the finest French wines, California wine had well and truly arrived, 200 years after the first vineyards had been planted.

Spanish missionaries introduced the first grapevines to San Diego in 1769. The vineyards extended northwards with the establishment of the missions, but it was not until the Gold Rush that wine-making came into its own. Buena Vista Winery was founded in Sonoma in 1857 by Count Agoston Haraszthy, a Hungarian considered by many to be the father of the California wine industry. Over the next two decades European immigrants built wineries throughout Napa, Sonoma, Santa Clara and the Central Valley.

The most important element in wine-making is "terroir," a combination of soil type, climate and elevation. California provides exactly what is needed to produce the finest wine grapes possible, but its early wines were humble table wines, produced by European families who had been drinking these simple accompaniments to their meals for generations. California wine-making never really developed beyond this before 1920.

The industry ground to a halt during the 13 years of prohibition and by 1933, when the law was repealed, it was in complete disarray. Some of the more enterprising wineries moved into production of communion wine, but many ceased operation completely.

Nevertheless, techniques and vine stocks improved over the ensuing years to such an extent that in the early 1970s California wines could compete with the best in the world.

California wine-makers are now very innovative, and are continually pushing the limits of their skills. New grape varieties are always being tested; the finest wines are still produced from the white Chardonnay grape and red Cabernet Sauvignon, but outstanding wine is produced from virtually every variety of grape available, including Sauvignon

Blanc, Pinot Noir, Chenin Blanc, Reisling, Merlot, Sangiovese and California's very own Zinfandel, which can have a light, almost Beaujolais-like quality, or can be big, alcoholic and chewy, like a massive Rhone wine.

The undisputed centre of the California wine country is Napa Valley. In this narrow valley there are 273 wineries, some dating from the 19th century. Every inch of territory is covered in vineyards, producing some of the very best wines in the world. Several of the great French wine producers have acknowledged the exceptional quality of California wines and have established their own wineries in the valley: Moët et Chandon, Tattinger and Mumm all have their own champagne houses

here, and the great Chateau Mouton Rothschild has joined forces with Robert Mondavi to produce Opus One, a Medoc-styled wine made to exacting standards in an amazing modern winery.

Other areas now rival Napa, and Sonoma County, long thought to be a poor relation of Napa, is producing wines that are the equals of their neighbors. The Russian River area, in particular, has exactly the right cool climate to produce exceptional Pinot Noir grapes, and the resulting wines from Dehlinger, Rochioli and Gary Farrell, among others, are difficult to beat.

Wine Country extends as far south as San

Diego County, and the Central Coast wineries, from Monterey down to Santa Barbara, are rapidly establishing themselves as worthy of serious attention.

Central Valley is the biggest producer of wine grapes in the state. Millions of gallons of wine are produced annually from its enormous supply. The wines are certainly no competition for the great wines of France, or of California, for that matter, but they are enjoyed in copious amounts throughout the world. Ernest and Julio Gallo are the undisputed leaders in the field; their winery looks more like a heavy industrial plant than the romantic image of a rustic building among the vineyards. Fortunately, even the Gallos are moving into the premium wine arena, producing high-quality wines for an increasingly discerning market.

California viniculture benefits from the marriage of scientific experimentation and the gut reaction most great wine-makers have to their craft. Unfortunately, the scientific element has had disastrous ramifications. The University of California at Davis, near Sacramento, has the world's most advanced course in eneology. Academics here developed a new improved root stock for vines, code-named AXR-1, which was widely adopted by the wineries. No one realised that it could not resist the dreaded phylloxera louse that almost destroyed the French wine industry in the last century. In Napa Valley alone, hundreds of acres of vines have had to be uprooted and burned, resulting in the loss of thousands of gallons of wine.

Most California wineries encourage visits from the public and have tasting rooms; many also offer winery tours. For any true wine-lover, visiting California is like going to heaven.

Reaping the rewards of a perfect climate: Alexander Valley's harvest

San Francisco Peninsula &
Monterey Bay

From San Francisco south to the lively college town of Santa Cruz and on around the Monterey Bay to the city of Monterey, this Pacific coast tour reveals strawberry and flower fields, lush apple orchards and a spectacular, deserted shore, revealing California's agricultural riches and undeveloped beauty.

2 DAYS • 261 MILES • 420KM

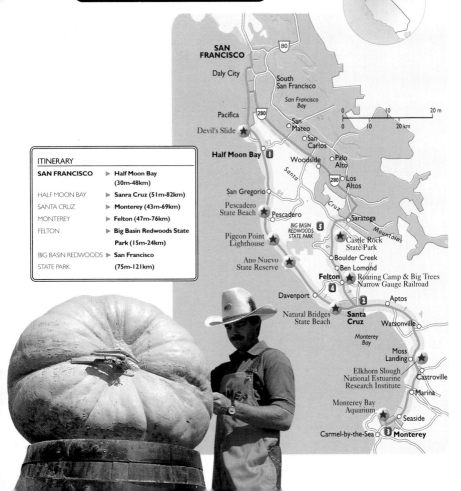

ITINERARY		
SAN FRANCISCO	►	**Half Moon Bay** (30m-48km)
HALF MOON BAY	►	**Sanra Cruz** (51m-82km)
SANTA CRUZ	►	**Monterey** (43m-69km)
MONTEREY	►	**Felton** (47m-76km)
FELTON	►	**Big Basin Redwoods State Park** (15m-24km)
BIG BASIN REDWOODS	►	**San Francisco**
STATE PARK		(75m-121km)

Map labels:
SAN FRANCISCO
Daly City
South San Francisco
San Francisco Bay
Pacifica
280
Devil's Slide
San Mateo
San Carlos
Half Moon Bay
Woodside
Palo Alto
Santa
San Gregorio
Los Altos
Pescadero State Beach
Pescadero
Saratoga
Cruz
BIG BASIN REDWOODS STATE PARK
Pigeon Point Lighthouse
Castle Rock State Park
Mountains
Ano Nuevo State Reserve
Boulder Creek
Ben Lomond
Felton
Roaring Camp & Big Trees Narrow Gauge Railroad
Davenport
Aptos
Natural Bridges State Beach
Santa Cruz
Watsonville
Monterey Bay
Moss Landing
Elkhorn Slough National Estuarine Research Institute
Castroville
Marina
Monterey Bay Aquarium
Seaside
Carmel-by-the-Sea
Monterey

A dizzy view of a spectacular route: Highway One, at Half Moon Bay

San Francisco Visitor Information Center, Benjamin Swig Pavilion, Hallidie Plaza, Market and Powell streets, CA 94101

▶ *Leave San Francisco on 19th Avenue, which crosses Golden Gate Park, and turn right at Sloat Boulevard. Pass the San Francisco Zoo and turn left onto the Great Highway, which becomes Skyline Boulevard. To the right are the cliffs of Fort Funston, a popular lift-off point for hang-gliders. Continue south to Hwy 1 and pass through Pacifica, one of California's newest towns, established in 1957, and a popular surfing community on the coast. The road becomes a series of breath-taking hairpin bends as it navigates steep cliffs with sweeping views of the ocean opening out around every curve. Take care at Devil's Slide, where the unstable hillsides periodically collapse into the sea, particularly after heavy rain. Continue to Half Moon Bay.*

Left: a dish fit to grace any giant's supper table – a monster Half Moon Bay pumpkin

❶ Half Moon Bay

Hallowe'en is the big event for this small coastal town, when thousands of visitors come to the annual Art and Pumpkin Festival. During the rest of the year the attractions include craft and antique shops, cafés and bakeries, and several restored 19th-century homes converted into bed and breakfast inns, in addition to the miles of rugged coastline and sandy beaches.

▶ *Continue south on Hwy 1 through Pescadero, founded by the Spanish in 1856 and now an artichoke-growing centre. Past Pigeon Point Lighthouse, built in 1871 and at 115 feet (35m) one of the tallest on the West Coast, the shoreline is increasingly deserted. At Ano Nuevo State Reserve there is a large elephant seal reserve and an easily accessible beach with millions of fossilised sea shells embedded in the rocks. Just before Santa Cruz, the Natural Bridges State Beach is a good place to witness the migration of thousands of monarch butterflies; near by, on Delaware Avenue, the Joseph M. Long Marine Laboratory of the University of California has an aquarium, touch-tank and sealion enclosure.*

BACK TO NATURE

The northern elephant seal was close to extinction in the late 1950s, when the Ano Nuevo State Reserve was established. This massive and decidedly ugly marine mammal made a spectacular recovery, and a large breeding colony of over 3,000 can been seen from December to April at this site 18 miles (29km) north of Santa Cruz. The males, which can weigh up to 3 tons/tonnes, leave after the pups are born, but at any time of the year there will be females with their offspring, basking in the dunes.

---

❷ Santa Cruz

Laid-back, counter-cultural values have become the trade-mark of this college town; in many ways, Santa Cruz today bears similarities to San Francisco's Haight-Ashbury in the 1960s. The presence of the University of California infuses the town with a high proportion of young people hell-bent on partying and surfing – all contributing to its relaxed atmosphere. Last century this was logging country, but in the early 1900s the town developed

The Giant Dipper, Santa Cruz, has been turning stomachs for 70 years

into a holiday resort, and in 1904 the now famous Boardwalk was built. Along Santa Cruz beach, the Boardwalk is the ultimate seaside entertainment center and the only original boardwalk amusement park still operating on the West Coast, with an antique merry-go-round, a 1924 wooden, Giant Dipper roller coaster that has carried over 25 million passengers, a ferris wheel, bumper cars and, of course, arcade games and candy floss.

Lighthouse Point, at the western end of the bay, is a popular surfing area, and the sea is usually teaming with tiny, wet-suited figures hoping to catch a big wave. On the ground floor of the lighthouse is the tiny Surfing Museum with a collection of old photographs and antique surf boards. Santa Cruz surfers have had their share of shark attacks, and the teeth marks in some of the displays graphically illustrate the ever-present danger.

The university was founded in 1965 and is spectacularly situated on 2,000 acres (809 hectares) of the Cowell Ranch, overlooking Monterey Bay. The Arboretum is particularly inter-esting for its Mediterranean garden and its outstanding collection of plants from Australia and South Africa. Many of the specimens are the only examples to be found in America.

▶ *Continue south on* **Hwy 1** *through Aptos and Watsonville, surrounded by strawberry fields and orchards, to Moss Landing. Colorful boats fill this weather-beaten little fishing harbor and close by is Elkhorn Slough National Estuarine Research Institute, where 1,400 acres (566 hectares) of salt marsh and tidal flats form one of the few undisturbed coastal wetlands remaining in California, home to over 150 species of birds, including golden eagles. Continue south, skirting Castroville, the "Artichoke Capital of the World" and passing the cheap motels that line the road at Seaside, into Monterey.*

❽ Monterey

Until the middle of the last century, Monterey was the most important town in California. Discovered by Cabrillo in 1542 (but not settled until 1770), it was first the Spanish capital of Alta California; it became the Mexican capital in 1822 and the American capital in 1846. The discovery of gold in 1848 moved interest away from Monterey to San Francisco. Whaling and then fishing became the main industries, until, more recently, tourism took over.

Fishing is still important, and at the Municipal Wharf commercial fishing boats unload their catches of tuna, swordfish, squid, salmon, halibut, cod, shark and anchovies – which are then cleaned and packed and sent off to market.

Fisherman's Wharf was built in 1846 for ships bringing goods around Cape Horn, and was used by whalers and sardine fishermen before becoming a tourist attraction with shops and fish restaurants. Several boat tours of Monterey Bay leave the wharf and the seals, sealions and sea otters provide non-stop entertainment. Across from the Wharf is the Custom House, California's oldest public building, erected in 1827. It was here that the American flag was raised for the first time in 1846 by Commodore Sloat. Inside is a display from a cargo ship of the 1830s.

Monterey's other great legacy from the height of the sardine fishing industry is Cannery Row. At its peak, the row housed 16 canneries that packed over 240,000 sardines, but the area went into steep decline after the sardine supplies mysteriously disappeared in 1948, and the fishing canneries closed. Thanks to John Steinbeck's novel Cannery Row, the street has seen a dramatic resurgence. It bears little resemblance, now, to the author's depiction, and the old buildings that remain house galleries, cafés and wine-tasting rooms. The highlight of the street is, without doubt, the Monterey Bay Aquarium, one of the largest and finest in the world, where 6,500 forms of marine life fill over 100 display tanks in a series of buildings that aim to capture the atmosphere of the original Cannery Row. There is a three-story mature kelp forest exhibit; a below- and above-water sea otter exhibit and a 90-foot (27m)-long tank replicating life in the Monterey Bay. In the latest exhibit, visitors view the 35-foot (10m) tall Outer Bay through the largest window in the world. The "indoor ocean" has more water than all the other aquarium exhibits combined.

RECOMMENDED WALK

The Path of History, through downtown Monterey, includes several good examples of the Monterey style of architecture. Stop at the visitor center at the Custom House, near Fisherman's Wharf, for a map and to pay a single, nominal entrance fee to all the buildings on the walk; these date from as early as 1770, and several were built during the mid-19th century, including California's first theater.

▶ *Return to Santa Cruz and take Hwy 9 north off Hwy 1.*

4 Felton
Up in the Santa Cruz mountains, just before Felton, is the Roaring Camp and Big Trees Narrow Gauge Railroad, on which an 1880s steam train carries passengers on a 6-mile (10km) trip through redwood groves. In Felton is a covered bridge dating from 1892, typical of the old California bridges, most of which have long since disappeared.

▶ *Continue north on Hwy 9.*

5 Big Basin Redwoods State Park
Beyond Felton is the Big Basin Redwoods State Park with several stands of 2,000-year-old redwoods in its 17,000 acres (6,880 hectares). The park extends as far as the Pacific Ocean, but its western side is accessible only from Highway 1. This vast area of forest offers genuine wilderness hiking; once off the main road it is difficult to believe that one of the most densely populated areas of California is only a few miles to the east. There is a profusion of camping sites and dozens of walking trails.

▶ *Follow Hwy 9 across Skyline Boulevard to Saratoga and continue along Saratoga Avenue to join I-280 north. I-280 passes through Silicon Valley, where many of the world's high-tech company*

FOR CHILDREN

Children love the bizarre and spooky atmosphere of the Winchester Mystery House, built at San Jose (off I-280) by Sarah Winchester, the eccentric heiress to the Winchester rifle fortune. She believed that she would live as long as the house continued to grow. When she died in 1922 there were 160 rooms covering 6 acres (2 hectares). Doors open onto blank walls, stairways lead nowhere, and ghost stories abound.

headquarters, including those of Apple, can be seen lining the freeway. From Los Altos the road climbs back to San Francisco, passing through some of the bay's most exclusive residential areas.

Enjoying life at Monterey, above the water at Fisherman's Wharf …

… and under the water, at the Aquarium in Monterey Bay

SCENIC ROUTES

Freeways are not normally the route chosen by anyone looking for great scenery, but Interstate 280 is an exception. Known as the Junipero Serra freeway, it cuts through the most beautiful part of the peninsula, from San Jose to downtown San Francisco.

CENTRAL COAST

Between San Francisco and Los Angeles, California Highway 1 hugs the coast, passing through some of the most dramatic scenery and interesting towns in the state. Fog-shrouded cliffs, crashing surf and wind-blown cypress trees have become symbols of this remarkable shoreline, and this is certainly the best way to drive between the two cities, if time allows. The road is narrow, long and tortuous, but the views are worth it.

Great scenery is not the only reason to visit the area. Several charming towns punctuate the coast, offering a variety of attractions; and perhaps the most intriguing place to visit along the route is Hearst Castle, at San Simeon. The area has also developed a well-earned reputation for its wines. Over the coastal range, the warm inland valleys offer perfect growing conditions for many varieties of grape, producing wines rivalling those of Napa Valley. The inland region lays claim to some of the most fertile soil in the nation, and around Salinas, the birthplace of writer John Steinbeck, fields of vegetables stretch as far as the eye can see.

Tour 21

John Steinbeck is most famous for his books about the Monterey Peninsula, particularly Cannery Row. This tour starts in the town of Monterey and heads south through Pebble Beach, Carmel and Point Lobos, through increasingly spectacular coastal scenery, to Big Sur. Farther south, at San Simeon, William Randolf Hearst built the most opulent and extravagant residence in California: Hearst Castle, complete with 38 bedrooms, 14 sitting rooms and two libraries. Four different tours are offered by the State Park Service. Continue through the artist's colony of Cambria to San Luis Obispo; from here the route returns north on the eastern side of the coastal range, passing through regions of vineyards and continuing past several missions built by Father Junipero Serra. Pastoral Carmel Valley leads back to Carmel and Monterey Bay.

Above: the lovely, gentle rolling landscape of Carmel Valley
Left: J. Paul Getty's Roman-inspired villa now houses the Getty Museum, near Malibu

Tour 22

The fabulous Getty Museum is the first stop on this drive from Santa Monica along the Pacific Coast Highway. Past Malibu and Ventura, the road winds along the coast to Santa Barbara, one of the most beautiful towns in the country sitting on a curving, sandy bay with the Santa Ynez Mountains as a backdrop. It then passes over the mountains into the Santa Ynez Valley and into a world of horses and wine (singer Michael Jackson has his ranch here), before dropping into Solvang which is as close to Denmark as you can get in America. The return to Santa Barbara takes you through La Purisima Mission State Historic Park and the colorful flower fields of Lompoc.

The Steinbeck
Loop

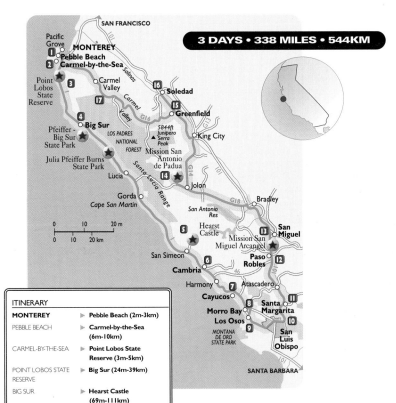

3 DAYS • 338 MILES • 544KM

Monterey Bay and Big Sur are set in one of the world's most dramatic and beautiful coastal areas. Coupled with the extravagant splendor of Hearst Castle at San Simeon, and the missions along El Camino Real, this tour represents some of the best California has to offer. It begins at Monterey, one of California's first and most successful settlements, where a walking and bike path follow the coastline for 3 miles (5km), passing rocky beaches and rich tidepools.

i *Monterey Visitor Center, 204 El Estero, CA 93940*

▶ *Leave Monterey on Ocean Drive and continue past Point Pinos Lighthouse and the Del Monte Forest at the Pacific Grove Gate to Pebble Beach.*

BACK TO NATURE

Every October, thousands of orange and black monarch butterflies congregate in a grove of trees at the end of Lighthouse Avenue in Pacific Grove, known as Butterfly City, USA. They come from as far away as Alaska and Mexico to spend the winter clustered together on the Monterey Peninsula.

❶ Pebble Beach

This private community lies within the Del Monte Forest and the famous 17-Mile Drive passes some of the most photographed seascapes in

America. Apart from beaches and Monterey pines, there are six world-class golf courses, two deluxe resorts and palatial residential estates. Wildlife abounds here and sealions, sea otters, cormorants and a host of other sea birds are everyday sights. Many of the knarled and wind-sculpted Monterey pines have reached stardom in their own right: most photographed is the Lone Cypress standing alone on a rocky outcrop above pounding surf. The only negative aspect to Pebble Beach is a fairly hefty entrance charge.

▶ *The southern gate at Pebble Beach exits in Carmel.*

❷ Carmel-by-the-Sea

Carmel is usually described as quaint, and with good reason: it is a picture-perfect little town full of art galleries, antique shops, designer boutiques and tea shops. If anything, it is almost too perfect: the tree-lined streets seem to be out of Disneyland, rather than a real

Standing firm above the sea: the Lone Cypress, Pebble Beach

community, and there are bans on traffic lights, neon signs and hot dog stands. Carmel is, nevertheless, a very popular, if expensive, destination, and having Clint Eastwood as its mayor has certainly helped its popularity. At the edge of Carmel is Mission San Carlos Borromeo del Rio Carmelo (usually known as Carmel Mission). This extremely well-restored piece of California's Spanish history is the final resting place of its founder, and the architect of the California mission chain, Father Junipero Serra. It is one of the most beautiful of the 21 missions and houses an interesting museum devoted to Serra. The only other site of note is the Tor House, built by poet Robinson Jeffers with his own hands, from rocks carried up from the beach, and now open for visits. The white sands of Carmel beach below Tor House provide a very pleasant stroll back into town.

▶ *Leave Carmel and turn south on **Hwy 1**. After 4 miles (6km) turn right into Point Lobos State Reserve.*

❸ Point Lobos State Reserve

This beautiful 1,276-acre (516-hectare) reserve, reputed to be the setting for Robert Louis Stevenson's *Treasure Island*, boasts tall stands of cypress trees, hidden coves, pristine beaches and strange sculpted rocks, re-designed by the crashing waves of the Pacific Ocean.

The area was immortalised by the great photographer Edward Weston and is a shrine to landscape photographers throughout the world. Marine life is abundant here, and the great success story is a thriving colony of sea otters that not too long ago were on the verge of extinction.

▶ *Continue south on **Hwy 1** for 20 miles (32km).*

❹ Big Sur

This wild section of coastline along Highway 1 is the jewel in the crown of California's coast. Big Sur is the name of a specific village on the coast, but it more generally refers to the stretch of coast between Carmel Highlands and Bixby Bridge. Dramatic cliffs rise from the Pacific Ocean; grassy promontories covered by wildflowers jut out over the surf; towering redwoods rise over coastal streams. Highway 1, the Cabrillo Highway, was carved and blasted out of the western slopes of the Santa Lucia Mountains over 100 years ago and, fortunately, the area has remained

unspoiled. There are a few shops and restaurants, notably Nepenthe, built as a honeymoon cottage by Orson Wells for his wife, Rita Hayworth; and close by is the Henry Miller Memorial Library, where Miller made his home in his later years when he wrote Plexus and Nexus.

The Julia Pfeiffer Burns State Park is home to the most southerly grove of giant coastal redwoods, along with cascading waterfalls, hiking trails and spectacular views along the coast.

▶ *Continue south on **Hwy 1** for 64 miles (103km) to San Simeon.*

❺ Hearst Castle

The gilded towers of newspaper magnate William Randolph Hearst's fantastic creation can be seen on a hilltop overlooking San Simeon. After one of the most magnificent natural sights of California comes what must certainly be the most extravagant man-made example.

A rich man's castle – William Randolph Hearst's opulent home

Outpost of an ancient volcanic range – Morro Rock

Hearst, with his architect Julia Morgan, took almost 30 years, from 1919 to 1947, to complete his fantasy castle. With over 100 rooms, it would cost 400 million dollars to build today. The architecture is an eclectic mix of Italian, French, Moorish and Spanish styles, and the interiors are an equally bizarre mix of antiques from around the world. At one time, wild animals roamed the gardens in what was then the world's largest private zoo. In 1941, Hearst's life was immortalised in the Orson Welles film *Citizen Kane*, and the house was frequented by many Hollywood personalities, including Charlie Chaplin, Greta Garbo and Clark Gable. But the bubble finally burst when Hearst died in 1951. Within six years the family had to donate the property to the State of California in return for a $50 million tax write-off. Hearst Castle is now a State Historic Monument, second only to Disneyland in popularity. The property is so vast that four different tours are offered of the house and gardens and reservations are highly recommended, especially in the summer.

▶ *Continue south on **Hwy 1** for 9 miles (14km).*

6 Cambria
Nestled in a valley lined with pine trees, Cambria is an artists' settlement with a somewhat contrived atmosphere, created with half-timbered buildings and many quaint gift shops pandering to tourists. If you can get past the tourist face of the town, there really is a thriving community of artists, and several of the galleries are worth browsing. The best bet, however, is to take a walk on one of the beaches searching for pebbles or jade, or to observe the large sea otter colony offshore.

▶ *Continue south on **Hwy 1** for 16 miles (25km).*

7 Cayucos
This old fishing town was founded in 1867 by Portuguese fishermen as a shipping point for dairy and beef products. It is noted for its long fishing wharf and the gentle waters of Estero Bay.

▶ *Continue on **Hwy 1** for 6 miles (10km).*

8 Morro Bay
Dominating the view as you drive down Highway 1 is the silhouette of Morro Rock, an enormous volcanic peak marking the westernmost point of a range of nine extinct volcanoes created 20 million years ago and known as The Sisters. This 576-foot (175m)-high sentry served as a landmark for Spanish explorers; today it is a protected nesting site for peregrine falcons. Beneath the rock stretches a 5-mile (8km)-long beach with 85-foot (26m)-high white sand dunes that serve as the habitat for a wealth of bird and plant life. South of town, opposite the entrance to Morro Bay State Park, the Morro Bay State Park Museum of Natural History has displays of some of the life that teems along the shore, including the peregrine falcon and sea otter. An observation deck gives a perfect view of the shore birds of the region. In town, seafood restaurants serve the freshest catch from the boat-filled harbour below Morro Rock.

▶ *Continue on **Hwy 1** for 4 miles (6km).*

9 Los Osos
Juan Gaspar de Portola named this area Valley of the Bears in 1769 because of the abundance of grizzly bears in the region. The bears are long gone, and it is now safe to follow the hiking trails that meander through Montana de Oro, one of California's loveliest state parks. Take the Los Osos Valley Road west until it turns into Pecho Road, which winds through the heart of this sanctuary.

▶ *Follow Los Osos Road east, then Foothill Boulevard east past the Madonna Inn to San Luis Obispo.*

10 San Luis Obispo
It is difficult not to like San Luis Obispo, a quiet, country town dominated by the agricultural students of California Polytechnic University. Be sure to stop at the Madonna Inn on the drive into town. Mr Madonna, who has a road construction business, built the first 12 rooms of the inn in 1958, this has now expanded to 109, and each room has a different theme, such as Jungle Rock or Floral Fantasy: the ultimate in kitsch. The men's room even has a waterfall cascading down for a urinal. If you survive this sensory experience, continue to the more refined atmosphere of

131

and white blossoms color the surrounding countryside.

▶ *Continue north on* **Hwy 101** *for 4 miles (6km).*

🔢 San Miguel

Mission San Miguel must be the most easily accessible mission in the state, lying within a few yards of the Highway 101 exit ramp and one of the more interesting missions in the chain. It was built by Father Fermin Lasuen in 1797 on the lush banks of the Salinas River. Brown-robed Franciscan monks still live here and there has been less restoration than at many of other missions: the interior is particularly elaborate and well preserved.

▶ *Continue north on* **Hwy 101** *for 11 miles (18km) to Bradley. Turn west on* **Hwy G18** *and drive for 21 miles (34km) to Jolon. Continue west on* **Hwy G18** *for another 5 miles (8km), entering Fort*

The 18th-century Mission San Luis Obispo de Tolosa

RECOMMENDED WALKS

The historic centre of San Luis Obispo is best seen on foot. A walking guide to the town is available from the San Luis Obispo Country Visitors Bureau, 1039 Chorro Street, Suite E.

quiet streets lined with Victorian homes that make up the bulk of the town. San Luis Obispo Creek wanders through the central plaza close to the Mission San Luis Obispo de Tolosa, built by Father Junipero Serra in 1772 and unremarkable except for the fact that it is the birthplace of the red roof-tiles that have become synonymous with Spanish mission architecture. Three fires ravaged the mission before the fathers decided to replace the thatched roof with a less flammable material and settled for tiles made from local clay. These were so successful that by 1784 they had been adopted by all the California missions. Near by is the County Historical Museum.

FOR HISTORY BUFFS

In 1925, at a time when the mass production of cars was changing the nation's travel habits, a hotel at 2223 Monterey Street in San Luis Obispo had its name changed to the Milestone Motel, and became the first "motorists' hotel" – or motel – in the world.

▶ *Take* **Hwy 101** *north inland for 10 miles (16km).*

🔢 Santa Margarita

Vineyards and cattle ranches characterise this area, where horses graze on golden hillsides dotted with ancient California oaks. The whole landscape is typical of central California.

▶ *Continue north on* **Hwy 101** *for 20 miles (32km) to Paso Robles.*

🔢 Paso Robles

Wine-making in this region dates back to 1797 and there are now 25 wineries operating here, with over 6,000 acres (2,428 hectares) of vineyards. Most of the wineries have tasting rooms and many offer tours. The town was named after the numerous oak trees that grow here; almond orchards are now as prominent, and during the spring their pink

Hunter-Liggett, a US military training base.

14 San Antonio

The most remote mission in the chain, San Antonio de Padua, is incongruously located in the middle of a huge military base. Built by Father Junipero Serra in 1771, it was the third mission in the chain and has, for the most part, been reconstructed. The first attempt at renovation was destroyed in the 1906 earthquake and the present work dates back to 1948, but its isolation gives a feel of what the missions must have been like when they were built – in spite of the tanks and heavy artillery that now rumble by just a little too close. In the spring the whole area is covered in wildflowers.

▶ *Return on Hwy G18 to Jolon and turn north onto Hwy G14 for 18 miles (29km) to King City, turn north on Hwy 101 for 9 miles (14km).*

15 Greenfield

This agricultural town is surrounded by many of the crops common to this part of the state including alfalfa, apples, berry farms, vineyards and chilli peppers. A brief tour of the area provides a good general introduction to the Californian farming industry.

▶ *Continue north on Hwy 101 for 10 miles (16km).*

16 Soledad

The oldest settlement in the Salinas Valley was established in 1791 with the founding of a mission. By the late 19th century it had become a dairy community, and it is now a major agricultural produce center with a distinctly Mexican feel – due, no doubt, to the high population of Mexican agricultural workers. The mission, which lies to the west of town, is one of the smallest in the chain, and has undergone extensive restoration.

▶ *Return south on Hwy 101 to the Elm Avenue west exit. Elm Avenue becomes Aroyo Seco Road, continue until reaching Carmel Valley Road, turn right and follow all the way through Carmel Valley to Hwy 1.*

17 Carmel Valley

Clint Eastwood owns a ranch in this peaceful valley of green, rolling hills, studded with oak trees. Even when the coast is shrouded in fog, the sun is often shining on the valley; all along it are fruit orchards, nurseries, strawberry fields and even artichoke fields. About 6 miles (10km) past the town of Carmel Valley are the Begonia Gardens, which reach their peak during July and August.

▶ *Continue west along Carmel Valley to join Hwy 1 by Carmel. Turn north and return to Monterey.*

Tranquil Carmel Mission, the resting place of Father Junipero Serra

TOUR
22

Southern
Central Coast

Some of the most sought-after property in Southern California is included in this tour, from Malibu to Santa Barbara to the Santa Ynez Valley. The rich and famous tend to gravitate to this area, which is less than two hours' drive north of Los Angeles – and with good reason. The towns are delightful and the climate is perfect; add to this beautiful beaches and rolling hills with vineyards and horse ranches, and the appeal becomes fairly obvious.

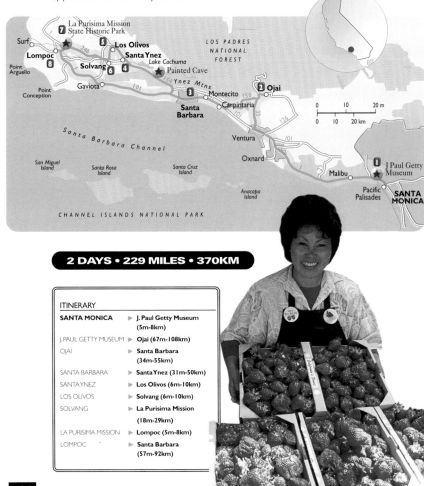

2 DAYS • 229 MILES • 370KM

ITINERARY

SANTA MONICA	▶	**J. Paul Getty Museum** (5m-8km)
J. PAUL GETTY MUSEUM	▶	**Ojai** (67m-108km)
OJAI	▶	**Santa Barbara** (34m-55km)
SANTA BARBARA	▶	**Santa Ynez** (31m-50km)
SANTA YNEZ	▶	**Los Olivos** (6m-10km)
LOS OLIVOS	▶	**Solvang** (6m-10km)
SOLVANG	▶	**La Purisima Mission** (18m-29km)
LA PURISIMA MISSION	▶	**Lompoc** (5m-8km)
LOMPOC	▶	**Santa Barbara** (57m-92km)

Map labels:

La Purisima Mission State Historic Park 7
Surf
Lompoc 8
Point Arguello
Point Conception
Gaviota
San Miguel Island
Santa Rosa Island
Los Olivos 5
Santa Ynez 4
Solvang 6
Lake Cachuma
Painted Cave
Ynez Mtns
Montecito 3
Santa Barbara
Carpintaria
Santa Cruz Island
Santa Barbara Channel
CHANNEL ISLANDS NATIONAL PARK
LOS PADRES NATIONAL FOREST
Ojai 2
Ventura
Oxnard
Anacapa Island
Malibu
Pacific Palisades
J. Paul Getty Museum 1
SANTA MONICA

ⓘ *Santa Monica Convention and Visitors Bureau, 520 Broadway, Suite 250, Santa Monica, CA 90401*

▶ *Leave Santa Monica on the Pacific Coast Highway, driving . along a beautiful coastline past Pacific Palisades to Topanga Canyon Boulevard. High on the right is the world's richest museum.*

❶ J. Paul Getty Museum

This extravagant replica of a Roman villa owned by Julius Caesar's father houses one of the world's most priceless collections of art, which has eclipsed the beach and the surf as the main reason for visiting Malibu. The antiquarian art collection is particularly strong, with a large number of outstanding Greek and Roman sculptures. Overall, the collection is quite eclectic, covering several centuries of painting and drawing, as well as illuminated manuscripts, 19th- and 20th-century American and European photography, furniture and porcelain.

Malibu is a favored address for many Hollywood stars, but is not particularly interesting. After the Getty Museum, the beaches and mountains are the main attraction, and although Malibu State Beach is known as the best surfing area in the state it is also good scuba-diving country.

FOR HISTORY BUFFS

Mission San Buenaventura was originally built in 1782 as part of Juniprero Serra's chain. The building that occupies the original site, on a delightful plaza in Ventura's town center, is a modern restoration, but it contains many relics dating back to the late 18th century. Close by, at 100 East Main Street, the Ventura County Museum of History and Art has outstanding collections of Chumash Indian treasures and an impressive display of artifacts from the Mexican-American war.

▶ *Continue along the Pacific Coast Highway, past several golden beaches. After Mugu Point the road swings inland to Oxnard, where strawberry stands are a common sight during the season. Continue through Oxnard; the Pacific Coast Highway joins **Hwy 101**, which continues to Ventura, where the 1782 Mission San Buenaventura sits in the center of town. Leave Ventura on **Hwy 33** and drive north 15 miles (24km) to Ojai.*

❷ Ojai

The Ojai Valley was settled 2,000 years ago by Chumash Indians; its present-day settlers are artists, writers and New Age thinkers, who enjoy the peace and clean, clear air of this small coastal mountain town. The colonnaded main street is filled with art galleries and antique shops, and less materialistic visitors can seek out the Krishnamurti Foundation or the Krotona Institute of Theosophy. The idyllic valley was used as the location for Shangri La in the 1937 film Lost Horizon.

La Purisima Mission, near Lompoc, rebuilt to its original 1787 design

▶ *Leave Ojai on **Hwy 150** and follow it back to the coast to rejoin **Hwy 101**. Turn north and pass Carpinteria State Beach, which has inviting sand and the safest swimming on the coast, thanks to an offshore reef. Continue up to Santa Barbara.*

🖪 Santa Barbara

Sitting on a curving, sandy bay, with the Santa Ynez mountains as its backdrop, Santa Barbara is one of the loveliest towns in the nation. Add to this a near perfect climate and you have the closest an American town gets to paradise. Red-tiled roofs, white-washed buildings and palm trees give the town a strong Mediterranean atmosphere, which hints at its Spanish origins. Santa Barbara Bay was first explored by the Spanish in 1602 and by 1786 the town was a growing Spanish stronghold. The Spanish element is still seen everywhere in the town's architecture and new develop-ment is strictly controlled by

building codes that were estab-lished in 1925 to maintain the character of the town for future generations. In the same year Santa Barbara was flattened by a massive earthquake, so most of its buildings are no more than 70 years old. The mission remained standing, however, and the grandest established by the Spanish, is often called the Queen of Missions. Founded in 1786, it sits on a knoll high above the town, its design based on the work of 1st-century Roman engineers. There are restored rooms and a museum recording the mission's history and in the adjoining cemetery are the unmarked remains of 4,000 Chumash Indians.

Santa Barbara's oldest build-ings are downtown. El Presidio de Santa Barbara State Historic Park, still being excavated and restored, has two of the build-ings that were part of the origi-nal Spanish fort blessed by Father Junipero Serra in 1782: El Cuartel, the second oldest surviving building in California,

Stearns Wharf, Santa Barbara, the boundary between town and sea

and La Canedo Adobe. A recon-structed chapel and padre's quarters complete the site.

The grandest building in town is the County Courthouse, built in 1929 in the exaggerated mission-style architecture adopted after the 1925 earth-quake. This Spanish-Moorish castle has fine Tunisian tilework, hand-painted frescoes and exceptional murals, making it one of the great public buildings of the West. An elevator goes to the top of the El Mirador Bell Tower, which gives unparalleled views of Santa Barbara and the bay.

The waterfront is separated from town by Hwy 101 but Stearns Wharf, the oldest pier on the West Coast, is an extension of Santa Barbara's main street, State Street. It was built in 1872 and has the usual mixture of souvenir shops, restaurants and seafood stands. To the west of the wharf is Santa Barbara Yacht

Harbor and, to the east, Palm Park where a trail of art is spread beneath the palm trees every Sunday for the Santa Barbara Arts and Crafts Show. Joggers, roller-bladers and cyclists fill the space for the rest of the week.

BACK TO NATURE

Go to the end of Santa Barbara's Stearns Wharf to see once-endangered brown pelicans trying to sneak fish from the fishermen. Until 20 years ago, these big marine birds were on the verge of extinction. Control of pesticides rectified the situation, and they are now as common as seagulls.

▶ *Leave town on State Street and drive north for 10 miles (16km) on* **Hwy 154** *over the Santa Ynez Mountains. Turn right on Painted Cave Road, which winds its way to the*

RECOMMENDED WALK

The Red Tile Walking Tour covers 12 blocks of downtown Santa Barbara and includes over a dozen points of interest, such as the earliest building in town and the Spanish-Mediterranean buildings that replaced losses from the 1925 earthquake. Maps of the tour are available from The Visitors Center at 1 Santa Barbara Street.

Chumash Painted Cave State Historic Park. A screen covers the entrance to the cave but you can catch a glimpse of brightly colored, 1,000-year-old abstract paintings used in rituals by the Chumash. Return to **Hwy 154** *and continue north across the San Marcos Pass and past Lake Cachuma.*

The exquisitely painted altar of Mission Santa Ines, in Solvang

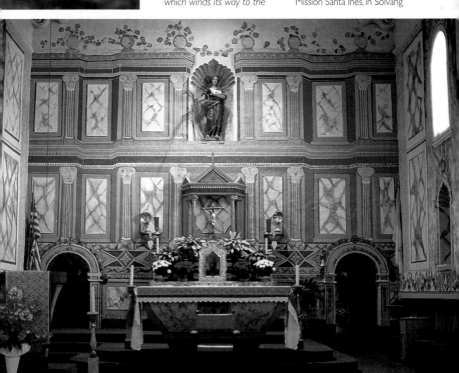

FOR CHILDREN

The Santa Barbara Zoological Gardens can be seen in about 30 minutes, but the 700 animals, miniature train ride and petting zoo are beautifully presented and, unlike most zoos, on a scale that children can enjoy. They are located at 500 Ninos Drive off Cabrillo Beach Boulevard.

❹ Santa Ynez Valley

Celebrities trying to escape the city head for Santa Ynez. Michael Jackson built his Neverland Ranch here, among the Arabian horse farms and vineyards. In recent years, this has become a prime wine-growing region, with more than a dozen wineries scattered around the picturesque country roads, many establishing a growing reputation with wine aficiona-

▶ Continue on **Hwy 154** to Los Olivos.

❺ Los Olivos

Once a major stop for Butterfield Stage Lines, Los Olivos attracts visitors today with its restored 19th-century buildings, including Mattei's Tavern, which was the original stagecoach inn. To sample the wines of Santa Ynez visit the Los Olivos Tasting Room at 2905 Grand Avenue for a "one-stop" comparison.

▶ Take Alamo Pintado Road out of Los Olivos and drive south to Solvang.

❻ Solvang

This Danish Disneyland was built in 1911, complete with windmills, half-timbered houses, thatched roofs and wooden storks. Supposedly, two-thirds of the population of 3,500 are of Danish descent; the shops are

dos. The largest is Firestone Vineyards, at 5017 Zaca Station Road. The town of Santa Ynez, on Hwy 154, at the north end of the valley, is a sleepy community with a white steeple church dating back to 1897. The Valley Historical Society Museum and Parks-Jane Carriageway House have exhibits that illustrate the 19th-century settlement and history of the valley.

Above: Santa Ynez Valley, the perfect antidote to city life
Right: children still flock to Hans Christian Andersen, whose bust stands in the Danish community of Solvang

CHRISTIAN ANDERSEN

filled with Danish porcelain and brassware, and cafés offer aebleskivers and Danish buttermilk pancakes. Despite a slightly phoney feel, as though it were manufactured for tourists, the town was, in fact, established by Danes, when a group of immigrant educators from Minnesota selected the area for a folk school. The Bethania Lutheran Church still holds services in Danish on the first Sunday of every month. Just to the east of the main business district is Mission Santa Ines, built in 1804 and one of the best restored of all the California missions, with a brilliantly painted altar and a colonnaded courtyard filled with flowers. A small museum in the mission building displays bibles and song books.

▶ *Leave Solvang on **Hwy 246** and drive through Buellton. Continue for 17 miles (27km) to Mission La Purisima Concepcion.*

7 La Purisima Mission

The original buildings at this mission, which were erected here in 1787, have long since been destroyed. Everything on the present-day site is a reconstruction, but so well executed that there is an impressively authentic atmosphere. Animals graze in the fields, crops are growing in the kitchen garden, tables are set, pans are on the oven and the store's barrels are overflowing with corn and beans. Costumed interpreters contribute to the most informative of the mission visits available in the state.

Lompoc's fields in full bloom, bringing a fiery flash of color to the surrounding countryside

▶ *Take **Hwy 246** to **Hwy 1** and turn left to Lompoc.*

8 Lompoc

More than half the world's flower seeds are grown in the fields around Lompoc and for nearly half of every year, from May to September, they are ablaze with color, as thousands of acres of fields are in bloom. A 19-mile (30km) self-guided tour has been designed to allow visitors to enjoy the spectacle to the full: maps of the Valley Flower Drive are available from the Chamber of Commerce.

▶ *Take **Hwy 1** back to Santa Barbara.*

THE FAR NORTH

Any journey north in California soon leaves the big cities and crowded freeways behind. Once past Sacramento, you enter a vast wilderness area, bigger than the state of Ohio, but with a population of little more than 250,000. This region extends from the giant redwood forests on the coast to the volcanic lava fields of remote Modoc County and up to the Oregon border, and in between are mountain ranges, active volcanoes, alpine lakes, white-water rivers and dense forests. Mount Shasta, 14,162 feet (4,361m) high, has permanent glaciers; 10,457-foot (3,187m) Mount Lassen still vents steam, and boiling mud pots at Bumpass Hell rival those at Yellowstone.

One of the great advantages of this region is that it attracts relatively few visitors, even in the national parks. Everything is on an enormous scale; back-country roads lead off into wilderness areas bigger than many counties in other parts of the state. You can drive all day and see only a few cars, which in California is quite exceptional.

This is certainly a place to get away from it all, and any number of outdoor activities are offered, from house-boating on Lake Shasta to mountain-climbing, llama-trekking or gold-panning. The only towns of any size in the region are Eureka, on the coast, and Redding, in the heart of the Shasta Cascade country. Eureka is an interesting, Victorian town; Redding has a good selection of lodging and dining establishments. Both are perfect bases from which to explore the region.

Although there are no real dangers here, the remoteness of the roads demands a reliable vehicle; otherwise it may be a long wait for someone to drive by and get help. During the winter, sudden snow storms can close roads completely, and care should be taken not to venture into the back country when weather prospects look uncertain.

Tour 23

The so-called Redwood Empire extends from San Francisco all the way to the Oregon border. The mighty redwoods, the tallest trees on earth, grow along this coastal region and although they have been decimated by logging, several major forests are still in existence. California Highway 1 continues its spectacular journey up the coast past Muir Woods National Monument, 45 minutes from downtown San Francisco; Point Reyes National Seashore, Bodega, where Alfred Hitchcock filmed The Birds, and on to an old Russian fort on the Sonoma coast. Passing through increasingly wild scenery, the road continues to the charming artists' colony of Mendocino, skirts numerous secluded beaches and runs through redwood forests to the perfectly preserved Victorian town of Ferndale. From Eureka, the major town on the north coast, Redwood National Park is a short drive north. The return route, on the inland highway, passes through the vineyards of

Left: Mount Tamalpais, Mill Valley, with San Francisco in the distance

Mendocino County and Alexander Valley on the way back to San Francisco.

Tour 24

North of Redding, California is as wild and challenging as any area in the country. This tour heads north across Lake Shasta, created to generate electricity with the enormous Shasta Dam, the second tallest in the world. The dam can be visited on a short side trip. As the scenery becomes increasingly dramatic, the route passes Castle Crags before the white summit of Mount Shasta comes into view, looming over the highway. To the north are high, wide open spaces and the old gold town of Yreka, which still feels like a frontier settlement. From Yreka the road continues south past the remote Marble Mountains and through the forests of the Trinity Alps. The tour then returns towards Redding, stopping at the restored Chinese Joss House in Weaverville, and continues east from Redding to Lassen Volcanic National Park, rivalling Yellowstone in the variety and drama of its thermal displays. It then proceeds past

Lassen Volcanic National Park's eerie, steaming landscape

Burney Falls to the southern side of Mount Shasta and the old lumber town of McCloud, before returning to Redding across Lake Shasta.

Tour 25

This tour samples some of the more attractive and accessible areas of California's North Country. Starting in Sacramento, it crosses the agricultural basin of the northern Central Valley and continues to Napa, on the southern fringe of the Wine Country. The old, historic town of Sonoma was the birthplace of the modern wine industry, and from here the tour continues through vineyards to the orchards of Anderson Valley and the Mendocino wineries en route to the coast. The journey reaches its prettiest section from Elk to Mendocino and continues up to Fort Bragg, returning inland past Clear Lake, the largest body of water entirely within California. After passing through the orchards of Capay Valley the tour heads back to Sacramento.

The Redwood
Empire

4 DAYS • 700 MILES • 1128 KM Redwood forests, rugged cliffs, secluded beaches and old logging communities line this spectacular drive along California's northern coast. Highway 1 is tortuous and the going is slow, but the tour returns more speedily through the vineyards of the warm valleys.

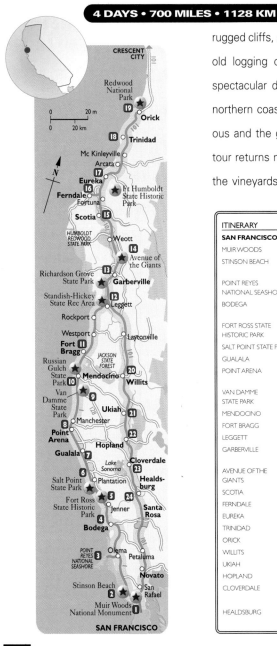

ITINERARY		
SAN FRANCISCO	▶	Muir Woods (13m-21km)
MUIR WOODS	▶	Stinson Beach (5m-8km)
STINSON BEACH	▶	**Point Reyes National Seashore (14m-22km)**
POINT REYES NATIONAL SEASHORE	▶	Bodega (35m-56km)
BODEGA	▶	**Fort Ross State Historic Park (19m-30km)**
FORT ROSS STATE HISTORIC PARK	▶	**Salt Point State Park (10m-16km)**
SALT POINT STATE PARK	▶	Gualala (20m-32km)
GUALALA	▶	Point Arena (18m-29km)
POINT ARENA	▶	**Van Damme State Park (31m-50km)**
VAN DAMME STATE PARK	▶	Mendocino (3m-5km)
MENDOCINO	▶	Fort Bragg (11m-17km)
FORT BRAGG	▶	Leggett (45m-76km)
LEGGETT	▶	Garberville (25m-40km)
GARBERVILLE	▶	**Avenue of the Giants (13m-21km)**
AVENUE OF THE GIANTS	▶	Scotia (29m-47km)
SCOTIA	▶	Ferndale (18m-29km)
FERNDALE	▶	Eureka (20m-32km)
EUREKA	▶	Trinidad (25m-40km)
TRINIDAD	▶	Orick (21m-34km)
ORICK	▶	Willits (184m-296km)
WILLITS	▶	Ukiah (24m-39km)
UKIAH	▶	Hopland (14m-22km)
HOPLAND	▶	Cloverdale (16m-26km)
CLOVERDALE	▶	Healdsburg (18m-29km)
HEALDSBURG	▶	**San Francisco (69m-111km)**

ℹ️ *Redwood Empire Association, 1 Market Plaza, Spear Street Tower, Suite 1001, San Francisco, CA 94105*

▶ *From San Francisco, drive north across the Golden Gate Bridge on Hwy 101. Exit onto Hwy 1 at Mill Valley, follow Hwy 1 to Muir Beach and follow the signs to Muir Woods.*

❶ Muir Woods

Sequoia sempervirens, the ancient coastal redwoods, can grow to over 360 feet (110m) and live for 2,000 years, and they are found only along a narrow coastal strip of California, between Monterey and the northern border. The trees in Muir Woods are the closest to San Francisco, only a 30-minute journey from downtown hotels. This ease of accessibility generates more traffic than at the more northerly redwood groves, but seeing the trees with people is better than not seeing them at all.

The 502-acre (203-hectare) National Monument was named for naturalist John Muir, and six of the 27 miles (43km) of trails are on a level stretch of the forest floor, making this one of the most accessible redwood groves.

▶ *Return to Hwy 1 and continue north for 5 miles (8km) to Stinson Beach.*

❷ Stinson Beach

Stinson Beach is the name both of a small town, with a distinctive arty feel, and of the finest stretch of sand on the North Coast. The 4,500-foot (1,372m)-long beach is one of the few in the area that are safe for swimming, and the water is warmed by the shoal of Bolinas Bay. The beach is part of the Golden Gate National Recreation Area and during the summer it is so popular with San Franciscans looking for an easy weekend escape that it can be impossible to park. If swimming doesn't appeal, the fishing is very good, and there are numerous nearby hikes on Mount Tamalpais rising above the town.

Audubon Canyon Ranch overlooks the Bolinas Lagoon, just north of Stinson Beach. This 1,000-acre (304-hectare) bird sanctuary in the redwoods is home to nesting egrets and great blue herons from March to July each year. There is also a small museum dedicated to the wildlife of the area.

▶ *Continue along Hwy 1 and continue north for 12 miles (19km) to Olema. Turn left on Bear Valley Road to Point Reyes Visitor Center.*

❸ Point Reyes National Seashore

Point Reyes is separated from mainland USA by the San Andreas fault. Geologically, it sits on the Pacific plate, and during the 1906 earthquake the Point Reyes Peninsula moved 20 feet (6m) northward. The epicenter of that earthquake was at Olema, close to the park, and an earthquake trail and exhibit is based in Bear Valley, near the main visitor center. The windswept peninsula covers over 66,000 acres (26,710 hectares) with over 100 miles (160km) of trails and a 100-mile

Sharks and whales share the waters of Point Reyes National Seashore

long coastline. It is the foggiest and windiest spot between Mexico and Canada – so warm clothes are always advisable. This is a good location for watching whales migrate from Alaska to Mexico, and some historians claim that it was here that Sir Francis Drake first landed in the Golden Hinde in 1579, at what is now called Drake's Bay.

Tomales Bay, formed by the San Andreas Fault, separates the Point Reyes Peninsula from the mainland. The 13-mile (21km)-long stretch of water is a breeding ground for great white sharks and swimming is discouraged – but there are excellent fishing and bird-watching opportunities. Inverness, on the south side of the bay, has several small shops, galleries and restaurants along its single street overlooking the water. The town of Point Reyes

Russian fur traders once occupied wooden Fort Ross, now rebuilt

Station is the agricultural center of West Marin and has a thriving arts and crafts community.

▶ *Continue north for 32 miles (51km) on **Hwy 1** through Tomales to Bodega Bay.*

❹ Bodega
This tiny village a short distance from the coast was where Alfred Hitchcock made his chilling film The Birds. The old school house still looks as it did in Hitchcock's day and next door stands the picturesque village church. Bodega Bay, on the coast, was discovered by the Spanish in 1775 and developed into an important fishing harbor. Fishing still plays a significant part in the economy, though sports fishing for salmon has now overtaken the commercial business.

▶ *Continue north on **Hwy 1** for 20 miles (32km) to Fort Ross.*

❺ Fort Ross State Historic Park
The wooden buildings of Fort Ross can be spotted from the tortuous bends of Highway 1. During the 19th century this was the North American outpost for Russian fur traders; the Russians arrived in 1812 and during the next 30 years decimated the sea otter population almost to the point of extinction. The fort was devastated by fire and earthquakes but has been painstakingly restored to its original appearance. A recorded audio tour directs visitors around the buildings which include a tiny Orthodox chapel and are furnished with displays of contemporary artifacts.

SCENIC ROUTES

From Jenner, at the mouth of the Russian River, Highway 1 climbs spectacularly to follow the coast, high above steep cliffs and crashing waves, as it winds up past Fort Ross to Salt Point. All along this section of road are sweeping views of the rugged coastline.

▶ *Continue north on **Hwy 1** for 10 miles (16km) to Salt Point.*

❻ Salt Point State Park
Waves crash over weird sandstone formations here, and batter clumps of sea palms, creating the impression of a miniature tropical island in a hurricane. An underwater park, rich with abalone, attracts scuba divers, and there is a pygmy pine forest and, a short distance inland, the Krause Rhododendron State Reserve, at its spectacular peak between April and June.

Just north of Salt Point, with an equally beautiful coastline, is an extensive private development named Sea Ranch. Many architectural awards have been won by the houses built here to a design that ensures minimum impact upon the environment. Some houses are available for

Colorful shopfronts brighten the pretty town of Point Arena

short rentals, and there is also a lodge and restaurant. Six marked trails lead to the sea shore: the Black Point Trail is the most dramatic.

▶ *Leave Sea Ranch; Gualala is immediately to the north on Hwy 1.*

7 Gualala

The Gualala River was a favorite fishing haunt of Jack London, who used to cast for steelhead here. This former lumber town still retains much of its turn-of-the-century character but, apart from an attractive stretch of coastline, there is little to occupy your time here. A few art galleries include one devoted exclusively to fine photography, and there are two interesting hotels: the Gualala Hotel, built in 1903, and, just outside town, St Orres, whose onion domes reflect the Russian influence in the area.

▶ *Continue north on Hwy 1 for 14 miles (22km) to Point Arena.*

8 Point Arena

Point Arena is typical of the small towns that extend up the Mendocino coast, one of the prettiest in the state. It was originally a logging community, but little happens here now, and this is principally a pleasant rest stop en route to the north. A public pier and boat launching facility serve both commercial and sports fishermen. Point Arena Lighthouse was first built in 1870, but the present 115-foot (35m)-tall structure was built in 1908, after the original was badly damaged in the 1906 earthquake. It was the first steel-reinforced concrete lighthouse in America. Both the lighthouse and its museum are well worth a tour.

▶ *Drive north on Hwy 1 for 34 miles (55km) to Little River.*

9 Van Damme State Park

Dozens of little coastal parks dot the highway, and this park is typical. Located on the scenic Little River, it offers campsites, safe but cold swimming, hiking trails and skin-diving. Close by is a forest of dwarf conifers. Hard soil prevents deep root systems

and poor drainage adds to the problem resulting in trees only 1 foot (0.3m) high that elsewhere reach a height of 50 feet (15m).

▶ *Continue for 3 miles (5km) on Hwy 1 to Mendocino.*

10 Mendocino

If there is time to visit only one town on the north coast, this should be the one. In many ways it is not typical: a cluster of wooden gothic houses cling together on a bluff overlooking the Pacific Ocean, resembling a New England fishing village more than a Californian town. In fact, the entire village was established by New England loggers in the mid-19th century, and is now on the National Register of Historic Places. In recent years it has been the location for many films and television shows, including the television series Murder She Wrote – supposedly set on Cape Cod.

Mendocino has become an important artists' colony, and the village is bursting with art galleries, including the highly respected Mendocino Art Center. Kelley House Historical Museum and Library features changing exhibits in a restored 1861 residence, and is the best place to learn about the history of Mendocino (it also acts as an unofficial tourist center). Across the road, the Ford House has displays on the history of the logging industry and a model miniature village of Mendocino as it looked in 1890.

RECOMMENDED WALKS

The only satisfactory way to see Mendocino is on foot, and the visitor center at the Kelley House has maps of a suggested walking tour through this immaculate town.

▶ *Continue on **Hwy 1** for 10 miles (16km) to Fort Bragg.*

Harbor seals take time to bask along the shore near Mendocino

⑪ Fort Bragg

This 100-year-old sea port retains its commercial atmosphere, with lumber mills and freight yards marring the otherwise scenic setting. At the south end of town is Noyo Harbor, where there is a thriving commercial fishing fleet and charter boats are available for sports fishing. The ornate Guest House Museum was built in 1892 to house visitors to the reigning lumber company. It now houses exhibits that illustrate the area's logging, shipping and general history. Fort Bragg's highlight is the 19-acre (8-hectare) Mendocino Botanical Gardens, where magnificent blooms cover the bluffs.

▶ *Continue north on **Hwy 1** to Rockport where the road turns inland to become **Hwy 101** (the Redwood Highway). After 46 miles (74km), enter Leggett.*

FOR CHILDREN

Fort Bragg is the headquarters of the Western Railroad Skunk Trains. Laid in 1885 as a logging railroad, the Skunk line now offers scenic excursions to the town of Willits. Trains originally ran on gas, giving rise to the comment: "You can smell 'em before you can see 'em," and the line's name.

---

⑫ Leggett

Leggett marks the official start of journeys through the forests of coastal redwoods. A short distance north of the town is a drive-through tree, set in a private grove: its tunnel, quite big enough for a car, was formed when the tree was damaged by fire. A little further north is the Standish Hickey State Recreation Area, which has ample camping space available

but only one mature redwood in its dense forest. A better bet is the Smithe Redwoods State Preserve, where you can hike to a waterfall or take a footpath down to the Eel River.

[i] *Leggett Valley Chamber of Commerce Tourist Information Center, Highway 1, PO Box 218, Leggett, CA 95455*

▶ *Continue north on **Hwy 101** to Garberville.*

13 Garberville

This southern gateway to Humboldt County gained notoriety for its prominence in marijuana cultivation. At one time the economy of the town was said to revolve around this lucrative cash crop, and there is still a distinct flavor of the 1960s in the bars and cafés in town.

▶ *Continue north on **Hwy 101** for 6 miles (10km) to Phillipsville and turn onto **Hwy 254**.*

14 Avenue of the Giants

A 33-mile (53km) stretch of road running through Humboldt Redwoods State Park is home to 60 percent of the tallest trees in the world. The road winds along beneath these giants, along the banks of the Eel River, and passes a number of redwood attractions, including the Shrine Drive-Thru Tree, One Log House, Chimney Tree, Immortal Tree and Eternal Tree House.

▶ *Re-join **Hwy 101** and continue north for 3 miles (5km) to Scotia.*

15 Scotia

Owned and operated by the Pacific Lumber Company since the late 1880s, Scotia is one of the few company towns left in the United States. Don't miss the self-guided walking tour through the world's largest redwood lumber mill, for an in-depth look at the timber industry.

▶ *Continue north on **Hwy 101***

for 16 miles (26km) and turn west at Fernbridge. Cross the Eel River to reach Ferndale after a further 4 miles (6km).

16 Ferndale

The entire town of Ferndale has been designated as a State Historic Landmark and a National Register Historic District. Visitors can step back 100 years and take a horse-drawn carriage ride down the main street, which has remained largely untouched since the 1890s. This is perhaps the best

A truck negotiates the "trunk road" through the Drive-Thru Tree

and most complete example of California's Victorian era in existence. In spite of earthquakes and natural disasters, Ferndale has remained surprisingly intact and authentic.

▶ *Return to **Hwy 101** and continue north for 18 miles (29km) to Eureka.*

17 Eureka

Eureka has more Victorian buildings than any other incorporated city in California: over 10,000, each one with more ornate detail than the next. The Carson Mansion is the best example of this 'gingerbread' style of architecture, and as such is reputed to be the most photographed Victorian house in the world. It is certainly extremely striking, located in a commanding position on 2nd and M streets. Built by pioneer lumber baron William Carson between 1884 and 1886, years of depression for the timber industry, the mansion was effectively a

---

SPECIAL TO...

One of the state's most unusual events takes place in Ferndale every May. The annual World Champion Kinetic Sculpture Race attracts all manner of bizarre human-powered vehicles that speed over land and water to gain the crown. Recent examples of the competing vehicles are displayed in Ferndale's museum on Main Street.

Gingerbread architecture at its best: the Carson Mansion, Eureka

acre (253-hectare) park set on a headland covered by forests and meadows, with beaches, sea stacks and a rim trail that is particularly beautiful at sunset.

▶ *Continue north on* **Hwy 101** *to Orick.*

⑲ Orick

Orick is the gateway to the Redwood National Park. The main road through this tiny town is lined with souvenir shops selling bears, windmills, deer, totem poles, furniture, clocks and more – all made out of redwood.

The park itself encompasses 106,000 acres (42,898 hectares), with 8 miles (13km) of coastal roads and more than 100 miles (160km) of trails. A taste of the park can obtained by travelling a few miles north of Orick, and a shuttle departs from the information center in town to take visitors to the Tall Trees Grove where the world's tallest known tree measures 367.8 feet (112m).

▶ *Return south on* **Hwy 101** *for 182 miles (293km) to Willits.*

job creation scheme, financed by Carson specifically in order to avoid laying off his best workmen. Today, the Carson Mansion houses a private club.

Samoa lies just across the Humboldt Bay via Highway 255 and the Humboldt Bridge; the primary attraction here is the last operating lumbercamp-style cookhouse in the West. The Samoa Cookhouse first started serving mill workers in 1893, and today visitors can dine at the long communal tables and experience the world of the lumberjack. In the restaurant's museum and dining room are early culinary items, as well as various historical mementos from the early years of the lumber and logging industries.

▶ *Continue north on* **Hwy 255** *to join* **Hwy 101** *at Arcata. Turn north on* **Hwy 101** *for 15 miles (24km) to Trinidad.*

⑱ Trinidad

Trinidad fishing village is one of the oldest settlements on the north coast. Its site was discovered by a Portuguese navigator in 1595; the present town, which dates from 1850, sits on a bluff overlooking the ocean. Trails lead down to beautiful, rocky beaches, the pier is still a working commercial fishing dock, and a working replica of the original 1870 lighthouse warns vessels of the rocky coast. A marine lab aquarium operated by Humboldt State University provides an introduction to the sea life of this part of the coast.

Patricks Point State Park, just to the north of Trinidad, is a 625-

BACK TO NATURE

In the early 1920s there were no more than 100 Roosevelt Elk in the Orick area, and practically none elsewhere in California. A refuge was established in 1948 at Prairie Creek State Park and today it is estimated that the population has grown to over 2,000. Every November, gray whales begin their 4,000-mile migration from Alaska to Mexico, swimming along the Californian coast. The migration continues until early February, when they return with their calves to Alaska. The northern coast of California juts out into the Pacific further than any other point in the continental United States, making this the best area for whale-watching. The whales usually swim closer to the coast on their way down, so November to February are the best months for sightings.

20 Willits

This small lumber town, the eastern terminus of the Skunk Train (see page 157), has seen better days. Closure of several businesses has hit the economy hard, but Willits is still a pleasant community. Near the train station is the Mendocino County Museum, full of pioneer period artifacts and Indian basketry.

► Continue south on **Hwy 101** for 22 miles (35km) to Ukiah.

21 Ukiah

Ukiah has been the seat of Mendocino County since 1859, when the population of the Russian River Valley was little more than 100. Near town, on Vichy Springs Road, naturally carbonated water comes bubbling out of the ground at 90°F (32°C) to fill 130-year-old outdoor tubs and an Olympic-sized swimming pool. Jack London, Teddy Roosevelt Robert Louis Stevenson and Mark Twain all bathed here. In town, the Sun House is an excellent example of "California Craftsman" redwood architecture, and the adjoining Grace Hudson Museum houses Pomo Indian artifacts.

i Mendocino County CVB, 320 S State Street, PO Box 244, Ukiah, CA 95482

► Continue south on **Hwy 101** for 14 miles (22km) to Hopland.

22 Hopland

It would be easy to drive straight past Hopland without noticing it at all, but there are good reasons to stop, such as the Fetzer Vineyards Tasting Room, where you can sample the wide range of wines made in the area. Across the road is the Hopland Brewery Brewpub and Beer Garden, which opened in 1983 as the first brewpub in California since Prohibition. Or turn off onto Highway 175 to reach the Fetzer Valley Oaks Food and Wine Center and visit their organic gardens, where you can see scarlet Nantes Touchon carrots, 110 varieties of tomato, 26 varieties of basil and every type of edible flower imaginable. Many of the vegetables are heirloom varieties, once on the verge of extinction.

► Continue south on **Hwy 101** for 16 miles (26km) to Cloverdale.

23 Cloverdale

At one time this was the northernmost citrus-growing area in California. Now it is the center of an emerging grape-growing industry, and just south of town is the Asti Winery, established in the 19th century as a cooperative community by Italian swiss immigrants. A citrus fair is held at Cloverdale every February.

► Continue south on **Hwy 101** for 16 miles (26km) to Healdsburg.

24 Healdsburg

This appealing town, built around a traditional square, is the center of one of California's premium wine-growing areas. Its setting, in the Alexander Valley, on the edge of both Dry Creek and the Russian River regions makes it a wine-lovers' dream. The downtown plaza has a small museum and the Sonoma County Wine Library – but the 50 wineries within 15 minutes of town really steal the show.

► Return to San Francisco, 64 miles (103km) south on **Hwy 101**.

Trinidad's replica 1870 lighthouse

Shasta
Cascade

3 DAYS • 453 MILES • 729KM Redding, the starting-point of this tour (a five-hour drive north of San Francisco), is the gateway to the Far North, a wild region where old Gold Rush towns cling to the slopes of Mount Shasta and the remote Trinity Alps, and weird volcanic landscapes still bubble and steam – between eruptions.

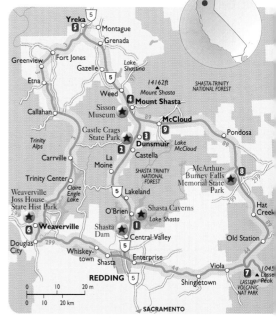

i *Redding Chamber of Commerce,
747 Auditorium Drive, CA 96001*

▶ *From Redding, drive north to
Lake Shasta.*

❶ Lake Shasta
The highway crosses this huge
lake, whose 370-mile (595km)-
long shoreline and 30,000-acre
(12,141-hectare) expanse make
it the largest man-made lake in
the state. The dam that created
it is the second biggest in the
world – three times taller than
Niagara Falls – and can be
reached on Highway 151, 5
miles (8km) west of I-5. At the
visitor center, a film describes
the construction of the dam,
which diverts three rivers to irri-
gate Central Valley's agricultural
land. I-5 crosses the Pit River
Bridge, the world's biggest
double-decked bridge, which
carries a railway line as well as
the highway.
  Lake Shasta is a mecca for
water sports enthusiasts and a
popular destination for houseboat holidays, and for landlubbers there is a boat trip across
from O'Brien, on the eastern
side of the lake, to the Shasta
Caverns, which feature interesting stalactite and stalagmite
formations in the limestone
caves. After the boat trip there is
a bus ride 800 feet (244m) above
the lake to the cavern's entrance.

▶ *Continue north on* **I-5***.*

*Left: boating on Lake Shasta
Above right: the Castle Crags,
created in the age of glaciers*

❷ Castle Crags State Park
After 25 miles (40km) the
forested mountainsides give way
to a group of 2,000- to 6,000-foot
(609 to 1,829m)-high glacier-
polished crags towering over the
Sacramento River. The Castle
Crags were formed 225 million
years ago, when they were
forced up through a blanket of
serpentine and glacial debris;
they are the oldest rocks in the
area, considerably older than the
relatively recent volcanic
creation of Mount Shasta.

▶ *Continue north on* **I-5***.*

❸ Dunsmuir
At the old railroad town of
Dunsmuir, 19th-century steam
locomotives and rolling stock
háve been converted into motel
units at the Railroad Park
Resort.

▶ *As* **I-5** *continues north, mighty
Mount Shasta looms into view,
dominating the landscape.*

❹ Mount Shasta
The tiny town of Mount Shasta
sits at the foot of its giant name-
sake. Only 3,000 inhabit this
outdoor pursuits center, which is
also home to a fish hatchery that,
until 1979, was the biggest in the
world. The Mount Shasta State
Fish Hatchery and Sisson
Museum was built in 1888 on a
site chosen for its proximity to
fresh water and the railroad, the
old hatchery is now a museum
with extensive displays on the
geology and human history of

the Mount Shasta region.
Behind the museum, a new
hatchery produces 5 to 10
million trout a year to stock the
streams and lakes of California.
Mount Shasta's 14,162-foot
(4,316m) peak is only the sixth
highest in the state, but it is
certainly the most impressive,
and can be seen towering over
the landscape from 100 miles
(106km) away. Five glaciers
tumble down the mountains,
and at the summit are bubbling
hot springs where, according to
Indian legend, the Great Spirit
dwells. The mountain is popular
with both mountaineers and the
more spiritually inclined, who
believe in the mystic powers of
the peak. About 7,000 climbers
attempt to reach the summit
every year – but only about half
of them make it to the top.
Shasta was a favorite mountain
of John Muir, who founded the
Sierra Club, and first climbed it
in 1874.

▶ *Continue north on* **I-5***, past
Weed, through high, wild, open
landscapes with very sparse
habitation.*

5 Yreka

Yreka is a surprisingly big town for such a remote area, founded in 1857 soon after the discovery of gold in the area and given the Indian name for Mount Shasta. Wild West lawlessness, internecine Chinese wars and a fire in 1871 were not enough to destroy the town, and many 1850s buildings have been restored. If the traffic disappeared, Miner Street, in the center of town, would look little different now from 100 years ago. Several Victorian homes have also been restored and are preserved in a nationally registered Historic District; some operate as bed and breakfast inns.

exhibit of restored buildings from the pioneer period in an 1800s village setting.

> **FOR CHILDREN**
>
> During the summer, the Blue Goose Steam Train leaves from the depot in Yreka on a tour through high cattle-ranch country, and visits the old railroad town of Montegue. There are great views of Mount Shasta during the three-hour journey.

▶ *Leave Yreka on **Hwy 3** west and drive through the Scott Valley for 17 miles (27km) to*

6 Weaverville

During the early 1850s over 2,500 Chinese settled at this Trinity County seat to prospect for gold. Their legacy is the Weaverville Joss House State Historic Park and the 1873 Temple Amongst the Forest Beneath the Clouds, beautifully restored to its original splendor.

▶ *Take **Hwy 299** east back to Redding, passing the Whiskeytown Lake recreation area on the way. Continue past Redding on **Hwy 44** for 50 miles (80km) and turn south onto **Hwy 89** through Lassen Volcanic National Park.*

Yreka has shed its turbulent past but retains its Victorian elegance

The Siskiyou County Courthouse, at 311 Fourth Street, has displays of gold in various forms from Yreka's glittering past, and the nearby County Museum, at 910 S Main Street, contains exhibits from the region dating from prehistoric times to present day. Outside there is an impressive

*Fort Jones, with views ahead of the Marble Mountains, that connect with the Trinity Alps. From Fort Jones, continue for 12 miles (19km) to the old mining supply town of Etna. Another 13 miles (21km) along **Hwy 3** is Callahan, a one-block town; continuing south, the road passes through the forests and mountains of the Trinity Alps and joins **Hwy 299** at Weaverville.*

7 Lassen Volcanic National Park

Known to native Americans as Fire Mountain, Broken Mountain and Mountain-Ripped-Apart, Lassen Peak is the southernmost volcano of the Pacific northwest's vast Cascade Range. It sits within a huge caldera formed by the collapse of its mother mountain, 30,000 years ago. Lassen is much more famous, however, for its much more recent behavior: surprise volcanic eruptions, culminating in a dramatic blast of steam and smoke that tossed five-ton boulders into the sky in 1915. These theatrics created such a thrill throughout the US that the peak and its breathtaking setting were protected as a National Park in 1916.

Lassen has easy access during the few short months when the main road traversing the park is not blocked by snow. Many of the park's most notable features are either visible or accessible from the road. Three of the world's four types of volcanoes are here, in addition to boiling lakes, mudpots and sulphurous steam plumes. The best place to appreciate Lassen's fiery presence, not to mention the wild flowers along the way, is at Bumpass Hell, where the careless Mr Bumpass lost one of his legs to a boiling mudpot.

▶ *Leave Lassen Park by returning to Hwy 44 and continuing north on Hwy 89.*

🎱 McArthur-Burney Falls
Teddy Roosevelt called these 129-foot (39m)-high falls, west of Highway 89, "the eighth wonder

Right: McCloud and Mount Shasta
Below: Bumpass Hell

of the world" – but don't hold your breath! Though they are one of the most scenic waterfalls in the state, they are no Niagara Falls. A trail from the car park leads to the foot of the falls and during the morning beautiful rainbows form in the mist.

▶ *Continue north on Hwy 89 around the southern flank of Mount Shasta to McCloud.*

🎱 McCloud
This queen of the lumber mill days was a company town where the workers were paid in script, which they spent at the company store, and their houses were built from the lumber that they had milled. McCloud has

changed very little since it was founded in 1827 and gas lamps still light the streets at night.

▶ *Continue west on Hwy 89 for 10 miles (16km) and turn onto I-5 back to Redding.*

Capital to
Coast

Leave California's capital, passing through the northern Central Valley, and head for the wine country. The Sonoma and Alexander Valleys lead to the Anderson Valley's fruit orchards, far off the beaten track. The tour then leads up the rugged Mendocino coast to Fort Bragg and returns to Sacramento via Clear Lake, the largest body of water entirely within California.

3 DAYS • 433 MILES • 695 KM

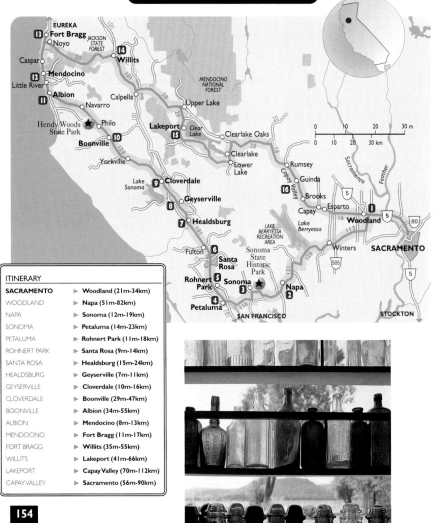

⌐i Sacramento Visitor Information
Center, 1104 Front Street,
Sacramento, CA 95814

▶ Leaving Sacramento, take I-5
North for 15 miles (24km).

❶ Woodland

What was once a typical little
farming community has grown to
become the seat of Yolo County,
but just off the main street is a
reminder of the past, in the form
of the old Opera House, originally built in 1885 and burned in
1892. It was rebuilt in its present
form in 1896 and there are regular tours and special performances. Near by is a fine
example of an early 20th-century
courthouse.

▶ Take Hwy 113 south and exit
on Hwy E6 west to Winters.
Continue west on Hwy 128
past the southern tip of Lake
Berryessa and turn left onto
Hwy 121. Continue into
Napa.

❷ Napa
(See page 116)

The town from which the world-
famous wine valley derives its
name is a world away from the
vineyards and expensive country
clubs a few miles north of town.
Like so many northern
Californian towns, this was a
Gold Rush center during the
1850s. The old historic downtown area on the bank of the
River Napa has good examples
of 18th- and early 19th-century
architecture, maps of suggested
walking tours are available from
the Napa Valley Conference and
Visitors Bureau, 1310 Napa
Town Center, CA 94559.

Napa is also the base of the
controversial Napa Wine Train,
restored in the late 1980s to offer
three-hour, 36-mile (58km)
round trips to St Helena, in the
heart of Napa Valley, while lunch
or dinner is served in restored
Pullman dining cars. Many vintners opposed the intrusion of the
train into the previously peaceful
vineyards, but commerce once
again won over environment.
Disembarkation from the train is

not allowed in the valley and it
apparently does nothing to ease
the notorious traffic congestion
on Highway 37.

▶ Leave Napa on Hwy 12 and
continue west past the "neo-
chateau" of Domaine
Carneros on the left. Continue
for 5 miles (8km) past the
winery and turn right onto
Napa Road to continue into
Sonoma.

❸ Sonoma
(See page 119)

It was in Sonoma Plaza in 1846
that the Bear Flag was raised to
declare California a republic;
less than one month later it was
replaced by the Stars and
Stripes. The history of the
Republic is preserved with the
help of displays of furniture and
clothing dating from the period
and shown in the Depot
Museum, itself housed in the
original town depot.

The City Hall in Sonoma

On the north side of the
attractive town square is Sonoma
State Historic Park, a group of
old adobe buildings including
the Toscano Hotel and Sonoma
Barracks, both of which are open
for tours. Also included in the
park is the home of General
Vallejo, the founder of Sonoma,
where tours are offered throughout the week. Just off the Plaza
is the Mission San Francisco
Solano, the last in the chain of
missions that stretch up from
Baja California in Mexico, which
houses a collection of watercol-
ors of The Missions of California
by Jorgensen.

▶ Leave Sonoma driving south
on Hwy 12. Turn right onto
Hwy 121, at the stop light at
the junction with Hwy 116,
turn right. Follow Hwy 116
through Lakeville into
Petaluma.

4 Petaluma

Riverside Petaluma retains a small-town America atmosphere: its streets needed little help to give the necessary 1950s look when the town was used as a location for American Graffiti and Peggy Sue Got Married. Petaluma grew up on poultry farming, and dairy farming but it has increasingly become a bedroom community for San Francisco. On the eastern edge of town is the Petaluma Adobe State Historic Park, where the restored 1836 two-story adobe building was at the centre of General Vallejo's vast land holdings.

▶ *Continue north on* **Hwy 101**.

5 Rohnert Park

Suburban Rohnert Park is another bedroom community, with the Sonoma Wine Information Center located just off the freeway, where interactive displays and literature cover most of the wineries in the county.

▶ *Continue north on* **Hwy 101** *to Santa Rosa.*

6 Santa Rosa

(See pages 118–19)
Fast-growing Santa Rosa boasts among its attractions a restored 1920s shopping area in Railroad Square and the intriguing Church of the One Tree, at Sonoma Avenue, a steepled church which, as its name suggests, was made from a single tree – a redwood chopped down in the 19th century. It now houses the Ripley Memorial Museum.

▶ *Continue north on* **Hwy 101** *for 17 miles (27km).*

7 Healdsburg

(See pages 118 and 149)
Strategically positioned between three wine-growing areas, Healdsburg is a good base for visiting wineries. It also has an excellent display of Pomo Indian artifacts at the old Carnegie Library.

▶ *Continue north on* **Hwy 101** *for 9 miles (14km).*

8 Geyserville

This small town sits in the heart of the Alexander Valley, one of California's most important wine regions, and Chateau Souverain's hop kiln design winery can clearly be seen from the west side of Hwy 101.

▶ *Continue north on* **Hwy 101** *for 10 miles (16km).*

9 Cloverdale

(See page 149)
This grape-growing center is a pleasant town with several restaurants and plentiful accommodation. It holds a citrus fair every February.

SCENIC ROUTES

The section of road from Cloverdale to Boonville along Highway 128 winds through high, rolling hills typical of northern California. Clinging to the hillside, the route gives beautiful vistas at every turn. Winter rains turn the hills bright green for a few months during the spring, but they soon revert to their normal golden color in the heat of California's summer.

▶ *From Cloverdale take* **Hwy 128** *for 27 miles (43km) through beautiful pastoral scenery to Boonville.*

10 Boonville

This secluded farming community is best known for the local language it invented in the 1880s: "Boontling" has a vocabulary of about 1,000 words, and the local paper still publishes a column in the language every week. Boonville is at the head of an important wine-growing region, and the Anderson Valley Brewing Company, a local micro-brewery, produces some of the best beer in the state. The Anderson Valley Historical Museum is housed in the little 1891 Conn Creek School House, and displays lumber industry relics and Indian artifacts.

▶ *Continue on* **Hwy 128** *through the Anderson Valley, where apple orchards climb up the valley until Philo, when vineyards take over. Drive another 30 miles (48km) to the coast.*

BACK TO NATURE

Just north of Philo, in the Anderson Valley, Hendy Woods State Park contains a grove of giant coastal redwoods towering more than 300 feet (91m) above the valley floor. Several walking trails meander through the forest and there are also camp sites available.

11 Albion

Albion is a tranquil fishing village, once one of a century-old series of "dog hole" ports, where steamers navigated between craggy inlets to pick up loads of timber.

▶ *Continue north on* **Hwy 1** *for 8 miles (13km) to Mendocino.*

12 Mendocino

(See pages 145–6)
This handsome village was built by New England loggers in the 19th century, and now has a large and active community of artists. A model of historic Mendocino and a display on its history are shown at Ford House.

▶ *Continue north on* **Hwy 1** *for 11 miles (18km) to Fort Bragg.*

13 Fort Bragg

(See page 146)
Fort Bragg is a working lumber town and harbor, with an impressive show of flowers in the 19-acre (8-hectare) Mendocino Botanical Gardens, set on bluffs overlooking the sea.

▶ *Return down* **Hwy 1** *to Noyo and take* **Hwy 20** *east for 34*

miles (55km) to Willits. The
*road passes through Jackson
State Forest which has over
52,000 acres (21,000
hectares) of redwoods,
Douglas fir, hemlock and
bishop pine trees.*

14 Willits
(See page 149)
Willits is the terminus of the
Skunk Train and home of the
Mendocino County Museum,
where items illustrate the area's
Indian and pioneer history.

▶ *Drive south on Hwy 101 for
17 miles (27km) to Calpella
and turn east onto Hwy 20 for
19 miles (30km) to Upper
Lake. Turn south onto Hwy 29.*

15 Lakeport
The "lake" in question is
Clearlake, the largest natural
body of water entirely within
California, which, though off the
beaten track, provides boating,
water skiing, sailing and fishing.
Lakeport, the county seat, is the
first town on Highway 29, in an
area of pear and walnut orchards

and a growing wine industry.
The Historic County
Courthouse is a regional history
museum with recreations of
rooms from the turn of the
century and exhibits of Pomo
Indian culture. South of
Lakeport, Highway 281 hugs
the western shore of the lake
and continues to Lower Lake,
where the Anderson Marsh State
Historic Park interprets 10,000
years of Native American
history, culture and archaeology.
Its headquarters are in an 1870s
restored ranch house surrounded
by 500 acres (202 hectares) of
freshwater tule marsh that
provides a winter home for bald
eagles and other rare birds.

▶ *Drive north on Hwy 53 for 8
miles (13km) to Hwy 20 and
east on Hwy 20 for 18 miles
(29km). Take Hwy 16 south
for 33 miles (53km) to Capay.*

16 Capay Valley
Pastures and almond orchards
make this part of the drive
particularly scenic in the spring,
when the hillsides are emerald

Sunset over Clear Lake

green and the almond trees are
covered in pink blossom.
Highway 16 runs south through
the farming communities of
Rumsey, Guinda, Brooks and
Capay, and has a number of idyllic picnic sites. The road follows
Cache Creek as it flows the
length of the valley, providing
fishing and swimming in the
spring and summer. Along this
route look for turn-of-the-
century homesteads with sturdy
wooden houses, windmills and
long-obsolete tank houses. On
the approach to Brooks, the 1868
schoolhouse stands by an even
older oak tree and in town you
can play "HighStakes Bingo" at
the Cache Creek Indian
Rancheria. The southern gateway to Capay Valley is Esparto,
where an almond festival is held
every February.

▶ *Continue on Hwy 16 through
rich farmlands for 15 miles
(24km) to Woodland and then
on I-5 for 15 miles (24km)
back to Sacramento.*

ACCOMMODATIONS

If possible, it's best to reserve in advance if you plan to stay in a city hotel or inn. Nevertheless, in many parts of the state, you may find rooms in roadside motels simply by looking out for a likely place and stopping. The inexpensive Motel 6 and EZ-8 chains are good bets for reasonable accommodation. All motels have parking lots, but some may have only basic facilities, with no restaurants or room service. Hotels vary widely in price and facilities, and some may not have parking spaces.

An increasingly popular accommodation option in California is the bed-and-breakfast inn, which is often a restored 19th-century house serving huge breakfasts (cooked or Continental) in communal dining rooms. Again, prices vary and some inns may not offer private bathrooms. Smoking and pets are generally not allowed: check beforehand.

Camping is popular and widely available in the State and National Parks, many of which are fully booked well in advance. Reservations can be made up to two months ahead through MISTIX (tel: 800/444-7275). Campgrounds vary from the basic, with very little except wide open spaces, to comfortable sites which provide washing, eating and even shopping facilities. Naturally, the price rises accordingly. Anyone planning to camp in the wild outdoors, beyond even the campgrounds, needs a wilderness permit (available from park rangers' offices) and adequate supplies, including emergency rations of food and drink; a first-aid kit including bandages and diarrhoea tablets; maps; a whistle; insect repellent; a waterproof groundsheet and sleeping bag and sun protection. The ranger should be given details of your whereabouts and your planned route and schedule, and all campers should be sensitive to the environment and wary of snakes and/or bears.

Youth hostels provide an alternative budget option, many in the most popular walking and hiking regions. Members pay slightly less than non-members and anyone planning to use a hostel should reserve in advance during the peak season. Most hostels have kitchen facilities and a night curfew, and all forbid smoking, drinking and drug-taking. For information on youth hostels in California you can contact the following local offices:
Central CA Council, PO Box 28148, San Jose, CA 951159 (tel: 408/298-0670)
Golden Gate Council, 80 Beach Street, Suite 396, San Francisco, CA 94109 (tel: 415/771-4646)
Los Angeles Council, 1502 Palos Verdes Drive, Harbor City, CA 90710 (tel: 213/831-8846)
San Diego Council, 1031 India Street, San Diego, CA 92101 (tel: 619/239-2644).

CALIFORNIA CALENDAR OF EVENTS

January

• Tournament of the Roses, Pasadena. A spectacular parade down Colorado Boulevard, with lavish floats, music, and extraordinary equestrian entries, followed by the Rose Bowl Game. Call 818/449-4100 for details or just stay home and watch it on TV (you'll have a better view). January 1.
• Gold Discovery Celebration, Coloma. A celebration of the fateful day that rocketed California to riches, with gold-panning demonstrations, musical entertainment, Gold Rush skits, and historic house tours. Call 916/659-7533 or 916/622-6198. January 24.

• AT&T Pebble Beach National Pro-Am, Pebble Beach. A PGA-sponsored tour where pros are teamed with celebrities to compete on three world-famous golf courses. Call 408/649-1533. Lasts a week; dates vary.

February

• Chinese New Year Festival and Parade. The largest Chinese New Year Festival in the United States is San Francisco's, which includes a Golden Dragon parade with lion-dancing, marching bands, street fair, flower sale, and festival food. Call 415/982-3000.

L.A.'s celebration is colorful as well, with dragon dancers parading through the streets of downtown's Chinatown. Chinese opera and other events are scheduled. For this year's schedule, contact the Chinese Chamber of Commerce at 213/617-0396. Late January to early February.
• National Date Festival and Riverside Country Fair, Indio. Coachella Valley dates and produce are featured at this annual desert festival, which also includes an Arabian Nights Pageant and camel and ostrich races. Call 619/863-8247 for details.
• Fresno Country Blossom Trail. A 67-mile driving tour featuring the fruit and nut orchards in full bloom. Call 209/233-0836. Occurs from late February to late March.

March

• Return of the Swallows, San Juan Capistrano. An annual event with a parade, dances, and special programs. Call 714/248-2048 for details. Mid-March.
• Snowfest, Truckee. A 10-day winter carnival with parades, ski challenges, polar-bear swim, children's carnival, and fireworks. Dates vary. Call 916/583-7625.

• Russian River Wine Road Barrel Tasting, Healdsburg. The vintners showcase wines still in the barrel, about-to-be-released vintages, and also some old gems from their cellars. Tastings are free and food is available to enhance the wines. Each year by February 1, a list of participants is released with the featured wines. Send a SASE to RRWR, P.O. Box 46, Healdsburg, CA 95448 or call 707/433–6782. First weekend in March.

• Ocean Beach Kite festival, San Diego. Kite building, decorating, and flying are all demonstrated and contested. Phone 619/224–0189 for details. Early March.

• Redwood Coast Dixieland Jazz Festival, Eureka. Three days of Jazz featuring 12 of the best Dixeland groups, including a variety of jam sessions, Call 707/445–3378. Last weekend in March.

• American Indian Festival and Market, Los Angeles. A showcase and festival of Native American arts and culture at the L.A. Natural History Museum, The fun includes traditional dances, storytelling, and a display of arts and crafts

as well as a chance to sample ethnic foods. Admission to museum includes festival tickets. For further details, call 213/744–33114. Late March.

April

• San Francisco International Film Festival. One of America's oldest film festivals, featuring more than 100 films from more than 30 countries. Tickets are relatively inexpensive, and screenings are very accessible to the general public during two weeks early in the month. Call 415/931–FILM.

• Red Bluff Roundup Rodeo, Red Bluff. A two-day rodeo with saddle-bronc riding, steer wrestling, bareback riding, brahma bull riding, team roping, and calf roping. Call 916/5271000. Usually second or third weekend in April.

• Toyota Grand Prix, Long Beach. An exciting weekend of Indy-class auto racing and entertainment in and around downtown Long Beach, drawing world-class drivers from the United States and Europe. Contact the Grand Prix Association at 310/436–9953 or 800/752–9524. Mid-April.

• Fisherman's Festival, Bodega Bay. Fishing Vessels, decorated with ribbons and banners, sail out for a Blessing of the Fleet, while landlubbers enjoy music, lamb, and an oyster barbecue, and arts and crafts fair, and a boat parade. End of month (dates vary).

• Asparagus Festival, Stockton. The spring harvest festival is celebrated with food and a variety of entertainment. Call 209/943–1987. Late April.

• Renaissance Pleasure Faire, San Bernardino. One of America's largest Renaissance festivals, this annual happening, is a re-created Elizabethan marketplace with costumed performers and living history displays. For ticket information, phone 88/523–2473. Weekends from April through June.

• La Jolla Easter Hat Parade. Prizes are awarded in several different categories. Call 619/454-2600 for more information. Easter Sunday.

• Ramona Pageant, Hemet. A unique outdoor pageant that portrays the lives of the Southern California Mission

Shasta Cascade, Yreka

Indians. The play was adapted from Helen Hunt Jackson's 1884 novel Ramona. Call 909/658–3111 for details. Late April to early May.
• Del Mar National Horse Show. Horse and rider teams compete in national championships. Held at the Del Mar Fairgrounds. Call 619/792–4288 or 619/755–1161 for more information. Late April to early May.

May
• Cinco de Mayo. A week-long celebration of one of Mexico's most jubilant holidays takes place throughout the city of Los Angeles. The fiesta's Carnival-like atmosphere is created by large crowds, live music, dances, and food. The main festivals are held in El Pueblo de Los Angeles State History Park, downtown; other events around the city. Phone 213/628–1274 for information.
There's also a Cinco de Mayo celebration in San Diego, featuring folklore music, dance, food, and historical re-enactments. Held in Old Town. Call 619/293–3161 or 619/220–5422 for more information.
• Redondo Beach Wine Festival. The largest outdoor wine-tasting event in Southern California. For exact dates and this year's locations, contact the Rendondo Beach Chamber of Commerce at 310/376–6912. Early May.
• Luther Burbank Rose Parade and Festival, Santa Rosa. Marching bands, floats, food and roses everywhere honor horticulturalist Luther Burbank. Call 707/542–ROSE. Mid-May.
• Venice Art Walk, Venice Beach. An annual weekend event which gives visitors a chance to take docent-guided tours, visit five artist's studios, or take a Sunday self-guided art walk through private studios and homes of more than 50 emerging and well-known artists. Call 310/392–8630, ext 342. Mid-May.
• Russian River Wine Festival,

Healdsburg. Five hours of superb tasting of wines, Sonoma Country food specialities, and signature dishes from local chefs. Music and crafts, too, all on the Healdsburg Plaza. Call 707/433–6782. Usually third Saturday in May.
• Great Monterey Bay Squid Festival. The squid in all its glory is the focus of the celebration here, which maintains that "a day without squid is a day in hell." Squid-cleaning and squid-cooking demonstrations are followed by a taste of the squid, which—as shown here—can be used in virtually everything but ice cream. Festival fare includes arts and crafts, educational exhibits, and the usual entertainment. Memorial Day weekend. Contact the festival at 408/649–6547.
• Avenue of the Giants Marathon. A scenic marathon along redwood-lined Avenue of the Giants and Humboldt Redwoods State Park, starting about 40 miles south of Eureka. Call 707/443–1226. Dates vary.
• Calaveras Country Fair and Jumping Frog Jubilee, Angel's Camp. The event inspired by Mark Twain's story "The Celebrated Jumping Frog of Calveras County." Entrants from all over the world arrive with their frog participants. Also children's parade, livestock competition, rodeo, carnival, and fireworks. Call 209/736–2561. Third weekend in May.
• Cross-Country Kinetic Sculpture Race, Arcata. Wild and crazy human-powered amphibious vehicles in a three-day race from Arcata to Ferndale across mud, sand, roadway, and water. Call 707/725–3851. Memorial Day.
• Bay to Breakers Foot Race, Golden Gate Park, San Francisco. One of the city's most popular annual events, it's really more fun than to run. Thousands of entrants show up dressed in their best Halloween-style costumes for the approximately 7½-mile run

across the park. Call 415/777–7770. Third Sunday of May.
• Carnival, San Francisco. The Mission District's largest annual event is a week-long series of festivals that culminates with a parade on Mission Street over Memorial Day weekend. More than a half-million spectators line the route, and the samba musicians and dancers continue to play on 14th Street, near Harrison, at the end of the march. Call the Mission Economic and Cultural Association at 415/826–1401. Memorial Day weekend.

June
• Music in the Mountains, Nevada City. A 3-week classical music festival. For information, call MIM at 916/265–6124. Dates vary.
• Playboy Jazz Festival, Los Angeles. Bill Cosby is the traditional Master of Ceremonies, presiding over top artists at the Hollywood Bowl. Call 310/246–4000. Mid-June.
• Pony Express Celebration and Re-Ride, Folsom. Horses and riders follow the same route that the Pony Express took, starting in Missouri and ending with a major celebration in Folsom, about 20 miles east of Sacramento. Much of the route parallels Hwy. 50 in El Dorado County. Call 916/621–5885 or 916/985–2707. Dates vary.
• Lesbian and Gay Freedom Day Parade. It's celebrated all over the state, but San Francisco's party draws up to half a million participants. The parade's start and finish has been moved around in recent years to accommodate road construction but traditionally it begins and ends at Civic Centre Plaza, where hundreds of food, art, and information booths are set up around several sound stages. Call 415/864–3733 for information. Usually the third or last weekend of June.
• Mariachi USA Festival, Los Angeles. A 2-day family-orien-

tated celebration of Mexican culture and tradition at the Hollywood Bowl, where festival-goers pack their picnic baskets and enjoy music, ballet, folklorico, and related performances by special guests. Phone 310/451–5044. Late June.
• Hot Air Balloon Classic, Windsor. Hundreds of brilliant silken balloons float silently across the sky above, while gawkers enjoy a food and crafts fair. Call 707/838–7285. Late June.
• Rough and Ready Secession Celebration and Chili Cookoff, Rough and Ready. This event celebrates the town's secession from the Union in 1850 in protest against a mining tax. It soon rejoined on the 4th July. Food, entertainment, and more. Call 916/432–4186 or 916/273–4328. Usually fourth Saturday in June.

July
• Independence Day. It's celebrated all over the state, of course, but it's terrific in Pasadena, which offers Southern California's most spectacular display of fireworks following an evening of live entertainment at the Rose Bowl. Phone 818/577`–3100 for further information.
• Festival of Arts and Pageant of the Masters, Laguna Beach. A fantastic performance-art production in which live actors re-create famous Old Masters paintings. Ticket prices range from $10 to $40. Call 714/497–6582 or 800/487–FEST. Early July through late August.
• Carmel Bach Festival. A 3-week festival honoring Johann Sebastian Bach and his contemporaries. It culminates in a candlelit concert in the chapel of the Carmel Mission. Call 408/624–1521. Dates vary.
• Gilroy Garlic Festival. A gourmet food fair with more than 85 booths serving garlicky food from almost every ethnic background, plus close to 100 arts, crafts, and entertainment

booths. Call 408/842–1625. Last full weekend in July.
• Mammoth Lakes Jazz Jubilee. A 3-day festival featuring 15 bands on 10 different stages, plus food, drink, and dancing—all under the pine trees and stars. Call 619/934–2478. Dates vary.
• Shakespeare at the Beach, Lake Tahoe. A bewitching experience of the Bard at Sand Harbor on the shore beneath the stars. Call 702/832-1606. Three weeks in late June and August.
• International Surf Festival, Los Angeles. Four beachside cities—Hermosa Beach, Manhattan Beach, Redondo Beach, and Torrance—collaborate in the oldest international surfing festival in California. Competitions include surfing, boogie boarding, sand-castle building, and other beach-related categories. Contact the International Surf Festival Committee at 3109/376–6911 for information. End of July.

August
• Sonoma County Showcase and Wine Auction. Four days of wine tasting and celebrations plus a wine auction. Held in the Sonoma County Wine and Visitor Centre and at different wineries. Call 707/586–6911. usually first weekend in August.
• Old Spanish Days Fiesta, Santa Barbara. The City's biggest annual event, this five-day festival features a grand parade with horse drawn carriages, two Spanish marketplaces, a carnival, a rodeo, and dancers. Call 805/962–8101. Early August.
• Nisei Week Japanese Festival, little Tokyo, Los Angeles. This week-long celebration of Japanese culture and heritage is held in the Japanese American Cultural and Community Center Plaza. Festivities include parades, food, music arts, and crafts. Call 213/687–7193. Mid-August.
• California State Fair, Sacramento. At the California

Exposition grounds, a gala celebration, with livestock, carnival food, exhibits, entertainment on 10 different stages, plus thoroughbred racing and a 1-mile monorail for panoramic views over the scope of it all. Call 916/263–3000. Late August to early September.

September
• San Diego Street Scene. This historic Quarter is transformed into an urban food and music festival. Call 619/557–8487 for more information. Early September.
• Sausalito Art Festival. A juried exhibit of more than 180 artists. It is accompanied by music provided by Bay Area jazz, rock, and blues performers and international cuisine enhanced by wines from some 50 different Napa and Sonoma producers. Parking is impossible; take the Red & White Fleet (415/546–2628) ferry from Fisherman's Wharf to the festival site. Call 415/332–3555 for information. Labor Day weekend.
• Monterey Jazz Festival. Top names in traditional and modern jazz. One of the oldest annual jazz festivals in the world. Call 408/373–3366. Mid-September.
• San Francisco Blues Festival, on the grounds of Fort Mason. The largest outdoor blues music event on the West Coast. Local and national musicians perform back-to-back during two marathon days. Call 415/826–6837. Usually in mid-September.
• Los Angeles County Fair. Horse racing, arts, agricultural displays, celebrity entertainment, and carnival rides are among the attractions of the largest county fair in the world, held at the Los Angeles County Fair and Exposition Center, in Pomona. Call 909/623–3111 for information. Late September.
• Cabrillo Festival, San Diego. A week-long fair commemorating the exploration of the West Coast by Juan Rodriquez

Cabrillo in 1542. A reenactment of the event takes place at the Cabrillo National Monument. Call 619/557–5450 for more information. Late September.

• Catalina Island Jazz Trax Festival. Great contemporary jazz artists travel to the island to play in the legendary Casino Ballroom. The festival is over two consecutive 3-day weekends. Call 619/458–9586 or 800/866–TRAX for more information. Late September or early October.

• Watts Towers Day of the Drum Festival, Los Angeles. Performances from Afro-Cuban folkloricos to East Indian tabla players. Phone 312/847–4646. Late September.

• Tuolumne County Wild West Film Festival and Rodeo, Sonora. A gathering of Western film stars and rodeo legends, plus arts and crafts, entertainment, rodeo, and awards dinner. Call 209/533–4420. Last weekend in September.

October

• Gold-Panning Championships and Historic Demonstration Day, Coloma. Gold-panning contests, foods, crafts, music, and tours. Living history demonstrations of spinning, weaving, cooking and doll-making. Call 916/622–6198. Dates vary.

• Sonoma County Harvest Fair. A 3-day celebration of the harvest with exhibitions, art shows, and annual judging of the local wines. At the Sonoma County Fairgrounds. Call 707/545–4203. Dates vary.

• Pumpkin and Art Festival, Half Moon Bay. Features hundreds of artisans' booths,

pumpkins carvings, music, and a contest for the largest pumpkin. Colorful in the extreme. Call 415/726–9652. Dates vary.
• Annual Bob Hope Celebrity Golf Tournament, riverside. Bob Hope is the honorary chairman of this annual event. For ticket and other information, contact the Riverside Convention and Visitors Bureau at 909/787–7950.
• Western Regional Final Championship Rodeo, Lakeside. Top cowboys from 11 western states compete in seven rodeo events including calf roping, barrel racing, and bull riding, team roping, and steer wrestling. Held at the Lakeside Rodeo Grounds, Highway 67 and Mapleview Avenue, Lakeside. Call 619/561–6070 for more information. Mid-October.
• Whale festival, Long Beach. Join in building a life-size whale from sand, and enjoy a family sand sculpture contest, food, crafts, children's activities, entertainment, booths on sea life and issues, and a watermelon feast. Call 310/548–7562. Late October.
• Halloween, San Francisco. The City by the Bay celebrates with a fantastical parade which is organized at Market and Castro, and a mixed gay-straight crowd revels in costumes of extraordinary imagination.

November
• Doo Dah Parade, Pasadena. An outrageous spoof of the Rose Parade on the Sunday before Thanksgiving, featuring participants such as the Briefcase Parade and a kazoo band. Call 818/449–3689.
• Hollywood Christmas Parade. This spectacular star-studded parade marches through the heart of Hollywood the first or second Sunday after Thanksgiving. For information, phone 213/469–2337.
• San Diego Dixieland Jazz Festival. More than 30 bands perform entertaining, foot-

stomping jazz at the Town and Country Hotel. Call 619/297–5277 for more information. Late November.

December
• Truckers Christmas Light Convoy, Eureka. Big rigs decorated and festooned with lights compete for cash prizes in this lumber town. Call 707/444–2323 or 707/442–5744 for dates and time.
• Old Town Holiday in the Park, San Diego. Costumed park docents lead candlelight tours of historic homes in Old Town. Call 619/220–5422 or 469-3174 for ticket information. Early December.
• San Diego Harbor Parade of Lights. Lighted boats cruise from the southwest end of Shelter Island, through San Diego Harbor to Seaport Village. Early December.

GETTING AROUND

Motoring
Accidents
1 Set up warning signs
2 Call police, Highway Patrol and ambulance if required
3 Take names and addresses of all involved, names and numbers of insurance policies and make and licence plate of other vehicle
4 Take names and addresses of all witnesses
5 Under no circumstances admit to or sign any statement of responsibility

Breakdowns
The American Automobile Association (AAA) is a member of a worldwide association of motoring organisations (AIT) and, as such, makes certain services available to visitors from member organisations. AAA operates a nationwide road service number: call 1–800-222–7764 or 1–800-400–4222 (24-hour) and you will be given information for obtaining emergency assistance.
    Should you break down on a highway, lift up the hood

(bonnet) of your car and remain in your vehicle until the Highway Patrol arrives. Do not open your doors or windows to anyone else. If you spot another driver who seems to need help, contact the police (dial 911).
    Some precautions can be taken, especially by those driving their own cars, before setting off on a drive, to avoid unnecessary trouble. Have the car's oil level checked every time you fill the tank, and check tire pressure regularly. Tires should be fully inflated, without any worn or uneven patches, before you set out on your journey. Also have the coolant level checked, and make sure there are no leaks in the radiator. Ideally the brakes and brake fluid should also be checked, and you should have plenty of antifreeze, especially if you plan to travel into skiing areas, in which case snow chains for tires are advisable (and, in some places, obligatory).
    Make sure all lights are working and that there is washing liquid supplied for the windshield.

Car Rentals
All the major car rental companies are represented, but better rates can usually be obtained from local companies, that are listed in the Yellow Pages. These are generally not based in airports, but they will provide a free shuttle service to their facility.
    None of the major companies will rent to anyone under the age of 25. It may be possible to find a local company that will do so, but be prepared to pay a loaded insurance premium. The best idea is to shop around before deciding which car rental firm to approach, and to make sure that you understand the conditions that apply to each firm's policy. For instance, some may charge an extra fee for renting a car in one place and leaving it in another; some may include a full gas tank in

Practical Information

the overall price, others may not – and so on.

It is also advisable to find out whether your own insurance would cover damage to a rented car, and what the details are of Collision Damage Waiver (CDT).

Car rental companies with offices in California include:
Alamo (tel: 800/327–9633)
Avis (tel: 800/331–1212)
Budget (tel: 800/527–0700)
Dollar Rent a Car (tel: 800/421–6868)
Hertz (tel: 800/654–3131)
National Car Rental (tel: 800/328–4567)
Thrifty Car Rental (800/367–2277).

Documents
Drivers need a valid licence from any country signatory to the 1949 Geneva Agreement. Car registration numbers and proof of insurance must be carried.

Route Directions
The following abbreviations for U.S. roads have been used throughout this book:
Hwy – Highway
I – Interstate

Rules and Regulations
Recently the power to impose speed limits was transferred from the Federal Government to individual states. This is still in a transitional period, but on many rural freeways the limit is now up to 65mph (105kph). Road signs always clearly indicate specific limits and they are strictly enforced.

Drivers and passengers must wear seat belts, and children under 4 years old or lighter than 40 lb (18kg) must sit in approved safety seats.

Rail Travel
Amtrak operates rail services in California, with a particularly scenic line running along the coast – the Coast Starlight, that runs from Seattle to Los Angeles or on to San Diego via Oakland, Salinas, San Luis Obispo, Santat Barbara and the

Malibu coast. Book ahead for this popular trip. Visitors from outside the U.S. can buy the USA Railpass, allowing 15 or 30 days' unlimited travel on Amtrak lines. Amtrak offices in San Francisco and Los Angeles sell passes within the U.S. to holders of foreign passports.

Travelers with disabilities should specify their needs when reserving seats with Amtrak: some stations are not well-equipped with facilities – and there may be discounts available.

Air Travel
(See also Travel to the U.S. from Overseas.)
Several airlines operate regular flights within California, including:
American Eagle (800/433–7300)
America West (800/235–9292)
Skywest (800/453–9417)
United (800/241–6522)
USAir Express (800/428-4322)

Bus Travel
Traveling by bus is inexpensive but time-consuming, and bus stations are often located in unsavory parts of town. Greyhound operates bus lines between all the major cities in California, but some routes (such as those between Los Angeles and San Francisco, for example) are as expensive as air fares. Travelers from outside the U.S. can buy Ameripass tickets, giving bus travel for seven, 15 or 30 days and available from Greyhound offices.

The Green Tortoise bus line operates between Los Angeles and San Francisco, and is geared towards younger travelers (tel: Los Angeles 213/392–1990; San Francisco 415/821–0803).

Alternative Travel
San Francisco probably provides the best public transport system in California, its best-known option being the bay ferries: the Red and White boats, that link San Francisco, Angel Island, Tiburon and Vallejo (tel: 800/445–8880), and

the Golden Gate Ferry Service, sailing between San Francisco and Sausalito (tel: 415 332 6600).

Underground trains operated by The Bay Area Rapid Transit company (BART) run between 33 stations in the San Francisco Bay area, and are generally a quick means of travel.

San Diego's Tijuana Trolley makes regular journeys to the Mexican border and between San Diego neighborhoods.

Safety
Be aware that certain areas of certain towns and cities are not safe for tourists. The best course of action is to talk to staff at the travel agency, tourist information center or car rental company and ascertain which neighborhoods should be avoided. If possible, equip yourself with a map showing the safe areas clearly, and be sure of the directions to your destination.

If you are involved in a motoring accident in an area that may be dangerous, stay in the car and keep doors and windows locked until police arrive on the scene. If you are bumped from behind, or if something is wrong with the car, head straight for a service station rather than stopping in an unknown area.

Never leave expensive equipment such as cameras or mobile phones visible in the car – keep them locked in the trunk (boot). Try to park in well-lit or monitored parking lots, and to fill the tank in daylight.
See also **Motoring: Accidents**, page 163.

HOLIDAYS
1 January – New Year's Day;
Third Monday in January – Martin Luther King Jr. Day;
Third Monday in February – Presidents' Day);
Last Monday in May (Memorial Day);
4 July – Independence Day;
First Monday in September – Labor Day;

Second Monday in October –
Columbus Day;
11 November – Veterans Day/
Armistice Day;
Last Thursday in November –
Thanksgiving Day;
25 December – Christmas
Day.
The Tuesday following the
first Monday in November is
Election Day.

LIQUOR LAWS

Liquor and grocery stores, as
well as some drugstores, can
legally sell packaged alcoholic
beverages between 6am and
2am. Most restaurants, night-
clubs, and bars are licensed to
serve alcoholic beverages
during the same hours.

The legal age for the
purchase and consumption of
alcoholic beverages is 21; proof
of age is strictly enforced.

RESTAURANTS

Eating out is not a problem in
California: the range of styles,
prices and locations is breath-
taking. The state's speciality is
California Cuisine, a
Mediterranean-influenced
style that uses fresh, healthy,
local ingredients (vegetables,
fruit, seafood) in original
combinations to produce beau-
tiful dishes (at high prices).
Examples of establishments
serving California Cuisine are:
Chez Panisse, 1517 Shattuck
Avenue, Berkeley (tel:
510/548–5525)
Four Oaks, 2181 N Beverly
Glen Boulevard, Los Angeles
(tel: 310/470–2265)
Spago, 1114 Horn Avenue,
West Hollywood, Los Angeles
(tel: 310/652–4025)
Terra, 1345 Railroad Avenue,
St Helena (tel: 707/963–8931)

Apart from this, California
has virtually every conceivable
type of cuisine on offer, from
fast food to Mexican, Japanese
to French, Indian to
Indonesian, and everything in
between.

TAXES

Sales tax is levied on goods and
services by state and local
governments and is not
included in the price tags you'll
see on merchandise. These
taxes are not refundable.

TRAVEL TO THE U.S. FROM OVERSEAS

Several airlines fly regularly
from Europe to the US, either
direct to California or to states
with connecting flights. All
major airlines offer cheaper
fares for advance purchase on
the APEX (advance purchase
excursion) scheme.
Non-U.S. airlines with flights
to California include:
British Airways (tel: London
(0345) 222 111)
Virgin Atlantic (tel: London
(0293) 747 747)
Aer Lingus (tel: Dublin (01)
844 4747; Shannon (061) 415
556)
Qantas (tel: Sydney (008) 177
767)
Air New Zealand (tel:
Auckland (0800) 737 000;
Christchurch (643) 379 5200)
Air Canada (tel: (800) 268 7240)

VISITOR INFORMATION

For information on the state as
a whole, contact the California
Office of Tourism, 801 K
Street, Suite 1600, Sacramento,
CA 95814 (tel: 800/862–2543),
and ask for their free information packet. In addition, almost
every city and town in the state
has a dedicated tourist bureau
or chamber of commerce that
will be happy to send you
information.

To find out more about
California's national parks,
contact the Western Region
Information Center, National
Park Service, Fort Mason,
Building 201, San Francisco,
CA 94123 (tel: 415/556–0560).

WHEN TO GO

California's climate is so varied
that it is imposible to general-
ize about the state as a whole.
San Francisco's temperate
marine climate means relatively mild weather year-round.
In summer, temperatures rarely
top 70°F (pack sweaters, even
in August), and the city;s
famous fog rolls in most
evenings. In winter, the
mercury seldom falls below
freezing, and snow is almost
unheard of. Because of San
Francisco's fog, summer rarely
sees more than a few hot days
in a row. Head a few miles
inland, though, and it's likely to
be clear and hot.

The Central Coast shares San
Francisco's climate, though it
gets warmer as you get farther
south. Seasonal changes are
less pronounced south of San
Luis Obispo, where temperatures remain relatively stable
year-round. The northern coast
is rainier and foggier; winters
tend to be mild but wet.

Summers are refreshingly
cool around Lake Tahoe and in
the Shasta Cascades – a perfect
climate for hiking, camping,
and other outdoor activities and
a popular escape for residents
of California's sweltering
deserts and valleys who are
looking to beat the heat. Skiers
flock to this area for terrific
snowfall from late November
through early April.

Southern California is usually
much warmer than the Bay
Area, and it gets significantly
more sun. This is the place to
hit the beach. Even in winter,
daytime thermometer readings
regularly reach into the 60s and
warmer. Summers can be
stifling inland, but Southern
California's coastal communities are always comfortable.
Don't pack an umbrella. When
it rains, Southern Californians
go outside to look at the
novelty. It's possible to
sunbathe throughout the year,
but only die-hard enthusiasts
and wet-suited surfers venture
into the ocean in winter. The
water is warmest in summer
and fall, but even then, the
Pacific is too chilly for many.

The Southern California
desert is sizzling hot in
summer; temperatures regularly top 100°F. Winter is the
time to visit the desert resorts
(and remember, it gets
surprisingly cold at night in
the desert).

INDEX